CW01237418

Faithfully Yours
Sharrad H. Gilbert

RHODESIA—AND AFTER

BEING THE STORY

OF THE

17TH AND 18TH BATTALIONS OF IMPERIAL YEOMANRY

IN SOUTH AFRICA.

BY

SHARRAD H. GILBERT.

65th Squadron I.Y.

WITH THREE MAPS AND FORTY-EIGHT ILLUSTRATIONS.

AUTOGRAPH EDITION.

LONDON :
SIMPKIN MARSHALL, HAMILTON, KENT & Co., LTD.
1901.

TO
MY COMRADES
OF THE TWO BATTALIONS
I DEDICATE
THIS BOOK.

PREFACE.

BEFORE leaving with my Squadron for South Africa, I had arranged to contribute to the Press a series of Articles descriptive of the life we should lead, and the varied vicissitudes and adventures through which it would be our fate to pass.

A number of these Articles were written and despatched; and appeared in the pages of an English newspaper.

But, encouraged by the flattering interest they aroused amongst the friends at home into whose hands they fell, and partly to meet the wishes of many of the comrades with whom I was serving, I decided to venture where, perhaps, I should have feared to tread; and to issue the whole series in volume form after our return, should I escape the dangers of a bitterly contested campaign.

I was further impelled to this course, as the rapid movements and scanty leisure of the Squadrons after their removal from Rhodesia to fields of greater military activity farther South, rendered the writing and safe despatch of these Articles too uncertain for one who had in addition to fulfil the many and trying duties of a private soldier.

Such is my apology for writing this book.

In passing through strange lands and savage tribes and customs, through weird and unfamiliar scenes, it would seem difficult to the traveller that they should ever be forgotten.

But as the years go by, he feels with keen regret that these memories lose their freshness. Pressed aside by newer thoughts and faces, the minor incidents are dimmed and are in time forgotten. Only those things which made the deepest impress at the time remain. Yet these memories are not dead. They are but dormant. The sight of a picture, the chance allusion in the social circle will bring back in a flood with undimmed freshness the forgotten events of days long past. And are there any sweeter pleasures than these? They tear men's minds from presentcare. They make men young again.

May I hope that this book will thus play the part of the magician's wand. That the sight of its pictures, the perusal of its pages, will keep green the memory of the happy days —happy despite the lack of luxury; and of the hardships and trials manfully surmounted on the sun-scorched sands of the South African veldt.

Such is its aim.

In a map of the late South African Republics, and even of the greater part of Cape Colony too, the first thing to strike the casual observer is the seeming bewildering combinations of 'fonteins' and 'gats' and 'puts' and 'kuils' which meet him at every turn. But—if we except those places which have derived their names from some person who has lived in their vicinity, or been connected with them in some other way—this bewildering variety can be condensed into a list of words which does not run to many scores.

And when known, these hitherto meaningless Krankuils, and Zeekoegats and Paauwpans possess a fascination all their own. Though 'Elands Laagte' has no lack of interest —though its name makes some to throb with sorrow, others with memories of pain, and all with pride, do they but bear the name of Englishmen—its interest is in nowise abated when one knows it takes its name from the vast herds of graceful antelope that roamed its valleys, not so many years ago. And visitors to the Capital of the late Free State will hardly demur at the pretty significance of its name, 'The Flowery Spring.'

Even the soldier, when, at the end of a long day's trek, he flings his weary body down at some Zeekoegat, would, if he had a spark of the sportsman in his veins (and what Englishman has not) feel his interest in things revive, did he but know that there the unwieldy 'hippos' were wont to gambol in the water-holes : or when scrambling down the rocky pass of some Buffels Hoek, surely it would lighten his labour to know that down that self-same path have countless herds of buffalo risked their necks. Perhaps, when the bitter memories of this war have softened, and the fusing of the races has begun, 'twill be better to think but of the pretty Kaffir meaning of 'Amajuba' Hill, and forget its present dread significance.

I have said enough to explain the presence of the Glossary at the end of this book; and though I do not claim that it is in any way complete, I hope it will not be without its interest and its use.

I take this opportunity of gratefully acknowledging the kindly interest displayed in the preparation of my book by all those amongst whom it was compiled; of sincerely thanking those Officers and Men — too numerous to mention severally—who so willingly gave their photographs for the illustrating of its pages, or supplied me with information relating to facts and scenes where it was impossible for me to be present in person. Without this help the production of this book would have been impossible. I wish especially to acknowledge the valuable assistance I have received from the following members of the two Battalions— from A. H. Dickenson, J. B. McCartney and Frank S. Pickford of the 50th—J. M. B. Stuart of the 60th—from a series of articles in the *Irish Field*, kindly placed at my disposal by their author, J. J. Ennis, B. A. Trinity College Dublin, Barrister-at-Law, and from Sergt-Major T. H. Crofts, both of the 61st—Lieut. C. J. Dyke, of the 67th—J. Kidd and C. J. Wilson of the Scottish Sharpshooters—A. J. Faulkner and E. Norburn of the 71st — J. Black and J. S. Parkinson of the 75th. Also the courtesy and help accorded to me by the British South Africa Company.

I place this volume—a labour of love—in the hands of those for whom it is written—to whom it is dedicated—MY COMRADES. Many have returned to the cares of business, to the unending round of the farm, or the brain-wear of professional life.

Should but a stray hour in the aftertime of toil be lightened; should the 'trivial round' be brightened by warm memories quickened by the perusal of its pages, then will I be satisfied to feel my work has not been in vain.

THE AUTHOR.

HINCKLEY,
    LEICESTERSHIRE.
December, 1901.

CONTENTS.

PART I.—RHODESIA.

Chap.		Page
I	BEIRA—FROM THE SEA	13
II	IN THE BAY—BEIRA	22
III	ON AFRICAN SOIL	29
IV	THE CAMP IN THE JUNGLE	37
V	BAMBOO CREEK	56
VI	ACROSS THE RHODESIAN BORDER	66
VII	THE GOLDFIELDS HOSPITAL, UMTALI	77
VIII	THE BASE CAMP AT MARANDELLAS	86
IX	THE CHASTISING OF MAPONDERA	98
X	TREKKING ACROSS THE PLAINS	110
XI	BULUWAYO	124

PART II. —AFTER.

I	WATCHING THE ORANGE DRIFTS	137
II	A STERN CHASE AND A LONG ONE	145
III	GUARDING THE ZWARTBERG POORTS	154

Chap		Page
IV	IN SCHEEPERS' HANDS	164
V	THE ESCAPE	173
VI	THE DEFENCE OF THE JAIL	181
VII	THE CHASE OF DE WET	189
VIII	UNDER ORDERS FOR HOME	206

PART III.—THE STORIES OF THE SQUADRONS.

THE STORY OF THE 50TH I.Y.	220
THE STORY OF THE IRISH YEOMANRY	240
THE STORY OF THE 65TH I.Y.	267
THE STORY OF DUNRAVEN'S SHARPSHOOTERS	287

LIST OF CASUALTIES 331

ALPHABETICAL GLOSSARY OF SOUTH AFRICAN NAMES AND PLACES (DUTCH AND KAFFIR), WITH THEIR MEANING AND DERIVATION 341

LIST OF ILLUSTRATIONS.

	Page
Frontispiece (*Photo by Ivie. H. Allan, Graaff Reinet.*) To face Title page.	
Beira—from the Sea	16
Kaffirs carrying kit-bags onto the landing-stage—Beira	16
Entraining at Beira	33
Wood fuel on Beira-Salisbury line	33
Umtali—from the Hospital	81
A Rhodesian Kopje	86
Angoni Policeman at home	91
A Native Telephone	91
Dead horses round Camp—Marandellas	96
A bit of the Station-yard—Marandellas	96
Women bringing in Native Beer at a War-dance	102
Bivouac of the Native Police	107
A bit of Mashonaland	107
A Mashonaland Stream	113
The Salisbury-Buluwayo Coach	113
The effect of the first Rains	128
Shoeing-smith Brazier and 'Marmalade'	128
Firing across The Orange at Grootverlangen	144
The Karbonaatjes Kraal in Flood	144
The Orange River—from the kopje	144
Britztown	148
Meirings Poort	161
Exercising horses in the dry river bed	164
Dutch Girls watching the entry of the troops	164
The Armoured Train that played havoc with De Wet	196
Christian De Wet	205
The Veldt after the Storm	228
The Church-Prison at Boshof	228
Officers' Quarters on the veldt	237

		Page
A Farm in the Karroo	.. ..	257
Column on the march	.. ..	261
Horse-lines—Sepulilo Kraal	.. ..	268
A Halt in the Forest	.. ..	268
A Rough track—Lomaghonda	.. .. ..	268
Grazing-guard on the march to Buluwayo	.. ..	272
"D" Troop Maxim on the march to Buluwayo	.. ..	272
The Cook-house, Marandellas	.. .. ..	292
The top of Zimbabwe Hill	.. ..	292
The Temple walls, Zimbabwe	.. .. ..	292
Camp in the horse-paddocks, Beira	.. .. ..	292
Fort Tuli	.. ..	301
Gen. Carrington inspecting the horses at Tuli	.. ..	304
Crossing sandy river-bed with double team	.. ..	304
Trekking in the rains—Tuli to Buluwayo	.. ..	304
Column entering Beaufort West	.. .. ..	309
Column crossing the Gamka River	.. .. ..	316
Column halted in the Karroo	.. .. ..	325

MAPS.

(*The Maps were specially prepared for this book by Stafford Gilbert*).

Southern Rhodesia ..	(*folding map*)	..	Facing page 13
Cape Colony ..	(*folding map*) ..	..	" " 137
The Invasion of De Wet	(*full-page map*)	..	" " 191

Cover designed by the Author.

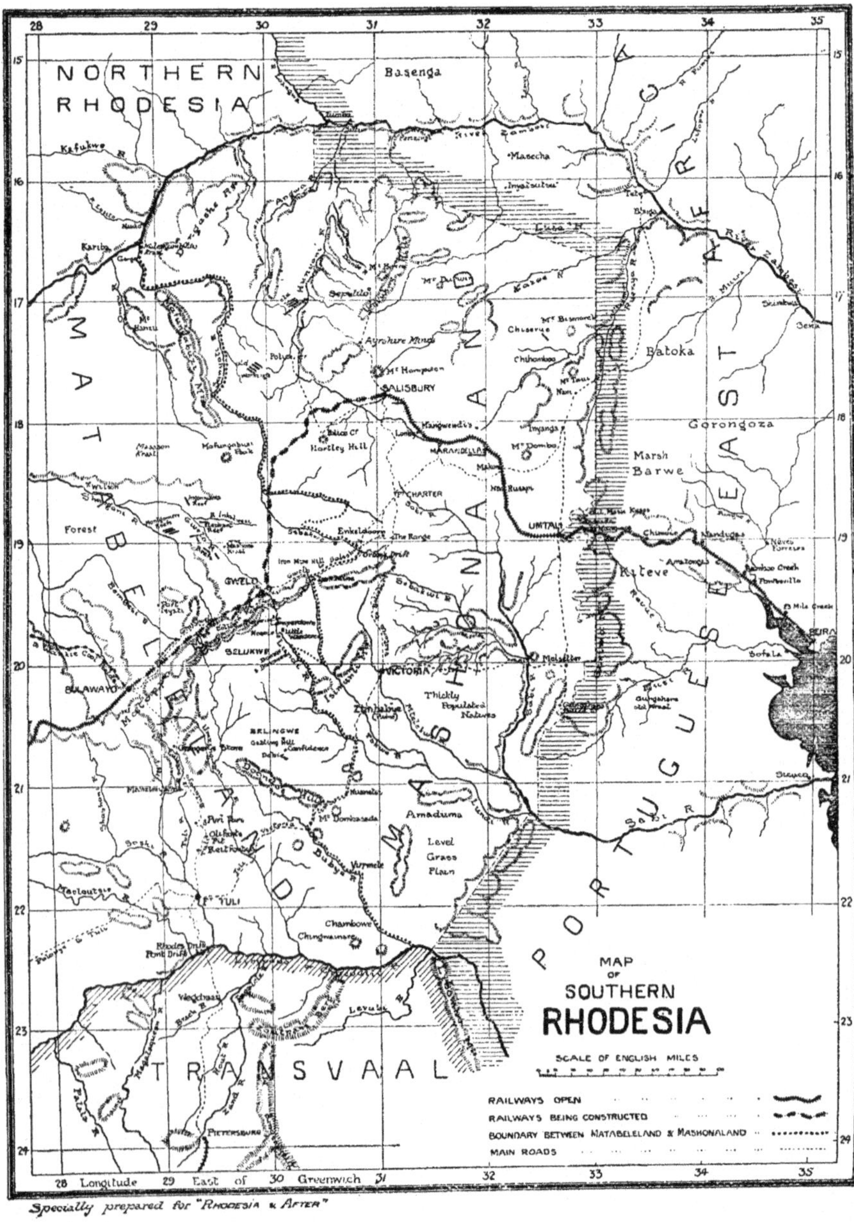

Specially prepared for "RHODESIA & AFTER"

RHODESIA.

CHAPTER I.

Beira—from the Sea.

A TOWN of corrugated iron and of three-storied erections constructed of unsubstantial wood. A town seemingly built for the necessity of the hour, instead of for the permanent habitation of man. A mushroom growth of huge showy hotels of bandbox newness, ending in a railway station on the left and a signal tower far away on the right. The whole backed and flanked by unbroken masses of rank vegetation of a rich green luxuriance, that could only be produced by the flat swampy soil of which the whole country around is composed.

Such is Beira—from the Sea.

Slowly the eye drinks in the strangeness and the details. We lie in a vast U shaped basin. On the extreme right, at the end of the U, the tall square landmark of the signal tower, painted in bold alternate stripes of red and white, and topped by mast and yard, is separated from the town by several miles of luxuriant tree masses, edged by a wide sandy beach.

Then a mile of dark buttressed sea-wall, at low tide splashed along its lower parts with dark green sea-growth, and at the full, beaten by a white surf line which now and again hurls far above the wall wisps and wreathes of foam, the very spray seeming to retain the muddy hue of the harbour water. Then another mile of sandy beach, partitioned by irregular rows of stakes planted to retain the sand from the voracious maw of the outgoing sea. Round the end of this the river winds out of sight, cutting it off from the further continuation of the shore line.

In the rear of the whole—seawall and beach—rise at frequent intervals large light-colored hotels, topped by tiled roofs of most aggressive brick-red tints, with gently sloping sides and gables. They are two and three stories in height, each floor surrounded by deep shady balconies, the graceful white pillars lending a light and picturesque air to the whole. When we consider the small white population of Beira, either the supply of hotels seems much in excess of the demand, or the white people of Beira must be of a wonderfully spongy nature. But the white population do not keep up establishments of their own, but nearly all live in these hotels, hence the existence of so large a number. In addition to these there are numerous French and American bars of much more shady repute.

The whole town looks like the motley assemblage of some huge exhibition or mammoth pleasure fair, for many of the hotels have in their grounds tall structures of outlandish shape and style — something between a Chinese pagoda and a miniature Eiffel Tower—from which their guests may enjoy the seascape.

And every building of any importance has its flag-staff. The French, judging from the ubiquity of the tricolour, seem to have planted a firm commercial foot in the place. The Portuguese colours—the National arms emblazoned in the centre of a parti-coloured flag in blue and white — are of course predominant. Each hotel flaunts its name from the top of a flag-staff, and the buildings of the trading companies are surmounted by their own particular colours. The names of the hotels are nearly all English, and the Beira Club boasts one of the largest buildings in the town. The intervals between the hotels are filled up with stores and other buildings, all of the same unsubstantial build.

One sees no horses, no oxen, no mules in Beira. The only means of locomotion are trollies pushed by boys, and masheelas (hammocks slung on poles). All the streets are interlaced with tram lines, and the trollies—small affairs to seat four, covered by a sunshade—keep up a constant lumbering noise the whole day long.

To the left of the creek stands the railway station—the terminus of the Beira and Salisbury line. To the left of that much resembles an immense building yard, for in that direction Beira is growing apace, and there are to be found buildings in every stage of erection, from the nearly completed hotel, with its roof gaily painted in yard-wide stripes of blue and white, to the plain corrugated iron stores and makeshift workshops of the men. From here man and his works give place to Dame Nature in her most abandoned mood, and on the south and west of the basin the thick-set cane-brakes and luxuriant growth of giant reeds advance right down to the water's edge, as though greedy of the mudstretches claimed by the tides. Here and there in rear of these are knolls covered with graceful palms—" lumps of leaves stuck on nothing," as one trooper not inaptly called them. And as each evening the malarial mists exhale from these steaming swamps, they are suffused by the rays of the setting sun, and the waters of the bay are tinged by the most gorgeous sunsets ; whilst the palms and scattered canes stand silhouetted in rich black outline against the flaming west. At low tide, treacherous sand-banks appear above the water in more places than one, and the ship that left the buoyed channel in coming in or going out would do so with results most certainly disastrous. There are no hills in the distance, but the eye roams over never-ending jungle and bushy tree tops to the horizon, which is not far distant owing to the flatness of the land.

But all this is but the framing of the picture. The real interest lies in the harbour itself—the huge oval basin of mud-colored water in which we ride at anchor. It is proverbially an ill wind that blows nobody any good, and this war must mean great things for Beira. Never in its history has the harbour held such an assemblage of vessels as to-day, and more are arriving daily.

The *Galeka*, the largest craft in the bay, swings steadily at her anchor within half-a-mile of the shore. We are not the only troops here, for to the right and left of us are large weather-beaten liners, packed with khaki figures, Queenslanders, Victorians aud New Zealand Rough Riders. The very names of the boats, the *Maori*, the *Waimate*, the *Monowai*, smack of the land they hail from. There are huge towering cargo boats, their decks built from end to end with horse stalls

— one has seven hundred Hungarians, another carries Australian 'whalers,' two more arrive packed with 'bronchos' from the States, in the care of rough-looking cowboys*. Over to starboard is a monster steamer busily unloading steel railway sleepers and iron telegraph poles, telling of the newly-opened country to which we are going, and between us and the shore—almost within hail-a little English watch-dog, the gunboat *H.M.S. Partridge*, rides daintily on the tide. Her sailors, in spotless white uniform, are just refreshing her white sides with new paint; a broad red stripe runs from stem to stern, and her tapering masts, brightly polished brasswork and flaunting British ensign, makes her one of the prettiest pictures in the harbour. Behind their protecting shields, six 4-inch quick-firing guns show their teeth in various directions, death-dealing maxims peer from unexpected corners, while, raised above her upper works, stands the projector of a powerful limelight, ready at any moment of the night to lay bare the nefarious designs of contraband runners, and any other knavish tricks of the friends of our friend the enemy.

Farther away rides a black-hulled, rakish-looking Portuguese gunboat; on each side she shows a long 6-inch breech-loading gun, but, though of larger calibre than the British guns, they are of less modern make, and, to put it in the vigorous language of one of the *Partridge's* bluejackets, "We could wipe her into h—— before she knew it." Happily, our present friendly relations with her Government render the wiping operation unnecessary.

During the day the harbour is alive with small craft. There are boats from the transports carrying officers ashore or to pay visits to other vessels; noisy steam tugs tow strings of unwieldy lighters to the sides of the cargo steamers for stores or horses. The miniature steam pinnaces from the gunboats cut swiftly across the harbour, raising a cloud of foam from their bows, as they bury their heads into the swell of the incoming tide. Near our sides a couple of swarthy Zambesis propel a native canoe by short rapid dips of their spoon-like paddles.

---

* Many of these cowboys joined one or another of the irregular corps, and did good work for us in the field. One of them, Abraham Guisert, a few weeks afterwards assassinated the British consul at Beira.

Photos by *C. W. McKechnie.*
BEIRA—FROM THE SEA.
KAFFIRS CARRYING KITBAGS ON TO LANDING-STAGE—BEIRA.

Another group sits astern of their craft singing a monotonous native song while the boat is carried along by a huge flimsy triangular sail, with the apex of the triangle at the bottom. The sides of these canoes slope inwards from the water's edge to the gunwale, having along the top a long slit just wide enough for a man to sit in, and at the side floats a log, fastened as an outrigger to preserve the equilibrium of the fragile craft. But every boat in the harbour—except perhaps when manned by a crew of Yeomen for the sake of exercise—is rowed by Kaffirs. The blacks are all called Kaffirs, though hailing from a score of different tribes, the distinguishing characteristics of which may in many cases be readily noted. Some of the crews of four or six oars are uniformly dressed—as far as the waist—in smart sailor-like jackets, gaily decorated with bright-coloured braid. But only as far as the waist. Every black, without exception, wears a gaudy-patterned cloth gracefully swathed round his waist, reaching just below the knees, and the legs and feet of all are bare. Note that crew. Each one dressed in a loose sailor jacket of spotless white, with four rows of khaki braid round deep collar, breast pocket and cuffs. Below that comes a waistcloth of deep blue, ornamented with huge sunflowers of flaming yellow. On each woolly head rests a bright crimson fez with a blue tassel hanging behind, while the deep chocolate legs and faces of the men complete a picture truly Oriental in its vivid color.

Parties of the Colonials came aboard to exchange greetings. They wear emu plumes in their hats, and black boots and leggings with their khaki clothing. They are burned almost as black as Indians, and from their magnificent physique and appearance seem to be the pick of the Colony. They always speak of England as 'home,' though born and living all their lives in the Colony, and their most cherished wish is to some day go 'home' on a visit.

This is what a correspondent—an officer—wrote home some weeks later concerning these Australians :—

"I have one regiment in my eye. I shall not name it, not because I should not like to proclaim it from the housetops, but because I have perhaps had more opportunity of watching it both on the line of march and in camp. They muster about

750 rank and file. Their discipline for the short time they have been together is beyond praise, and the spirit that pervades the regiment, from the Colonel to the cook, is such as many a regular regiment of the British army might well envy and emulate. For some time I asked myself what inspires this feeling, what makes this spirit? Very few of the men or officers had ever been in Great Britain. It was an emblem to them, only a thin imaginary cord holding two people under one banner. I had heard in past years that Australia might, if we at home did not please them, sever their connection, and, to quote a Colonialism, ' start on their own,' and somehow, I know not why, I believed it. This unfounded belief is, thank God, now shattered, and almost an impossibility. I was talking to a trooper one day, and I asked him why, as he had never been home (Great Britain is always 'home' to the Australian), he was so enthusiastic about our little island.

" ' Why,' said he, ' can't you guess?'

" I was getting at it now, and on the verge, as I found out, of the key that opened the lock.

" ' The Queen, God bless her,' said he. ' We would all ride to h—ll for her.'

" Every bushman living in a log hut, every workman, no matter his politics, hangs over his chimney-piece a picture of the Queen, and his wife teaches her children that that perhaps penny paper picture, cut out of some pictorial issue, is the embodiment of the greatest woman, the greatest Queen, and the best of mothers man has wot of, and she to them is not a sentiment, not a figure-head to cheer for, but a woman who sympathises with their lot in life, and I verily believe they think they only have to go home and lay their wants, if they have any, before her, and that justice, sympathy and kindness will be their reception, as of course it would be. I have tried to picture this extraordinary sympathy that exists between the Queen's personality and the Australian, and I have failed to convey its intensity. Mr. Cecil Rhodes landed at Beira on his way to Rhodesia, and there was a talk of his going to see the Australian contingent, and, much as he wanted to go, it was thought advisable that he should not, for, as the Australian said, 'We are fighting for the Queen, not for Rhodes.' I suppose there is not such a democratic country as Australia. The Colonel of a regiment told me that one of his greatest difficulties in instituting military discipline was the friendship that existed between officers and men, and so he established the system in camp that at the end of each troop line, the captain and subalterns were to mess together, and at the other end the sergeants messed. The Colonel had what was called a staff mess for his majors, doctor, adjutant and himself."

Fresh transports and cargo boats are arriving every day. On the deck of one are half-a-dozen long ambulance wagons, another—the *Cymric*—is packed with New Zealand Rough Riders. They are the 'Fighting Fifth,' and as they pass slowly by our stern they shout the Maori war-cry in response to our hearty British cheers. One stentorian voice flings out the challenge of their name, followed by the shout of the remainder. Thus it runs—

    LEADER. *Erima.*   ALL. *Patu tangata*
    LEADER. *Erima.*   ALL. *Kai tangata*
    LEADER. *Kokiria kia mate.*
    ALL. *Hi-ha! Hi-ha!* (pronounced *heeya*).

The translation is roughly—
    The Fifth! The Mankillers!
    The Fifth! The Maneaters!
    Charge to the death!
    We will! We will!!

It has a most weird, and, at the same time, blood-stirring effect on those who hear it. Each New Zealand contingent has its own war-cry, and with luck we shall in the near future hear it mingling in battle with our 'hurrahs.'

As she came within hail we asked them whence they came.
"New Zealand," they said. "Where are you from?"
"Old England," we yelled, as the distance slowly widened.
And a rough voice added, "An' Oireland."
The 61st were not going to let Ireland be forgotten.

But on Tuesday, May 10th, a visitor of another sort steamed into the harbour. This was the *Herzog*, the German vessel which was seized on suspicion at the commencement of the war. She had three tiers of promenade decks, and was crowded with French and German tourists—male, female and babies. As she steamed slowly by us to her anchorage, some of our young thoughtless spirits, who are always ready to cheer, even if a bumboat goes by, tried to raise a 'hurrah.' They were promptly suppressed. The Germans did not respond in any way, but intently regarded us through their glasses. They were only calling here before going lower down the coast. Possibly—yes probably, there are amongst them some who will later on act against us in the field. In the evening the commander of the Portuguese gunboat visited her in state— blue heavily laced frock-coat, large epaulettes, white duck trousers, massive sword and white cocked hat.

The horses are rapidly being put on shore from the steamers, and every day we send fatigue parties from each company to take them up to the corrals, three-quarters of a mile outside the town. The only road lies along the rails, winding in and out between the trucks and the engines. One man of the Dublins had his leg broken in negociating his unbroken Texan to the paddocks. Crushed between the railway trucks.

The police of Beira are very officious, and appear to delight in taking possession of the persons of anyone save those of Portuguese nationality. The other day they tried to arrest a six-foot Queenslander. He came upon two of them unmercifully beating a native. So, knowing little and perhaps caring less about the majesty of the law as embodied in the Portuguese policeman, he remonstrated with them on the inhumanity of their conduct.

Then they foolishly tried to arrest him too.

Most probably the treatment they received was bruited through the police barracks of the town, for I never afterwards heard of a Portuguese policeman attempting to lay his hands upon a Bushman. Certain it is that for some days one could distinguish upon the decks of the *Maori* two tall khaki-clad figures topped by the white helmets of the police force of Beira.

The following extract from the *Rhodesian Advertiser* explains itself:—

" On Sunday the long talked of bull fight took place at Ponte Gea (Beira), the object being in aid of the Church Building Fund."

This should provide ideas for those churches which are

casting about for fresh and original ways of wiping off their building or other debts.

There are bumboats with fruit and other commodities by the ship's side every day, though not so many as at Teneriffe, our calling place on the voyage out.

And so day succeeded day on the *Galeka* at her anchorage in the harbour at Beira. We knew not if we should have a day or a month here, so passed the time in buying wrist and ankle rings from the Kaffirs and in fishing from the stern.

Our officers lent us sea lines, we bribed the cooks for raw meat to serve as bait, and passed hours hanging over the rails. The only fish we caught were cat-fish, weighing from eight to twenty ounces. I caught either six or seven in less than two hours in my first attempt. It was a much better result than I have ever achieved in fresh water fishing. We did not eat the fish, but gave them to the Kaffirs, who were delighted. They are ugly, brown, flat-headed objects, with twelve long feelers projecting from their jaw, and they make a faint noise when dying.

Near the stern of the vessel were two small half-open sky-lights which ventilated the second-class bathroom. Just under the lights was the bath.

It was on one of these evenings that one of the Leicesters choose to indulge in the luxury of a bath. The water was deliciously cool and he lay back in utter content and splashed himself.

Suddenly, through the open sky-light, a large cat-fish came with a flop into the bath. As soon as it touched the water it waved its long feelers about and began to rush round. It looked like ugliness personified.

The man was dumb-foundered for a moment. He knew it couldn't be 'snakes' as we were allowed no intoxicants on board.

It must be an incipient attack of acute dementia.

Whatever it was, with a yell he sprang from the bath, and was outside the door almost before he knew what had moved **him.**

And a soft titter came from above.

CHAPTER II.

In the Bay—Beira.

THERE is a question which is purturbing us, a question which daily troubles our minds through the medium of our perspiring bodies. It intrudes itself upon us as we seek the deck awnings during the day; it worries us as we lay stripped in the streaming troopdeck at night. During the physical drill-with-arms it becomes literally the ' burning ' question of the hour, and we can hardly forget it in the cool siesta of the evening, when the banjo player tunes his banjo, and the sweet singers of the squadrons make melody for the sake of good fellowship, and for the passing of time.

When we left the shores of England, we left for a winter campaign. The authorities filled two kitbags for us with thick uniforms, and thick woollen underclothing, and thick woollen other things, and what the authorities did not give us, and in some cases what they did give us, our kind friends and solicitous relatives loaded us with over again. And now we are here, and we want the winter campaign to commence. The warm wollen clothing is all ready to don at a moment's notice. The tam-o'-shanters to keep our ears warm by day, the Balaclava caps for our comfort at night, the thick socks, the warm mits, and the worsted jerseys are all laid ready.

And the winter has begun, and instead of Balaclava caps we are ordered to wear our large sombrero hats during the middle of the day for fear of sunstroke. We must wear a handkerchief of some kind as a protection for our scorched necks, and the sunburnt Artillerymen who are with us, peer comically from underneath the brims of their immense sunhelmets as they pace the deck in shirt sleeves, or with no shirts at all.

And what we want to know is this ? If this is winter here, what in the name of all that's hot—(this isn't swearing, its only appropriate)—is it like when it is supposed to be summer ?

IN THE BAY—BEIRA.

This morning (May 7) we were honoured by a visit from Senhor Meyrelles, the Portuguese Governor of Beira. Over the bay came a large white boat with mahogany gunwales and shining brass rowlocks, impelled by six powerful oars which rose and fell with all but the precision of a man-of-war crew; over the boat a white awning stretched from stern to stern, and above this floated at each end the Portuguese colours. As she swiftly approached we saw she was manned by a crew of magnificent Mozambique natives of a very different cast of features to the Kaffirs who were loading the lighters alongside. They were dressed in spotless white uniform, with deep dark blue sailor collars, edged with three rows of white braid. Blue cuffs and breast pockets similarly braided. Below this, white waist cloths reaching just below the knee, left bare the dark chocolate-coloured legs and feet of the men. A touch of bright scarlet colour at the neck inside the open collar, and above the bare black woolly heads and round prominently boned faces and immense rolling eyes, and the picture is complete. The boat dashed alongside, and the party were received at the head of the gangway by the captain of the ship and the chief military officers on board. The Governor was a slightly-made dark man, with black moustache and short pointed beard, in navy blue mufti with a large white sunhelmet. The party also included several men and half-a-dozen ladies, a bevy of daintily-tinted muslins and lace. As the Governor left the boat the large flag at the bows was lowered, and as his foot touched the deck of the *Galeka*, a white ball of bunting danced upwards to the head of our foremast, and broke open to the breeze—the blue and white Portuguese colours—remaining there during his stay. They remained for luncheon and the boat went ashore. About two o'clock the boat was seen returning. It came leisurely round to the port side and made fast, whilst the oars were shipped, and the black crew lay about the seats in attitudes of ease. The broad chested coxswain looked like some dusky Eastern potentate, as he sat cross-legged upon the purple cloth which was spread over the stern seats, with one arm resting idly on the tiller, his white teeth gleaming and his large white eyes rolling along the sun-darkened rows of faces which looked down on him from the ship. A shrill pipe from the chief officer—the black crew spring to their places, and the gay party return to their boat, escorted by the captain and the colonel in command of the troops. The preceding order of things is reversed. The large flag is hoisted at the bows of the boat, the Portuguese colours flutter slowly down from our masthead, and the boat rows away to the tune of "Three times three" from hundreds of lusty British throats from the ship's sides and lower rigging. If the Governor of Beira has never heard a British cheer before, he won't forget this in a hurry. As the boat passes *H.M.S. Partridge*, a bugle rings out the "General salute," and so they pass onward across the harbour and are lost round a bend in the shore.

For some days the disgorging of stores has been going on from the holds of the *Galeka*. For days four derricks have been constantly swinging, and from early morning till dark, and even by the aid of the electric light (when sufficient lighters could be obtained) the cries of the sailors—'ook orn! 'awl up ee-asy! 'awl away! lower!—have mingled with our drill and with our food, have punctuated our pleasures and helped to pass the time while at our work. Each day the noisy tugs would tow to our sides strings of huge shapeless iron lighters—seeming all one capacious maw. Each morning crowds of cool-looking naked Kaffirs—or next to it—would descend into the dark depths of the holds, accompanied by the unfortunate ship's officer in spotless duck, without whose presence no work would be done. Each dinner-time the same crowd of Kaffirs—but steaming, perspiring, glistening oily Kaffirs—would ascend for their ration of rice, driven up by a limp-looking rag of a ship's officer, to descend again when the spell of ease was over.

And the ship seemed no lighter.

Hay by the scores of tons, bags of rice by the hundred, boxes of saddlery and horse equipment by the score, grim bundles of stretchers by the dozen, boxes, bales, bundles by the thousand, whose contents no one knew save those concerned; they all came to light from the dark depths below, gripped by the rapacious hooks, and swung aloft by the donkey-engines as though in child's play.

Surely enough stores here for an army; but still the work went on unceasing.

And the other boats in harbour were equally busy. Great square lighters, with flat tops, round which was erected a substantial fence of posts and rails, were towed to the side by the fussy black tug, and made fast. Then came the fun. These were the horse-lighters. See from the deck high above swings in mid-air a kicking, struggling animal, which with some difficulty is made out to be a horse. Head, tail, and feet hanging helplessly down, supported by a band under its belly, it looks the picture of an animal out of its element. But it swings over the side and is rapidly lowered towards the lighter. A pause, as it is poised above, and an active fellow clutches the halter which hangs from its head. A rapid signal, a sudden descent, and it finds it feet on a makeshift terra-firma. Then it has its turn. With two men hanging on its head, it kicks and plunges to its heart's content, till it chooses to think better of it, and to be coaxed and pushed into its place on the lighter, and the sling goes aloft for another kicking, struggling burden. And so, till the lighter holds thirty-five or forty half-broken bronchos, and is fetched ashore by the tug.

Whilst the unloading of the boat was proceeding the Kaffirs slept on board—on the roof of the stables, and they provided much amusement for the men. I have called them Kaffirs, and all blacks here are indiscriminately Kaffirs, but there are really three or four different races, the distinguishing traits of which can be easily noted. There are a group of Zambesi negroes. They are small-built slim looking men, and they have their front teeth filed to a point. By their side stands a tall, well-built black, with large holes in his ears. He is a Shangaan. Give a Shangaan a cigarette or a *cigar* while he is working—and the eye of the 'baas' is on him—and with a 'tank you' he will stow it till a more convenient season, not behind his ear but *through* it. This is absolute fact. There is one standing by that winch, in one ear is stuck a discharged brass Lee-Metford Cartridge case (it is plugged up and is full of snuff). In the other ear hangs an ordinary key-ring from which swings a moderately-sized rusty key, the whole hanging to his brawny shoulder. Many of them carry the empty cartridge snuffboxes. They seem favourite receptacles for the powdered luxury. The Kaffirs proper are a poor lot—Kaffir is a term of disgrace among the more aristrocratic tribes. Ask one of those ear-ringed negroes 'You Kaffir?' He will spring up affronted, and pointing energetically to his pierced ears, assure you 'Me Shangaan, me *no* Kaffir.' Some of the Shangaans wear little, black woolly moustaches, ragged and ill-nurtured, and small tufts of black beard on the chin.

And lastly, are one or two members of that indomitable fighting race, the Zulus. They have lost caste in their tribe—and are enforced to work and eat 'mongst the despised Kaffirs around. Nobly built fellows, proudly set even in their fall. Bearded like the Shangaans, their whole appearance at once differentiates them from the races around. Their hair near the forehead is interwoven in curious concentric circles with horse hair, and twisted strands of the same material encircle neck, wrists, upper arms, ankles, and above the calves. To these when in dancing or war costume they attach the ostrich plumes, made so familiar to us by the pictures of the last Zulu war. Perhaps, even now, they have been stowed carefully away in some dark recess of the kraal ashore, and after some extra degradation has been heaped upon them, these relics are brought forth, and sad memories indulged in of the times when *they* took an honoured place at the feast, or on the warpath.

Most of the blacks wore numerous twisted brass wire wristlets and anklets. These rings had been placed upon their limbs when they were 'picanninies' or babies, and never left them till manhood. They represented a kind of wealth. Of course, now their limbs were full grown it was impossible to remove the rings as they were. The men purchased these rings from the Kaffirs—they had to be cut off—and had them fastened round their own wrists as ornaments. The blacks were adepts at untwisting part of the wire and fastening it so that hardly a join could be seen. They would sing their native songs (?) and dance. At the end of each effort a shower of coppers and silver would reward the performer. One old Zulu was induced after much persuasion to try a war dance. It was a tame affair for a time, but as he waxed warm we thought it lively enough. For he looked so fierce, and jumped to such a height, throwing and warding off imaginary assegais with his shield, that the younger men began to look askance at him, and to edge a little farther away from the inner circle of the onlookers. Or we would get them to teach us their language, but you never knew whether they were talking Zambesi, Shanghaan, Kaffir, or mongrel Portuguese. Most likely it was a mixture of all the lot.

But enough of the Kaffirs. Never get to leeward of them if you can help it. And if you are compelled to have them round you, keep an eye on all your possessions, even to the sugar in your tea, or they will have it, and of the manner of its going you will know not.

But the welcome order to disembark has come at last. Four squadrons go ashore to-day, and the rest are to follow to-morrow. And there is pandemonium down below, for the men are packing their kit-bags. The tables are heaped in confusion, and the air is thick with the forcible language of the Leicesters blended with the rich brogue of the Ulsters and the Dublins.

Down the steps rushes a big-boned son of Erin.

" Did anywan here see two cakes o' soap I left outside me kit-bag at all?"

" Divil a cake. Ye haven't perchance heard of a tin of sardines I've lost?"

" I haven't. What kind av a tin was it at all? Should you know the tin if ye saw it?"

" An' indeed I shouldn't. It was the same kind as any other tin, and if I saw wan, shure it might belong to some other man who had bought some sardines as well as meself."

" Well, I haven't seen it. But what can ye expect at all if ye leave things about."

" An' shure what about the soap ye lost?"

And there is hilarity among the Irish, for their love of repartee is great.

The Babel goes on.

" There, that's done. Lend us yer towel, Tim "

" It's wet through. Besides I want to use myself."

And amongst the Leicesters there is a crash as a smuggled bottle of beer falls from the racks above.

" Hello, another ginger-beer gone."

" Ginger be blowed. It's *BEER!* "

The interest at once becomes general.

" What! no "—" Hold it sideways. Don't waste it. Drink,

man."—" But it isn't mine "—" Never mind. Hand it here. I'll pay the owner. There's not much spilt "—" Give us a drink "—" After me "—" Don't go too deep. *Whoa*!!"—" Oh, I say, old man, give us a smell "—" Why, you pig, you've emptied it." Sighs and groans.

And so all is confusion, save at one table set apart, where men are writing letters, for the *Galeka* takes our mails back with her. This table is almost hidden beneath a stratum of letter cases and note paper and nothing is heard but the scratching of pens and the muttered blessings of the rest as some sun-burnt Tommy emerges from his task, and thumps the table with ponderous fist in gumming down his envelope.

All day long it continues. Even after the advent of the electric lights and the swinging of the hammocks.

" There. Look at that, you clumsy pig."

" What's 'e done, Jimmy ? "

" He's t-t-t-tumbled out of his b-b-b-b-blooming hammock, and rolled across the b-b-b-blooming table, and upset my b-b-b-bottle of E-e-e-eno's Fruit Salt."

But on the morrow order reigned, and dressed in full marching order, the 65th paraded at 8.30 a.m. on the main deck, and were carefully inspected by the officer in command. But our troubles were not over yet. First one squadron left, and then another, and we were left till last. True we had permission to sit on the deck, and remove our rolled cloaks from our shoulders, but it was 2 p.m., and we had waited as patiently as we might for five-and-a-half hours before the paddle steamer, *Trevor*, came alongside for us. We now had an opportunity of admiring the graceful lines of the magnificent vessel which had been our home so long, and we gave three cheers for her captain and three groans for her cook as the distance widened between us. Rapidly we make our way across the harbour to the landing stage, and at a quarter-past two on Friday, the 11th day of May, of the year 1900, I first set foot on African soil.

* * *

And the wonder again grew. If this is the winter in Africa, what on earth is the summer like? And Old Sol answered in a silent, but unmistakable way.—

" If you wait here so long, I'll be happy to show you ! "

CHAPTER III.

On African Soil.

The Romance—from the transport deck—

AFRICA! Stanley's dark continent, the home of 'Jess' and of 'She.'
Northward those dark dense forests are threaded by streams whose sands are mingled with gold dust, where dusky Arab merchants trade glass beads and shoddy knives for ivory, white —*and Black*. They are the home of the rogue elephant, the monster man-crushing constrictor, the dreaded gorilla. They are the haunt of the pigmies and the worshippers of fetish. True, these things are some thousands of miles away, but fancy annihilates distance—imagination knows no mileage.

Over there in the eye of the sunset, lies Rhodesia, with all the charms of a little known and undeveloped land. The dream and the life-work — or part of it — of the colossal-minded Rhodes, the empire builder, the modern Warwick—whose hills are made of wealth waiting for the plucking; whose plains are roamed by the zebra and the giraffe, the eland and the wildebeeste, the blesbok, and the graceful antelope.

Turn southward, and there lie the rich plains of the Transvaal —the theatre of war. War! the field on which thousands of heroes are battling for empire—are playing the game, the chances of which are glory, or a no less glorious soldier's death—thousands clad in khaki as are we, and whose epoch making labours we have come to share. Over there are the stricken fields of Magersfontein, of Belmont, of the Modder. Over there the indomitable Baden-Powell is still making his gallant stand, and yes—somewhere over there lies Pretoria.

Nay, why go so far afield. Here at our feet these Portuguese jungles and forests are the home of big game. Its glades are filled with wild pig and with buck. Its creeks are haunted by the sluggish alligator, and do not the men of the horse guard return daily aboard with tales of horses startled by the scream of the hyena and the roar of the king of beasts himself?

Turn which way you will—the air is big with romance. For this is Africa, whose hidden wealth no one knows, whose dark secrets no explorer has yet fathomed.

The Reality—on land.

On the jetty the Company shook themselves to settle their equipment into place after the crowding of the steam tug in the run from ship to shore. Then they looked round, leaning on their rifles.

Their first sensation was one of heat. The second, one of disgust—mingled with heat. The third, well, there wasn't a a third. It was overpowered by the force of the breathless quivering heat. From the jetty to somewhere inland—one hadn't the energy to look where—ran a toy railway (I believe they call it a narrow gauge, twenty-four inches from rail to rail) unevenly raised above the surrounding surface on an embankment of sand. To right and left stretched a disused sewage farm, to all appearance. On every side dry black mud, looking treacherous even in its dryness. For the most part clothed with a coarse yellow herbage, not interwining and carpeting the ground as with civilized grass, but each root or clump standing a few inches from its fellows on its own little plot of dark earth, as though even they were sick of themselves and their surroundings. Dotted here singly, there in clumps, standing up dark and sapless from the sere and yellow herbage, are desolate looking stumps which in their season may or may not put forth leaves and become luxuriant tropical plants. For do not forget that this is winter. To us, as we passively endure the parboiling of the sun, it is a fact that is hard to remember.

Scoring the face of the land in all directions are gullies, winding 'nullahs,' dry watercourses, which in the wet season will be purling streams—of fœtid mud. Here and there stand beehive shaped Kaffir huts, of dried grass and bamboo, with steep heavily thatched roofs and deep overhanging eaves. Raised on piles on the low ground, and resting on the soil where it is higher, some boast a little courtyard filled with animal life. Here is a typical one. A lean sheep, two goats, half-a-dozen little black pigs, and innumerable fowls share the courtyard—and the hut—with their human owners. While chained to a pole in the centre an immense grey ape keeps solemn watch and ward over the whole of the happy family. Occasionally a native, of loftier aspirations than his peers, will ape the iron dwellings of his white neighbours and the result will be an artistic construction of nondescript, or rather of no shape at all, the materials of which at one time formed the outer coverings of bully beef and New Zealand mutton. And through it all, like a vivid yellow wale upon the black face of the earth runs the sandy embankment of the jetty railway.

The word is at last given to move, and under repeated injunctions from the officers not to hurry but to take things easily—an injunction hardly needed—we pick our way along the rails of the embankment. Past gangs of dusty legged Kaffirs pushing railway trucks; strings of Kaffirs carrying boxes of stores; parties of Kaffirs, shovel in hand, mending embankments. Past huge iron sheds in course of construction, studded all over with Kaffirs on roof and walls, like flies on a ceiling in summer; each individual Kaffir trying to outdo the rest of his tribe in making a din with a hammer; past Kaffirs at work and Kaffirs waiting for employment; old Kaffirs who grin, and young Kaffirs who stare; surely it is the plague of locusts over again, with the locusts by some process of evolution changed to perspiring Kaffirs.

The rail from the jetty was only a branch, and five hundred yards away joined the main Beira railway, on which we found our train waiting for us. Stripping off our equipment and our tunics, we marched back slowly for our kit-bags. But first, by order, handkerchiefs were knotted round necks (to protect the spine) and we transformed ourselves into the semblance of Italian organ-grinders by ruthlessly tearing down the sides of turned up sombreros, and pulling down the brims all round our heads. Their jaunty beauty was gone, and we regarded each other with disgust.

And truly every inch of shade is welcome. As we stand waiting, the sun doesn't shine as we in England understand it, the heat tumbles down in solid bucketsful. Such lavish generosity it has never before been our lot to experience, and it fairly overpowers us. Our sombreros provide a little shade—for our feet, and a man may look round in vain for his own shadow. If he lifts up his feet he will find he is standing on it. And we catch snatches of the talk of two Portuguese railway officials as they pass—

"Gude day. It ees quite windy to-day."

"Yes, quite a pleasant breeze."

Great Scott! and this is a windy day in Beira.

Slowly, with many halts, our belongings are transferred from the landing place to the train, and we are told off to our compartments, ordered aboard, and at last we are off. Our long sojourn on shipboard is over. The hammock will henceforth give place to the tent; the deck planks be replaced by the jungle and the veldt.

Take one of the wagons of which any of our English luggage trains are made up, I mean those low-sided trucks in which granite and other stone is carried. Cut it down to about sixteen feet by five. Put it on six little wheels placed away under the body until the truck far overhangs the rails on either side. (The truck is five feet wide and the rails but two). Over this put a flat corrugated iron roof. Board in the ends and leave the sides open and you have our travelling carriage before you. Put together a long string of these carriages, attach two comical little engines—made, by the way, at the Falcon Works, Loughborough, as the plates on them attest. In *each* carriage pack sixteen men in full marching equipment, thirty-two kit-bags, and sundry big boxes of store, for we carry three days rations with us, and you have complete a troop train on the narrow gauge section of the Beira-Salisbury railway.

To compress sixteen pairs of legs into this confined space is evidently impossible—at least with any degree of comfort. So in a few minutes each side of the train presents a long vista of dangling limbs clad in putties, boots and spurs. The plan has many advantages. It makes more room inside, catches any stray breeze that may be stirring, and affords a fine view of the country through which we pass. Moreover as we are on a

ENTRAINING AT BEIRA—*p. 32*—Photo by *C. Lucas.*
WOOD FUEL ON BEIRA-SALISBURY LINE—*p. 34.*—Photo by *P. S. Inskipp.*

single line there is no immediate danger of amputation from passing trains.

As we start, I attempt to jot down a few rough notes, but the bumping and the swaying is so violent that the pencil every moment makes short excursions in every way except the right one. So after vainly attempting to read the last three lines I have written I am compelled to relinguish my literary efforts till a more convenient season.

Leaving behind us the flats of Beira—quite willingly—in a few minutes we are passing the horse paddocks and we look curiously and perhaps a trifle anxiously at our future mounts. There are several thousands of them, long tailed, unkempt looking horses, but of beautiful bone and build: many of them more than half blood, with the making of flyers. Enclosed in huge paddocks, encircled by an eight feet barbed wire fence, loosely plaited in places with branches and grass, they stand or move restlessly about in great droves of many hundreds in a drove. But jealously guarded by deep bronzed Australians, who ride here and there at a loping canter with that careless lounging seat peculiar to the Colonial stockman. Many are the ugly gashes caused by that cruel wire as almost daily mad rushes are made by the unbroken animals; and more than once the horse guard have told us, a panic has broken out, followed by a stampede, and whole lengths of the fence have gone down like grass before the solid charging body of a thousand maddened horse. Farther on parties returning from water are passed, each man with four horses, and they wave their whips in salute as they swing by at an easy canter.

Then away from man and his works, across vast stretching plains covered with a long coarse grass, where the traveller on foot would in places be lost to view. At rare intervals the herbage is broken by clumps of noble trees of strange shape and foliage, and more frequently by shrubs whose palmate-shaped leaves proclaim their near relationship with the tenderly cherished daily-sponged palms that grace our tables at home.

We pass a sudden depression in the land, and the vegetation recedes, leaving a glimpse of black muddy morass to foretell the fate of the venturesome traveller who shall attempt to traverse these Portuguese swamps. Everywhere butterflies of gorgeous hue flit with jewelled wings from flower to flower, and more than one dashes through the open sides of the truck as we traverse the waving wastes.

Now we plunge into the jungle and do not leave its shades again until our destination is reached. In places like, and again strangely unlike, an English wood, some of the large trees, save for something foreign in the twist of their limbs and the contour of their tops, almost remind us of the familiar oaks and elms at home. But beneath is a thick interlacing undergrowth of luxuriant shrubs which flit by us in a bewildering feast of foliage, whose variety and form 'twould exhaust a botanical dictionary to describe. Huge grasses grow thickly on the banks, almost encroaching upon the rails, and every now and then we have to quickly draw back our heads as the sturdy bents sharply brush the carriage sides and sweep over the iron roof. The forest is thickly studded wfth huge conical anthills from fifteen to thirty feet in height. They are evidently of ancient construction as they are invariably covered with a thick growth of bamboo and large trees, the result probably of the freshly upturned soil. Occasionally the course of the railway has cut through these monuments of insect labour, leaving the clean cut section, and showing plainly the myriad vertical cells of the interior structure.

No coal is used on this line, the engines burn wood fuel, and every few miles a plentiful supply of logs are heaped up by the side of the line. Near each heap is a group of native huts of fragile build, whilst set apart stands a bell tent or a hut of better and more substantial make. It is the little settlement of the woodcutters and their white ' baas,' who at a salary of £30 a month, lives his lonely life in the fever-filled forest, and accomplishes his daily task—no easy one—of keeping his negro crew up to working pitch.

A slowing up of the train, and we stop at a small station, a couple of iron buildings and a neat enclosed garden filled with large leaved banana trees. Opposite is a large native kraal, and the negroes bring us large bottles of clear limpid water from the spring close by. We drink greedily. This is our first day in Africa; with another week's experience we should think twice before touching it, however tempting it may look. The negroes are great snuff-takers and wear round their necks little bottle gourds or the pointed end of a buck's horn to hold the much esteemed luxury. They make their snuff from a large black pod filled with handsome black beans, with scarlet tips, called a ' Kafir bean,' and if they get a discarded cigar end to grind up with this they esteem themselves the most fortunate of men.

But thrice welcome surprise to parched and thirsty men; near this station stands a dark skinned Portuguese with several bottles of limejuice for sale—genuine long flower-embossed bottles of Rose's limejuice. Our mouths water in anticipation. A dozen eager outstretched hands—

" Here, boss. How much?"

" Five sheeleens, sare."

" Five blazes! They elevenpence-halfpenny in England, you d——d Jew. I'll give you two shillings."

" No, sare. Five sheelens, sare."

The sight of the bottles is tantalising beyond endurance.

" Here, I'll give you three shillings."

A shake of the head, and a warning whistle from the engine.

" Four then."

But the man is obdurate, and eventually two bottles come into our carriage at five shillings a bottle. We are yet but new to South African prices. We have much to learn.

Once more we are off. Now we emerge from the jungle, crossing far-reaching park-like glades of golden-hued herbage broken by noble trees and wanton growth of shrubs. Large birds rise from the grass, startled by the train, and overhead flocks of pigeons swiftly cross the glade. Buried in the depth of the forest are negro kraals—collections of flimsy huts of plaited grass with high pointed roofs. Some are mere sloping shelters, while others have no walls, but consist simply of a roof supported by half-a-dozen bamboos.

And now the sun sets and darkness falls over the jungle. It grows rapidly cooler, and tunics are again donned as a protection from the malarial night mists. The negro huts we pass are illuminated by the fires burning in the centre of their floors, and from every part of the forest and the glade swells the evensong of the insect life and bell-like note of the frogs. It is the vesper hymn of the African jungle which nightly rises from the myriad life of the undergrowth and the swamp. On every side it fills the air with an unbroken undertone of sound; and as the strangeness of it grows upon us with the darkness, conversation is hushed, and an unaccustomed silence falls upon the men.

And so through the darkness, until our destination—called '23 mile peg'—is reached. There is no building or sign of life, simply a large water tank raised on high by the side of the line. We scramble out over the sides of the trucks and fall over each other in a narrow space between the train and a high, almost vertical bank, for we have stopped in a rather deep cutting. With some difficulty the baggage and stores are unloaded, and following our officers we scramble up the bank and stumble for nearly half-a-mile through long grass and across dry gullies, till we suddenly come upon tents, lines of them, showing in the light of the newly risen moon. They are the squadrons who have preceded us. By the time we have pitched our tents our belated tea is ready—corned beef and ship biscuit, with hot coffee. We are quite ready for it after our ride. Afterwards each man is served out with a quinine tabloid, and turning into our tents we roll ourselves in our blankets and are soon wrapt in dreamless slumber.

And so passes our first sleep on *terra firma*—our first night on African soil.

CHAPTER IV.

The Camp in the Jungle.

THEY called it " 23 mile Peg " on the maps, but the name was too ugly for the African Paradise we were encamped in. So we soon changed it to "Twenty-three Mile Creek" which sounded more romantic in our ears. The name of course explains itself ; we were twenty-three miles from Beira.

The station existed in name only, for there was to be seen nothing but a long siding, a water-tank and an iron bridge over the creek. At the side of the line was an open space worn bare of grass and beaten hard by many feet, for this had been an important native kraal. The population to-day consisted of but a few dozens, a miserable remnant who were employed as wood-cutters and water-carriers for the camp. And the dismantled huts of those who had gone stood deserted and forlorn amidst what were once well kept gardens, now but wastes of wanton vegetation where the pumpkin trailed amongst the ruins, and bore small white fruit, parodies on its former products. Some of these huts, now but broken frameworks, were clever examples of interlaced bamboo work.

From the open space a wide sandy path wound through a tract of fire blackened grass land, then passed by the guard house. This, which was used as a guard room and magazine, the stores being also piled up around it, made quite an imposing appearance amongst the native huts around it. It was a large square building of thick mud walls, through which window-panes, filled with very dusty glass, admitted a modicum of light to the interior. It had evidently been the former residence of some white man, who had lived here in some capacity or other ; what, it would be hard to say. The thick thatch roof far overhung the walls, and formed a deep cool verandah, admittedly the coolest place in camp during the heat of the day. At the back was a small lean-to bedroom, the broken and decaying frame of a bamboo bedstead—built into the wall and floor—still standing there. The house stood in a large garden filled with banana trees, some but a yard in height, others large and full grown.

But for nervous sentries the guard house had its terrors, for it was literally infested with immense grey rats, and many are the yarns told by the guards of the fearless precocity of those animals in the still hours of the night. On the first night the 65th Company furnished the guard, they had a prisoner handed over to them, and they describe with much glee the extreme alarm exhibited by the man, when on suddenly awakening in the night, he saw by the feeble rays of the lamp three large light grey rats, one on his face, the other two sitting on his chest and contentedly trying to make a late supper off the buttons of his greatcoat. A large fire was always kept burning in front of the guard house at night and answered a double purpose. It provided warmth for the guard—for the nights were cold—and scared away any wild beasts which might be prowling around.

Leaving the guard house, the path crossed a rather steep dry watercourse, and then passing through low undergrowth for a short distance opened into the immense glade in which stood the camp.

The camp itself varied very little from other camps, and save as a setting for the animated and picturesque life which pulsated through its lines, calls for very little description. Of course it consisted solely of small bell tents. There were no large marquees for officers' or sergeants' mess, canteens, concert tents and other luxuries of home camps. We were here on grim work intent, and the gaud and the glitter was replaced by sober-clad soldiers moving silent and phantom-like amidst surroundings of their own hue, with which they merged and became all but invisible. Removed a short distance away were the tents of the officers, and their mess room consisted of a large roughly built hut, with wide-stretching grass roof and no walls. Under this the tables and hammock-chairs were placed. Standing on the edge of the jungle, it also caught any shade afforded by the large trees on its borders.

But the chief glory of Twenty-three Mile Creek was its

THE CAMP IN THE JUNGLE.

splendid water supply. The distance from the camp to the creek was some three hundred yards and the path lay through the jungle, crossing several deep gullies, which had to be negotiated by means of the trunks of trees which had fallen across. To cross the rounded trunk of a tree in heavy boots with a bucket of water in one hand and the other hand full of pots and pans, and a ten feet ditch underneath, is not easy, but we became proficient in the exercise before we moved from the camp. The path ended at the creek, a shallow stream rippling over a bed of finest sand, teeming with small fish, clear as crystal and deliciously cool. To thoroughly understand our delight it must be remembered that for five weeks we had not known the taste of *cold* refreshing water. Soon after we sailed from Southampton the water—which was almost lukewarm throughout the voyage—became tinged with a reddish sediment. It was the rust from the new water-tanks. This tinge became more pronounced as the voyage lengthened, until during the last week or so, as we approached the bottom of the tanks, we were drinking water of the colour of deep sherry, but without its clearness. No water was taken in at Cape Town as it was thought it would last until we reached our destination. Of the way it did last, the following extract taken from my diary will eloquently tell :—

"*May 9th.*—Had our first experience of ship's beef to-day. I saw the casks opened last night, large pieces of meat swimming in brine, and thickly encrusted with salt. . . . We had practically no water on the ship. The drinking water was cut off at 7 o'clock this morning, also the washing water. The salt beef was the last straw. The men went in a body to the orderly officer with their meat. He showed it to the ship's officer who sent them back saying it was all right. Had a miserable dinner. Salted beef, bad potatoes, and no water, with a blazing sun to increase our thirst. During afternoon word was passed that the orderly from each table might fetch a bottle of iced water from the 2nd Class galley. There was soon a string of waiting orderlies that reached half-way past the stables. Before half of them were served word was passed along that the water had entirely given out.

" No tea at tea time, as there was no water to make any. Bread and butter only. Very dry meal, and men growled a great deal. . . . Later on some water was got on board, and at 7-45 p.m. tea was served. As the ' cookhouse ' sounded, from every part of the ship ironical cheers broke out, and the ' devil's tattoo ' was beaten on every tin pan that came to hand till the noise became absolutely deafening."

After this, one can understand the keen pleasure with which we hailed this unlimited supply of water which might have been drawn from the coolest English spring.

A few yards below the drinking place, over which a sentry always stood, the creek widened out and formed a bathing place for the officers. Lower down was another pool about five feet deep, and sufficiently long for a short swim. This was used by the men. So fascinating were the attractions of the creek that special hours for bathing were fixed, and men were prohibited from going into the water between the hours of 9-0 a.m. and 1-0 p.m., and after five o'clock at night. No soap was allowed to be used in the creek as the water lower down was used by the natives for drinking purposes. At first water was boiled for the men to drink, but the water of the creek being analyzed by the doctors was found to be perfectly pure, and the troops were allowed to drink it in moderation.

By the path leading to the creek stood a tree which, could it but be planted in English soil, would be a sight which people would come from all parts of the country to see. Imagine four slender trunks growing to a great height at the four corners of a square, and standing about five feet apart. These trunks were about two feet in diameter at the base where their buttressed roots branched out in all directions, in many places exposed to view by the summer rains. At every three or four feet each trunk threw out a short sturdy limb across to the adjoining one, with which it became incorporated, until all the way up on each side was a lattice work of diamonds and squares. The whole tree thus formed an immense vegetable chimney with massive openwork sides and a hollow shaft from crown to roots. At a height of sixty or seventy feet it branched out into a noble spreading crown of large-leaved foliage of darkest green. As the slanting rays of the sinking sun shone through the forest, piercing the tree from side to side and changing it into a black silhouette of Brobdagnagian lace-work, it became one of the most striking pictures in the jungle around.

THE CAMP IN THE JUNGLE.

It was not till many weeks afterwards, when we had left it hundreds of miles away, that I learned the life-history of the "Ladder Tree," as the men habitually called it.

Many years ago there grew in that spot a tall and stately tree which reared its shapely head in pride above the other trees of the forest. But pride goeth before a fall. The tree was of course covered and festooned with parasitic creepers as are nearly all trees in these African wilds. Each summer they hung down in chains of pendant flowers; each autumn saw them die, unheeded by the monarch of the woods upon whose limbs they hung. But there grew about the roots of the tree a creeper of a deadlier kind, a more insidious foe, which lived and flourished and did not die as did the other kinds. And year by year it grew higher about the trunk of the doomed tree, throwing strong tendrils from stem to stem, and locking the trunk more securely in its death-grip. At last the tree died in the unequal struggle and the parasite grew stouter and stronger in all its parts, and threw out branches and leaves in place of those of its victim. And the once stately tree decayed and crumbled to dust in the embrace of its destroyer, and in time there was nothing of it left, and the parasite stood alone, an empty living prison, and an object of wonder to all who passed that way.

Such is the life-history of the "Ladder Tree" of Twenty-three Mile Creek.

There were no parades on the day after we arrived, but part of the morning was occupied in putting straight the tents after the hasty pitching in the darkness, and a few other necessary duties. But our hearts were not in the work. Ever and again, as we almost mechanically performed our tasks, impatient eyes were cast in the direction of the dim, leafy recesses surrounding us. To be sure, we had been forbidden to wander more than a mile away from the camp. A mile, forsooth! Here were a thousand young adventurous bloods, freshly taken from desk or farm, who four months ago had as much idea of seeing an African forest as they had of exploring the mountains of the moon. It was preposterous. And so the officers must have realised, for no notice was taken of the many flagrant breaches of the regulation which took place.

For my part, even before rising I had firmly resolved that these mysterious forest glades should yield some of their secrets before the sun had set. So, gathering two boon companions, we armed ourselves with a pocket compass and stout flexible canes each terminating in a neatly cut fork,—for the benefit of stray snakes—and sallied forth in search of adventures. Crossing the creek at the watering-place, we scrambled up the opposite bank and were soon in a leafy ocean of strange plants and trees. Before we had penetrated many yards all sounds and signs of our comrades were left behind, and the camp might have been a hundred miles away for any sign of human life that showed. But what cared we? We were in a new world.

The spot we were in was but thinly timbered. Walking was difficult owing to the many creeping plants which caught the feet at every step, until we struck a negro path, leading away we knew not where, and this we followed in greater comfort. On every side were bushes of varying height and size. Some armed *cap-a-pie* in a panoply of long sharp thorns, others throwing aloft exquisite sprays of lightest foliage, which rose to their height, then curved earthward in languid grace, as though weary of the ardent wooing of the sun. Nimble creepers, laden with blossoms, threw themselves from shrub to shrub. Springing up amongst the larger plants and standing about two feet in height were olive green orchids thickly dotted with brown spots; whilst here and there a cactus covered with sturdy spines made us keep a wary eye open in the interests of our garments. Now, one of us, intent on some novelty in view, would suddenly sink through the carpet of matted creepers into a dry watercourse several feet in depth, and the silent forests would ring with the merry laughter of the others. In some of these ditches, we found great centipedes, nearly twelve inches in length, which I am sure ought to be re-named ' millepedes ' from the astounding number of legs they possessed. But, with all their legs, they were venomous-looking creatures, and we decapitated all we came across. I remember some years ago a gentleman lately returned from the tropics presented me with a quantity of foreign parti-coloured ' beans ' or large seeds, half black and

half bright vermillion. These seeds he told me were called
'native beads' and were gathered by the blacks and strung
together, forming necklaces with which they adorned
themselves. I had always included these amongst my choicest
and most curious possessions, and here in the forest they hung
around by scores, their pods turned black and burst open by the
sun, revealing to view the vivid touches of colour inside. It
was truly an *embarras des riches*.

There was a marked scarcity of bird life — in
this part of the jungle at least—and the few we did
see flitted from tree to tree in silence. That is the thing
which strikes you most in these forests—the absolute silence.
If when alone in their depths you stand still for a few moments
a feeling of awe comes over you, and the flutter of the wings of
a startled bird will cause you to start and look round. We did
not see any monkeys on that particular morning, though they
were met with many times during our stay. But everywhere—
in the air, on the ground, wherever a bare patch of sand was
warmed by the sun—were gorgeous butterflies. They rested on
the leaves to sun their wings, they feasted on every flower,
whose colours they emulated and rivalled. Time after time
did my companions impatiently wait for me, whilst I tried to
determine the family and group of some specimen by comparison
with those I have met at home. The 'blues,' 'fritillaries,'
sober-winged 'hair-streaks,' and 'admirals" both white and
red, I could recognise, also a minute 'blue' no bigger than a
house-fly. But the majority were entirely strange. There were
sulphur yellow wings with black velvety borders, large whites
merging into orange, 'admirals' with yellow bars in place of
white, 'blues' with tails like a 'hair-streak,' and one monarch
of all clothed in richest dark brown, with a large spot of metallic
blue set like a jewel in the centre of each wing. But I must
leave this fascinating subject, or my readers will wax as
impatient as did my companions, though I trust they will not
use the same expressions as they did.

The trees now grew more thickly, and our progress became
proportionately slower. On every hand lay large trees, just
where they had fallen, monarchs of the forest that had had their
day. Their dead branches formed entanglements through which

our way had to be broken; their trunks were but outward shells of bark through which our unwary feet crashed into beds of decayed and rotten wood as we thoughtlessly leaped from trunk to trunk. Two deep—three deep they lay where they had fallen perhaps years before. Crossing each other at every angle; here stark and bare, there covered with a pall of matted creepers, they presented a thorny path to our unaccustomed feet. Farther on large tracts were covered with gaunt leafless trunks charred and burned by the flames of recent bush fires. Stark and dead they stood and the mid-day sun took advantage of their bare tops and poured in a flood of light and heat, filling the newly-opened glade with myriads of many-hued insects, which filled the forest with a quiet murmur of humming wings as they darted from flower to flower in the very joyousness of living. Once more we pierced the dim shades, where the leafy ceil above us was so thick that the sun's hot rays were filtered of their heat and a welcome coolness laved the brow.

Round every large tree flourished a colony of bamboos. Notice yonder huge canes. From a base thick as an athlete's arm they taper higher and higher until, piercing the branches of the trees, they spring many feet above their topmost crests, and wave their crowns gracefully to the movements of the untrammelled breeze. A chaos of bushropes and parasitic creepers flung in wanton luxuriance from limb to limb, or hung in festoons, some gemmed with blossoms, others but trailing chains of vivid green. Large bunches of fern with overlapping leaves shaped like jagged fingers of seaweed, clung in clusters to the trees, appearing in most unexpected places. At last bursting through the final belt of vegetable maze that barred our path we came upon a scene of wild beauty which far surpassed all that had gone before.

At our feet a deep ravine, clean cut in the face of the land as by the savage blow of some gigantic sjambok, traced its sinuous course. At the foot of the precipitous banks, some twenty feet below, flowed the creek on its way campwards. It was the dry season and here and there in the bed of the stream its low waters had laid bare banks and bars of silvery sand. Between these islets the clear limpid current rippled and flowed with a gentle murmur until lost to view round a distant bend, whilst small white-bellied fish momentarily glistened in the sunlight as they darted over the shallow places to find a refuge in some dark pool underlying the steep banks and shaded by drooping rush and bamboo clumps. Along the edges of the ravine stood rows of forest monarchs, their branching tops filling the creek with chequered lights; their roots, washed into view by the rains of many summers, lined the sides of the creek, and buttressed and held together its steep banks by their spreading fibres. At intervals along its course, the stream was bridged from bank to bank by fallen trees. Many of these, falling short had buried their heads in the bed of the stream, whilst in places they lay so thickly as almost to choke its course. Up the steep bank the sand lay wreathed in heaps, encroaching amongst the tree butts far into the surrounding jungle, and plainly showing the height to which the waters rise in the season of the rains. Farther along the trees mingled their foliage above the stream, throwing the objects beneath into a deeper gloom shunned by the winged life which elsewhere darted and hovered over the face of the water.

This we saw, the whole enchanting picture framed and bordered by the luxuriant foliage of the primeval forest.

From this point we followed the course of the creek, making our way along its bed by means of fallen tree and sandbank. We had often to take to the jungle for some distance when the waters stretched from bank to bank in deep dark pools, into which as we drew near large grey rats and other strange beasts dived with a splash. It was necessary to keep a sharp eye upon these places as they were the haunt of the cruel alligator in the winter time. In the dark depths they would lay submerged, all but their eyes and snout, and patiently wait for any ill-fated animal which should stray within their reach. In one place the stream had been roughly dammed with interlaced bamboos, all but one narrow passage, in which was placed the end of a curious native fish trap. It was a conical rush-woven basket so constructed that fish could enter freely, but once in, exit was impossible until they were taken out by the black owner of the snare.

The farther we penetrated the wilder and more tangled became the jungle. We were now some miles from the camp.

Narrow tracks and paths ran down to the water's edge, and in the sand we saw numerous marks of delicate hoofs, crisp and clear as though made but half-an-hour before. Near the deer tracks, too, were larger and more significant 'spoor'— footprints larger than our outstretched hands, edged with the divided marks of toes. And upon a thorn-bush I found a tuft of tawny hair, whether from the deer or from the coat of the owner of the claws we were not versed in forest lore sufficiently to say. We looked at our flexible canes. Viewed under these circumstances they did not seem to be half the formidable weapons we had deemed them at the start. I consulted my watch.

"By Jove, didn't think it was so late. We shall miss tea if we go any farther."

"Yes, I think we had better turn back. I shouldn't like to miss my tea."

"Not on any account" said number three, relieved at our unanimity.

So, pulling out our compass, we made a bee-line for the camp. That is, figuratively speaking. For if any respectable bee had described the same line in his flight as we did in our stumbling course over tree trunks and round dense thickets, I am afraid his character for sobriety would have been lost for ever.

Though pitched in such an oasis of natural beauty, it was never forgotten that we lay practically on the Portuguese East African coast, a notoriously unhealthy one (we were but 18 feet above the level of the sea) and every precaution was taken against the attacks of the sun and of that silent insidious foe— malarial fever. Quinine was frequently served out to the men. No man was allowed out of his tent during the heat of the day unless wearing his sombrero, and tam-o'-shanters were compulsory after sun-down as a protection against the mists and the heavy dews. Men were encouraged to wear handkerchiefs round their necks on parade and were forbidden to sit on the grass after the sun had gone down. In particular, no refuse must be thrown or nuisance committed by day or night in any except the proper places. Thanks to these wise precautions, there was wonderfully little sickness in camp. During the first

THE CAMP IN THE JUNGLE.

day and night nearly everyone was attacked with sharp colic pains, and some men were really ill with them. But I believe this was in many instances caused by drinking the cold water of the creek whilst the sun was high and the body in a heated state. Severe diarrhœa was also rife amongst the men, and in a few cases this turned to dysentery. But otherwise there was practically no illness in the camp.

Our dress for parades was lax, to say the least of it, but it was eminently suited to the climate and to the work we had in hand. Stout riding breeches, heavy boots and puttees were a *sine qua non*, rendered necessary by the rough jungle we had to traverse. Above that we wore nothing but a shirt, with sleeves rolled up to the elbows and a bandolier across the shoulders. Also, if a man was wise, a handkerchief tied round the neck. That, with rifle, belt, and bayonet, and the sombrero with brims pulled well down, completed our costume and equipment for work in the jungle. But one thing was insisted on. It was immaterial whether a man wore braces or a simple belt ; he might wear a pink shirt or he might wear the regulation ' grey-back ' ; but there was one thing he must do : he must bring upon parade a specklessly clean rifle. This was our ' drill order,' and day after day we marched into the wild country round the camp and practiced attack and defence as adapted to the novel surroundings.

Sometimes we were working through long coarse grass in many places as high as our heads, and again through thick woodland where at a few yards distance a man would be lost to view amongst the close-set trunks. We had to work our way by compass and every precaution had to be taken to prevent detached parties from being left behind, when they would be lost almost to a certainty. On one occasion we came across traces which an officer, an old African hunter, said were made by zebras. On the same day, when crossing a narrow glade, we noticed a human skull suspended from the topmost branch of a dead bush — a native fetish of some meaning unknown. Naturally several of the sacreligious of the 65th laid their heads together and resolved to annex this skull as a desirable trophy for the front of their tent. But, on the following day, after tramping the jungle for nearly half-a-day, they had to return in disgust, as they were unable to find the right glade.

Or, marching across the railway to a large opening in the forest clear of trees, we would have battalion drill. The immense glade was covered with the usual coarse African grass, which as we entered it came nearly up to our knees. To our front it stretched away to the far border-line in one unbroken sheet as level as a hay-field. As the movements commenced we looked forward to having an easy time. But as we advanced farther into the herbage the ground dipped in hollows here and there and the deception of the level looking grass became painfully apparent. Instead of reaching to our knees in these places it rose above our waists and in more than one hollow it actually brushed our chins. The ground beneath, which we could not see, was covered with lumps varied here and there by small ant-hills, and through it all we were expected to keep our dressing and correct intervals. I remember we sometimes grumbled at the rough ground at home when at battalion drill, but what the choice spirits of the ' L ' Company would have said to this I fairly shudder to think. Over this ground we executed the old familiar manœuvres—the movements in column and quarter column, the deployments, the formations in echelon or in line and many others which forcibly brought back the happy days in camp with the 1st Volunteer Battalion of the Leicesters. It was all practice, but one can imagine it was no child's play with the sun pouring into the glade with its usual intensity. One day an officer—one of ' Our's '—had a narrow escape. The sharp eye of our company sergeant-major suddenly saw a large snake twined round a tall wisp of grass, with his head within easy striking distance of the officer's hand as it hung by his side. There was no time to give warning, but in less time than it takes in the telling, the poisonous reptile—for nearly all African snakes spell death—lay writhing on the ground, cut in two by Sergeant-major Hobden's ready sword.

A rigid guard was kept around the camp, especially at night. Each company contributed its daily quota to the guard. They mounted for twenty-four hours. It is related how a driver of one of the trains, which stopped at the place, had visited the camp, but on attempting to leave after dark he found his way barred by the sentry. Only a few yards away stood the train, the engine hissing impatiently to be off ; but the sentry was inexorable, he would listen to no blandishment or explanation. Eventually the driver had to return to the guardhouse and obtain the kindly escort of the corporal of the guard, who conducted him to his train. Some of the more remote posts were rather trying to nervous sentries, and many were the tales of round glowing eyes and lithe stealthy forms by which they had been visited during their lonely watch. One night a sentry discharged his rifle — they were always armed with ball cartridge. But all he bagged was an extra day's guard from the Colonel for alarming the camp. On another occasion the ' spoor ' or tracks of a lion were found all among the lines when morning broke. I do not suppose we should have slept quite as soundly had we been aware of the midnight visitor snuffing round the outside of our thin canvas walls.

At every hour of the day and night long trains, drawn and pushed by two or three engines and laden with men, horses and stores, passed our camp on their way northwards, and sometimes more food and stores would arrive for us, when a whole company would be turned out on fatigue, no matter at what hour, to carry the boxes up from the railway to the camp. More than once did we turn out of our beds into the chill night air to shoulder heavy boxes and stumble with them over the uneven ground in the darkness up to the camp.

The food at the camp was abundant in quantity but sadly lacking in variety. It was simply corned beef—' bully beef ' or ' embalmed beef ' were its pet names—and hard ship biscuits for breakfast, ditto for dinner and the same for tea. This diet, continued day by day for weeks, was apt to pall upon one.

It was scarcely to be expected that the same military discipline and bearing would be found so deeply inculcated amongst a force eighty per cent. of which had four months before never heard the crisp voice of the drill sergeant, as amongst regular troops who had lived for years in an atmosphere of pipe-clay ; and whilst on board the *Galeka* this laxity was to a certain extent overlooked. But once under canvas the reins were tightened and the men taught the difference between an officer, a non-commissioned officer and a trooper, and that rules and regulations were framed to be

D

observed, and not broken through like circus hoops. But there was very little crime, and court-martials were few and far between.

Snakes of all lengths—from eight inches (one of the most deadly) to four and five feet—were fairly numerous around the camp and our roving parties of amateur explorers seldom returned without one or more of these reptiles hanging from their canes. By the side of, and in the creek they were always to be found, and if you asked the natives about this species they would inform you in broken but very significant English— " he bite you—fifteen minutes you fineesh." They were not often met with in the camp itself. One day a large one was discovered coiled up under the bed on which lay a sick officer, and was promptly despatched. On another occasion a party of twelve of the 65th, of which I made one, had been told off for fatigue duty under a corporal. It was not work at which either honour or glory in any quantities were to be gained—in fact we were picking up the empty bottles and tins which had been carelessly thrown down around the guard house, and wheeling them away in a barrow. I was chatting to the man next to me and we both stooped to pick up an empty beef tin which lay near us half filled with dead leaves. He secured it first, when on lifting it a small greenish-black snake with silvery white belly—one of the eight inch kind—shot out from the tin and struck savagely at the man's face, less than two feet away. Of course we soon sealed its fate, and proceeded with our work, laughing at the promptitude with which the man had dropped the tin. Careless and free from care, such incidents lent a spice to our lives and we welcomed them as providing breaks in the monotony of drill and camp life routine. It was not till night and the darkness, when you alone lie awake amidst the regular breathing of your sleeping comrades, that the thinking comes, and you realise with a shudder how near you have been to death.

We had a pet in our tent—a self-installed one, if the truth must be known. It was a large dark grey frog, which had probably wandered from the creek and lost his ' return half.' I found him under my bed one morning just after reveille had sounded. This was the commencement of our acquaintance.

At first we were for pitching him out, but he looked at us so mournfully, in such a without-a-friend-in-the-world kind of way that we let him stay, and each morning it would be a matter of conjecture under whose bed he would be found. The bugler seemed to be his especial favourite, a liking which was by no means reciprocal. He stayed with us nearly a week, but one wet night he returned to his sorrowing relatives and we saw him no more.

On any patch of sun warmed sand, did but an old log lay near, you might stand and watch whole families of gaudy little lizards, if you approached softly enough. Moving swiftly as the light streaks which played on their lithe little bodies, they darted here and there upon the unwary flies. But one move of your foot and the place which seemed filled with them a moment before would be a mere patch of sand, hot with the rays of the sun.

I was fortunate enough on one occasion to witness a cure by a native doctor, though he was not clothed in the insignia of his profession—the elaborate if scanty costume of skulls, cross-bones, dried frogs, lizards, etc., etc., which is the tall hat and frock coat, so to speak, of the native medical practitioner. He was dressed in a waist-band and engaged in the menial occupation of chopping firewood for the cooks with an axe. The cook's assistant had been badly stung by a large ant-like insect and was making a fuss about it. Learning the cause of the outcry and also a description of the winged cause of it, the native chattered away to the man for a minute in Zambesi—probably exhorting him to " buck up and be a man "—and then disappeared into the edge of the jungle. In a few minutes he returned with three or four specimens of the same kind of insect that had inflicted the sting. Making a shallow hole in the ground he put the insects into it, piled hot embers round them, and charred and dried the bodies almost to an ash. Pounding this up, he made it into a paste and applied it to the wound, which had swelled considerably. In less than five minutes a watery discharge came from the place, and with this the pain disappeared. By evening the swelling had gone and the man had almost forgotten the fact that he had been stung. It was literally curing him with a hair of the dog that had bitten him.

On the 19th of May the two battalions were formed up in quarter column and the Colonel in command announced to us the glad tidings of "Mafeking's relief." We cheered as we had never cheered before, and the air was thick with flying hats for the gallant Colonel and his no less gallant men, who for more than seven long months had successfully resisted the most determined efforts of the wily enemy.

Three days later we had a distinguished visitor. This was no less than the Hon. Cecil Rhodes. He arrived by a special train from Beira, and, escorted by Colonel Parke, made a short stay and a tour of the camp on his way to Rhodesia. A tall, broad-shouldered man, his face seemed lined with care and looked much thinner than the preconceived idea I had of him, from the photographs I had seen.

I understand he made the remark, during his visit, that we had come out on 'a huge picnic'—a view which, taking into consideration our later experiences, was a most optimistic one, to say the least of it.

And each night as the darkness fell, the forest song began, and from every herb and every creek and pool, the grasshoppers and the frogs vied with each other in chanting the tale of another day completed, and another night begun. Many a time have we turned a little way into the jungle paths, and, seated upon the nearest fallen tree, have listened to the evensong of the insects, till with unspoken consent, conversation dropped away, and we sat filled with the harmony—and our own thoughts.

In the cool of the dusk, too, our own concerts were held under a large spreading tree in the centre of the camp, and the dark forests around echoed with the old familiar English songs; and seated around on our blankets we forgot for a time that we were aliens and parted from home by the width of half the world. Our concerts were more than once dimly lit by huge forest fires, which, though miles away, sent an unconscious tremor through the frame as the sky above flickered with their reflected flames.

At last the time came when we must say good-bye to this African Eden. Our kits had been packed for thirty-four hours waiting for the train which might arrive at any time.

THE CAMP IN THE JUNGLE.

The punctuality of these trains was of a very erratic quality. I wonder how those of our friends at home who fret and fume if their train is five minutes late would like to sit on their carpet bags for *twelve hours*, and not dare to go back to their homes, as the train might arrive at any minute. I think the following short extracts taken from my diary will explain better than any other language I could use how those of us who were not born patient had that virtue thrust upon us. They also throw an interesting sidelight on several other vagaries of these ' bantam trains ' :—

May 11.—Every few miles our engine had to stop for water. The driver once pushed things a little too far. Instead of renewing his supply at the tank he should have done, he ran on, thinking he could just reach the next tank. But his calculations were at fault. His train came to a full stop just 200 yards before he reached the tank, and the engine being uncoupled, all hands had to turn out and *push* it to the water.

May 18.—G—— and party went to the station in full marching order to proceed to Umtali by the train due here at 2 p.m. But it was 8-30 p.m. before it came. The other day our farriers had a still longer wait. They went down at 6-0 a.m. and the train did not come in till 6-0 p.m.

May 20.—A train taking up a company of New Zealanders and 100 horses stopped here for a few minutes. They had plenty of food but no water on the train, so we climbed down to the creek and filled their water-bottles. There was an engine at each end of the train, and the driver of the hinder one was partly drunk and in an evil humour. He had been causing a lot of trouble by not acting in concert with the other engine. A few miles before reaching here he broke his engine away and they could not climb the next stiff incline till he thought fit to come and help them. They have a four days' journey before them. I don't envy them. There will probably be trouble with the driver. The New Zealanders said they should have half killed him before now, but they were afraid he might refuse to drive the engine at all, and they would then be stranded at the next hill.

May 22.—I was on guard by the station. The sick are being sent farther north to-day, and at 5 p.m. they were brought down, two on stretchers. The 50th Squadron, who were also going, were marched down and sat on their kitbags waiting for the train. They waited till 8 p.m., but there was no sign of it. As the mists were rising, one of the tents was struck—the inmates being distributed amongst the other tents—brought to the side of the line and pitched as a protection for the sick. At 8-30 the train came and the sick were loaded up. But shortly afterwards the ' fall in ' sounded and the whole of the men in camp were marched in the darkness to the line a short distance from the station. The ambulance train had run into some trucks which projected too far from a siding and several of the carriages were off the line. The sick got out as well as they could, and those on stretchers were lifted out. Then after much delay and about two hours' hard work, the carriages were lifted by main force on to the metals, and the train went away. They had a narrow escape from going down a bank.

May 23.—We leave to-day. Train due at 11-30 a.m. Carried stores, camp kettles, etc., down at 10-0. At 11-0 struck tents and packed them on luggage trucks which were waiting here for the engines. Had dinner at 12-0. Most of us had packed our spoons away in kitbags expecting it would be bully beef. But it was boiled rice, so we manufactured temporary spoons from pieces of bamboo. As the train had not arrived by tea time, the camp kettles were fetched back, unpacked, and we had tea. The sun was very hot, and there was no shelter in the camp after the tents were down.

Eventually it did arrive, and at 8-0 p.m. on the 23rd of May we moved off from Twenty-three Mile Creek after a camp of twelve days' duration. The supply of the usual open wagons—described before—was not adequate enough for the company, so eleven of us were put in a small grain van—a box with iron roof and large door at the side, which had to be kept open all night to prevent the devoted occupants from suffocation. No seats, save kitbags ; no light save the fag end of a candle found in someone's haversack ; no food, save a tin of bully beef and four biscuits ; and no room to stretch our legs in sleep. We made ourselves as comfortable as the circumstances permitted, which was very uncomfortable indeed. Rumbling and shaking along—by high banks faintly lit by countless fireflies, like the lamps of a miniature city ; over the broad Pungwe river, the most unhealthy spot in the whole line, where five of the Scotch engineers gave their lives in the construction of the bridge ; past dark stations where we stopped, so the miles were slowly covered. Someone attempted to start a song but it quickly died a natural death ; which was just as well, as otherwise it would soon have died a violent one. At last, at 12-30 a.m., the train pulled up and coated figures stumbling by in the darkness apprized us that this was Bamboo Creek, our next camp. We fell in, with our two kitbags before us, all mixed up with the Hampshires who came in the same train. After being extricated from the other company—you couldn't recognise your dearest pal in the darkness—we slung our rifles, and shouldering our two heavy bags, stumbled for some distance along the rails, till turning aside, we found ourselves among tents, lines of them, evidently a large camping ground. The ground had once been occupied by bushes, which had been cut down, though as we found to our cost, the stumps had never been dug up. Reaching a bare patch at last we dumped down our belongings with a grunt of relief and went back for the tents. These were pitched with some difficulty, and sorting out our kitbags by the light of two dim lanterns, we unpacked our blankets, and, not waiting to search for the softest spot, were, at 3 a.m., soon stretched in a deep, well-earned sleep.

CHAPTER V.

Bamboo Creek.

ONE day, many weeks after we had left Bamboo Creek, I chanced upon the following sentence, written shakily in pencil, upon the walls of a Rhodesian Hospital:

"*Bamboo Creek, the white man's grave.*"

It was only the work of an idle moment, scrawled by some unfortunate when the fever had left him strength and the power to think. But for the truth of it let the little row of graves in the cemetery at Bamboo Creek bear witness; for the bitter proof of it go to the Umtali graveyard, to the last resting-place of the score of British and Colonial soldiers who lie there. To its fever-laden flats we owe the teeming hospitals of Umtali and Marandellas. Of Umtali, where over ninety men were crowded into a building intended to hold but fifty; of Marandellas, where in addition to the iron hospital of nearly forty beds, fifty large huts of mud and thatch had to be built to cope with the incoming sick. Many a man who saw his name among the pitiful list of those invalided home, owes to Bamboo Creek his shattered health and the wreck of the bright hopes with which he left his country and his home.

We arrived at the place in the dark on the day following a heavy rainstorm, and the dank earthy smell of the ground filled us with vague presentiments of the evils to come. We woke with the morning light and looked at it, and the sight of it after the luxuriant beauties of our last camping place filled us with loathing and disgust. A large stretch of black looking soil covered with rows and squares of dirty looking tents, bare hard trodden earth in the rising parts, soft and sticky black earth in the hollows. Bounded on the front by the railway, running between dykes and miscellaneous pits of smelling stagnant water crossed by planks; at the back by a belt of coarse yellow shoulder-high grass, save where it was burnt off, and the blackened tufts and stumps alone remained above the dark earth; on the right by a vast miry horse paddock; on the left by waste ground covered with a sparse growth of shrubby vegetation and a plentiful sprinkling of empty bottles and tins and the varied refuse of a camp.

The camping ground, before it was worn bare and hard by the feet of the many bodies of Colonial troops who had preceded us on this roundabout route to Rhodesia, had once been studded with trees of varying size. We had first discovered this in the small hours of the morning of our arrival, when, laden with heavy boxes of ammunition and stores, we had stumbled and tripped over the short stumps left standing by those who had felled them. To be sure, wide paths, well-defined in the daylight, wended from the gates of the camp to the locations of the various companies, but the daylight was not always with us, and the stumps were.

As a rule when a man feels sore with grievances and campaign worries; when he thinks his officers have sat upon him a little too unmercifully; or that he has had more than his fair share of fatigues, he at once feels better when he enters his tent, the canvas home where he can fling himself down, and kick out his legs, and growl to his heart's content amongst the hanging kits and water-bottles and the rest of his belongings, amongst the surroundings which from continual use have acquired a certain atmosphere of homeliness and rough comfort. But even this consolation was out of our reach. For if we sat down in our tents, we could only inhale the smell of the floor and curse the way our kits were getting soiled. At first we had cut down the long grass to make a covering for our floor to at least hide it from view, but this was forbidden, as the grass was calculated to harbour refuse, and it was considered easier to keep the tents perfectly free from this when the floors were bare of covering.

Upon the day following our arrival, a general parade had been ordered, and in the interest of the scene our sorrows were forgotten for a time. It was an assemblage typical of Britain in South Africa. There side by side with the Imperial Yeomanry from England and the Scotch company of Sharpshooters, stood the Irishmen from Dublin and Belfast; and facing us were the rows of deeply-bronzed faces of the sons of Greater Britain, the contingents from Australia and the land of the Maoris. It was the first opportunity we had had of seeing the Colonial bushmen on parade, and their stalwart and workmanlike appearance excited our admiration to the utmost. And when the Colonel commanding the troops announced that he had called us together upon the birthday of her Most Gracious Majesty the Queen, and asked both Britons and Colonials—common subjects of one sovereign—to join in giving three hearty cheers in Her honour, it was hard to tell who had the lustier lungs, the men from the old country or the men from the new.

We had barely been in camp a day before the grasp of the malarial fiend began to tighten around us. Men fell sick fast. Each day the number on parade grew smaller and smaller, and the dreaded malarial fever, which before was but a name to frighten the timid, had become a very real thing amongst us. The two or three small hospital tents soon grew full and an extra fatigue party was required whose duty it was to throw water on these tents to keep the interiors cool. The doctors were the hardest worked men in the camp, for their labours ceased neither by night nor day. The parade for the sick was held at 9 a.m. each day, and it resembled more the parade of the squadrons than of their sick. Soon the hospital tents could hold no more and the sick and the hale had to make the best of it in their own tents. Many a man could only reach his bed when entering his tent by stepping over one or two blanketed forms which lay supine and still through the days and the nights. The fever took away all desire for food, and to get them to take even the barest nourishment was a work of tact and patience. The majority of the men fought against it bravely and only gave in when on parade under the hot sun. It had become most unusual for a parade to pass without paying its toll to the long list of the sick. The 65th suffered heavily, but even they were not the worst. In one of the Yeomanry squadrons but two men remained fit for duty out of a full section of 28 men, and each day these men took their turn, one to stay at home as tent orderly whilst the other fell in on parade—the sole representative of his section. The camp was gradually becoming a vast hospital, and men wondered at the order which had brought us to this place, and wondered more as day followed day and no instructions came to move us.

The men were also attacked by acute diarrhœa and dysentry, and it cowed and saddened us to see the wan pinched faces that wandered about the camps, some crawling weakly alone, others too weak for that, leaning on the shoulder of their comrades. No man knew but that his turn would come next, and to be tied thus in a hotbed of disease, whose fangs fastened indiscriminately upon the strong and the weak, was infinitely worse than facing the mouths of hostile guns.

So day slowly followed day, each revolution bringing its spell of misery, each claiming its share of men for the overflowing hospital tents. Were we a camp forgotten? Should we be left here till of the squadrons none would be left to do the work and fill the duties? Men wondered.

Across the railway line were the 'flats,' stretches of burnt bush, where the numerous Kaffirs employed by the railway built their kraals and lived their squalid lives. Their chief, a sturdily built truculent looking black, with a face as ugly as they make them, was dressed—or partly dressed would perhaps be nearer the truth—in a straw hat, a blue pilot jacket, and a dirty coloured waist cloth. He had a peculiarly harsh voice, and upon the resumption of work after the mid-day rest, its strident tones would bring from the low doorway of each hovel a teeming crowd of partially clothed black men, who with the silent tread of many naked feet, passed to their work, each one casting a curious glance at the khaki clad stranger who watched them.

At one end of the 'flats' was the white cemetery of Bamboo Creek, a small square of ground, but thirty yards each way, fenced by rough posts and wire. When we came it held four graves, marked by white crosses of roughly-shaped wood with black paint inscriptions. When we left three more had been added, the graves of three ill-fated troopers of the Imperial Yeomanry, victims of the malarial fever of Bamboo Creek.

The food which tempted the fastidious appetites of the sick and pretended to satisfy the healthy ones of the hale was:

Breakfast, bully beef, biscuits and coffee.

Dinner, biscuits and bully beef.

Tea, bully beef, biscuits, and tea.

This we had on every day of the week without exception, from our first landing in South Africa. Our officers did what they could, and on many occasions gave tins of milk and jam to the men. Fortunately for us again, several sutlers had followed us from our last camping-place, and had set out their wares just beyond the gates, where a tin of condensed milk or a one pound tin of jam could be had for one shilling and sixpence, and other things in proportion, so if we had money we could vary our diet a little. We knew not who was responsible for our insipid diet, we only knew that our teeth ached with breaking adamantine ship biscuits, and that we loathed the sight of bully beef.

And in mockery came the recollection of the advice we received before sailing: " There are two great rules for the prevention of fever in Africa, and the chief of these is to keep the body well nourished with good and sufficient food."

The very surroundings of the camp were horribly appropriate; for previous to our coming, numbers of horses had died of ' blue tongue ' (the South African horse sickness), and the carcases were not buried, but dragged by oxen into the long grass half-a-mile from the camp, where they were left to the beasts and birds of prey, a cordon of evil-smelling carrion. Above in the blue vault sailed on slow motionless wings the vultures which fed on them, and which a regimental order forbade us to shoot or molest.

Truly fit guardians for the hell beneath them.

There was at least one loop-hole of escape from the death trap we were in, of which I oft-times availed myself. It was the jungle.

Away northward of the camp ran a narrow path. Through the burnt scrub, through the belt of overtopping jungle grass, and past the circle of dead horses, from which the black vultures flew with heavy satiated flight as you passed, and by which you tightly grasped your handkerchief to your nose. Another tract of grass, and then crossing the bed of a half-dry creek, all traces of man disappeared and you were in the real jungle, the luxuriant jungle of Portuguese East Africa. Giant palms towered above, bearing leaves large enough to thatch the side of a roof, each leaf armed along its edges with cruel saw-like spines, which effectually protected the bunches of hanging fruit from invasion. Here were trees clothed with creepers covered with masses of flowers in white and yellow; flowers whose tempting sweets drew clouds of butterflies of every imaginable hue. Here were narrow native paths winding through the tall grass and the trees, paths where the familiar voices of the camp were hushed, where reigned a stillness in which almost the beating of the heart was heard; a calm broken only by the constant hum of the insects and occasional mystic rustlings in the long grass which might mean nothing, but which, on the other hand, might mean a great deal. For Bamboo Creek was well known to be one of the best districts for big game in the whole of Portuguese East Africa, itself the happy hunting ground of the hunter of big game.

Many were the strange sights and sounds seen and heard by the night sentries, and retailed with bated breath in the mornings, and a visit to the body of a horse on the morning following its demise and funeral cortege showed in unmistakable signs the work of the large carnivora which haunted the jungles around.

I remember on one occasion I was busy with my net around a large blossom-covered bush near the creek I have mentioned, and there arose all at once a huge clatter from its banks as though a cyclone had wandered into half-a-dozen tin shops, mingled with unearthly yells and shouting. I stood undecided whether to keep my post or run for my life. Suddenly up from the banks burst several of our venturesome Yeomanry yelling at the top of their lungs, and one warrior banging the zinc lining of a biscuit case for dear life. When they had recovered sufficient breath, they explained that they had been chased by a huge reptile several times as long as themselves as they were crossing the bed of the creek. It was a large alligator, and after chasing them for some yards, it thought better of it, and plunged amongst the reeds which lined the banks, at which I did not wonder, for the pandemonium they raised was quite sufficient to frighten a much larger reptile than a simple African alligator.

At this season the creeks were very low, and in many cases were nearly dry beds. After the hot sun bath outside it was like entering another zone to break through the foliage and descend the banks of some dry creek. Overhead the arching trees met and plunged the bed below into a shade which seemed at first almost darkness to eyes fresh from the intense light above. Then for a cool stroll along the fine sand and rounded pebbles of the bottom, evading the occasional deep pools of dark still water which remained, and where every log had to be closely scanned before too near an approach was made. Birds cry and twitter amongst the shrubs along the sides, grateful for the coolness, and butterflies with boldly marked wings in black and yellow, only found in such places as these, rise in scores from the sand as you pass.

During our stay some of the men obtained permission to organise small shooting parties from the camp, and various kinds of buck were shot and brought in. Once or twice lions and zebra were shot at, but none were brought home as trophies.

The railway and station were always full of interest for an observing eye. The narrow-guage railway ended here, and the journey westwards was continued on the broad guage. The station and telegraph offices were in a long range of verandahed iron buildings, standing at the back of a shady grove of huge banana trees. These trees were planted in rows and some attempt at the picturesque had been made by arranging grottoes and circles of white spa rock around their base. Everywhere were Kaffirs in fifties and hundreds unloading stores and moving along large solitary railway trucks. As the truck slowly proceeds they all sing a monotonous chorus to one old villainous-looking black who sits on the front buffer and gives the time. This continues in an even droning rhythm until a hard bit of pushing is reached, when the voices increase in shrillness and become quite excited in tone, to return again to the same monotonous chant as the difficulty is overcome and the truck runs along easily to the pressure of a hundred bare black shoulders.

The rare arrival of a passenger train brings a cosmopolitan lot of travellers. Large bearded Englishmen, smaller sallow faced Portuguese, English officers and their sable retainers, rough looking miners, going to the Manica mines above, and a dozen other men and one or two ladies whose occupation could only be guessed at. Such were the passengers by one train I stood watching.

BAMBOO CREEK.

Some of the Kaffirs when their work is finished carry with them a curious musical instrument. Upon a flat hollow wooden box are arranged two rows of small iron strips, attached to the box by one end and raised an inch above its surface at the other. These are of different lengths and are tuned to the different notes. The instrument is held in both hands and the ends of the iron strips are twanged by the thumbs. The drowsy character of the music brought forth is a happy match for the monotonous singing of the instrumentalists.

Below the station stood the Bamboo Creek Hotel. This was within our bounds, though just beyond it was the Portuguese settlement where we could not go, partly because it was forbidden ground, and more so because there was a sentry always there to stop us.

But the hotel itself. Up four wooden steps, across a wooden railed-in verandah, and you step at once into the realms of Bret Harte, you have surely entered the saloon of some backwoods mining camp. You are on the *qui vive* for the blustering voice of the traditional mining bully and expect to hear the bark of the revolver of some Deadwood Dick of the penny dreadfuls.

A large matchwood boarded bar-room, at the far side a long counter, backed by the usual bar-room shelves and a glittering array of coloured bottles and flasks. The clink of glasses mixed with the hum of a score of conversations, a shifting population of slouch-hatted, shirt-sleeved, booted and spurred, and picturesquely dressed men, with brown faces and sun-scorched arms. At one end the click of billiard balls and the old familiar sounds of " No, in off the red " ; " Spot the ball, there " ; " Four to plain." The whole seen through reeks and wreaths of the smoke of bad shilling cigars and black cake tobacco. Behind the bar the sallow faces and the broken English of the attendants, here and there a soft-footed negro servant, passing silently, and every few seconds the crash of a broken bottle, for as fast as a bottle is opened and emptied it is not put back again into the racked boxes 'for return' as in England, but is flung through the open window at the back of the bar to join the broken dozens that have gone before.

All liquors are a shilling per glass. The bottle and glass are placed before you and you help yourself and pass the bottle back. The prices are rather different to those of the English smoke-room. Bottled beer is 2s. 6d. the half-pint, 4s. 6d. the pint bottle; draught beer is unknown; sodas are 1s. per bottle; clarets and wines 6d. per glass; cigars 1s. each. You can purchase Martell's three star whiskey at 10s. the bottle. Attached to the bar are dining rooms where a very good dinner of four or five courses—including such out-of-the-way dishes as African buck and boar's head—may be had for 4s. Many of us enjoyed here the first real square meal since we left England. The hotel catered for the officers of the camp, and their mess was held here every night.

But from bar-room, or jungle, or where you choose to go, there was but one return. To the fever-ridden camp, to the supine forms in the tents.

Our condition attracted the attention of the Rhodesian Press, and later on a leading article appeared in the *Rhodesian Herald* which created such a demand for that particular number that the article was reprinted in a subsequent issue in order that those who wished might read the fatal truths it unfolded.

I think I need not scruple to quote in full the article in question. It was written in connection with the burial at Salisbury of Lieut. Andrews, of the 70th Squadron of Sharpshooters, who died there from disease contracted in Portuguese East Africa :—

Reprinted by request.

In deference to repeated requests from members of the Rhodesian Field Force, we repeat the underneath article from our issue of the 11th inst. It appears that the demand for the papers far exceeded the supply, and we are confident our readers will bear with us in this act of courtesy to the men who are fighting for them:

"FIGHTING FAR FROM THE FRONT.

On Monday afternoon we had a melancholy reminder of the presence of the unseen enemy that has worked gaps in the ranks of our brave forces in the field. More deadly than the Mauser bullet, than the iron hail of the shrapnel, as the returns of our casualties show, is the fever foe. The units of the Rhodesian Field Force have beyond a doubt been subjected to a far severer health test than, exclusive of the Ladysmith garrison, have any others in South Africa. From the time of their arrival in Beira, the struggle began. They were many miles from the fighting front, but sickness sought them out in their paddocks, in the black oozy mud on which their beds were made, in the doubtful water which tempted their thirst under the hot sun. The Imperial Yeomanry were, if possible, more unfortunate than their fellows. They first became acquainted with the veldt some few miles from Beira. In the thick jungle adjacent to a swamp, where the drinking water filtered through the decayed undergrowth of many years, their camp was pitched. Bamboo Creek was hardly a change for the better, as the hospital returns and three newly-dug graves quickly showed. Climatisation under the circumstances was a dangerous process, and on the high veldt at Umtali the abnormally full sick list was evidence—although the corps is composed as it is of fine vigorous men, typical of the young blood of Britain—of the ill-effects of the delay in the low country. The gallant soldier to whom we have paid our last respects is one of a score or more of good men whose lives have been sacrificed. The movements of a large army are never without the scarring of sickness, but if a Commission of Inquiry into the health of the forces of the colony is deemed advisable by the House of Commons, some small part of its attention might advantageously be given to the case of the Rhodesian Field Force while in the transit from the ships to the base camp."

CHAPTER VI.

Across the Rhodesian Border.

FORTY-THREE men in an open truck. Most of them sick with dysentery and fever, and some unable to rise to their feet without the helping hand of a chum. With the forty-three their baggage. Also sharp-cornered boxes of biscuit, bully beef and miscellaneous stores. Where a man clambered in there he stayed, unless he climbed over the body of his neighbour. And this through two days and a bitterly cold night between.

But what cared we? We were leaving the fever-stricken camp of Bamboo Creek for the healthy mountain ranges of the Rhodesian border.

The order had come suddenly. By mid-day on Sunday our kit-bags and bedding were packed, and in our blue deck uniforms —donned to save the khaki from the engine sparks—we waited expectant. The hours rolled on and the day dragged to a close, and still we waited. Darkness came, and reluctantly we unpacked our blankets and lay down to sleep; not knowing then if the arriving train would turn us out at midnight.

It was near mid-day next day when it did come. Eight horse-boxes (seven of them filled with horses for the Rhodesian Artillery) and one open truck. The worst of the sick were put in the eighth horse-box, and the rest packed in the open truck. There was but room remaining for a fourth of the squadron, and when 'A' Troop was chosen, the disappointment of 'B,' 'C' and 'D' was pitiful to witness. And so at half-past twelve on the twenty-eighth of May we slowly steamed out of the miasmal fever pit of Bamboo Creek.

Past the Portuguese settlement—a collection of verandahed tin shanties arranged round an immense 'plaza' of bare earth, cracked and seamed with the sun, and planted round with bananas.

Then to the jungle. Mile upon mile of coarse sun-dried grass of straw-like size and nature, thickly sprinkled with small green-foliaged trees. Here and there the monotony broken by a vast stretch of fire-scorched veldt, the black earth but partially hidden by the blacker tufts of the grass roots, and over which, from the blackened trunks of trees, the dead foliage hung in red festoons, forlornly.

Once, as the engine snorted up an incline on the tree-bordered track, the hot air grew more heated and a sneezing epidemic seized the men. As we rushed onwards things grew worse instead of better, and, the incline breasted, the cause was not far to seek. Some miles ahead a fierce jungle fire was burning and it was the pungent smoke from this that made sport with our olfactory nerves. Above the tree-crests hung drifting clouds of smoke, and, even in the bright light of day, fierce tongues of flame would now and then show luridly above the wealth of undergrowth. Our road sloped gently downward, and for this we thanked our luck. Faster and faster we gather way, till the rattle of the wheels makes difficult coherent conversation, and we watch in silence the scene in front of us. Now the flames are easily distinguished as they lick with hungry tongues the smaller trees to their destruction. For many hundred yards it spreads and creeps along the side of the line, but the bare railway strip has barred its progress further westward. We are abreast of it—the bursting and crackling of reeds fills our ears, and our eyes are rendered all but useless by the pungent driving smoke. But the hungry roar of the flames is answered by a derisive shriek from the engine, and with a rush we emerge from the stifling fumes into the pure air of the forest on the farther side.

On, and less than half-a-mile away a native kraal stands in a clearing, and at the doors the savage owners sit shaping their weapons or curing the skin of some beast captured in the chase. They seem regardless of the fire raging within a short distance from their dwellings. Possibly they know that should danger threaten, they could easily carry their few household goods across the line, and—— well, if the village goes, a few hours' work will build another one.

Now the line gradually ascends to the Chiruvo Hills, and

patches of mopani and other large trees break the outline of the smaller jungle growth. The land is well watered, for the hillsides are seamed and broken by numerous water-worn valleys, and from the banked-up rail we look down upon deep dark leafy ravines where the leopard and the cheetah love to lurk, and from the banks fringing borders of rare fern and feathery palm droop in graceful curves to the life-giving stream below.

" What station's this, Johnny ? "

" Amatongas, sare. You wait feefteen minutes here, sare," and the courteous station-master — or his equivalent in Portuguese—waves his hands with a deprecatory little gesture towards where a dozen dusky sons of the soil are throwing up short-cut logs of wood into the engine-tender. Out we tumble, and almost before one can look round a wood fire is boiling arrowroot for the sick, and our busy cook comes staggering up with a huge kettle of oily boiling water from the engine wherewith to make tea for the hale. And the yellow-faced little Portuguese, who has fever written on his face if ever we saw it, fusses around and wonders at the energetic ways of the Englishmen.

A few of us explore the precincts of his wooden hut, and we regard with wonder and an irresistible desire to laugh the coiffure of a native dandy from a neighbouring kraal. His hair was gathered up in little bunches, each one bound round with a light-coloured grass except at the end where a little tuft of dark hair stood out in the quaintest manner imaginable. His head reminded me of nothing so much as a hill covered with miniature palm-trees, with light yellow stems and a tuft of black fuzzy foliage at the top.

We didn't laugh for fear of hurting the feelings of this black Beau Brummel, but we had to leave him and look at something else, or we should have done. Just then another native came up from the spring, bearing aloft a large calabash of clear cool water. The Portuguese assured us it was " ver gude," and we made a raid on it, but our officers would only let us drink it sparingly. What was ' gude ' for a Portuguese might spell ' fever ' for us. The sable water-carrier had gone in for a more durable kind of decoration. He was embossed. On forehead, cheeks and chest his flesh was raised in regular patterns of lines and spots—a kind of tatooing in relief. We were prepared in our wanderings to see *Nature* in her most abandoned moods ; but when this dusky savage smiled at us through features composed mainly of warts and wales, we were fain to admit that here her wonders were eclipsed by *Art*—and Fashion.

And, as we leave, the light fails rapidly, and the chill of the African night comes down on us like a pall. Close wrapped in cloaks we make our dispositions for the night. A keen wind rises and sweeps through the forest, and we grow too cold and cramped to sleep. The gradients are severe, and as the engine coughs and slowly mounts them, great fiery sparks and glowing flakes of tinder fly past or in amongst us. Far forward, perched upon the slightly convex roofs of the horse-boxes, one sees dim shapeless forms. They are our black ' boys.' One has ridden the whole day on the cow-catcher of the engine. Now, rolled from head to foot in their gaudily-tinted blankets, they are huddled in sleep, though how they manage to maintain their position upon the roof of the swaying trucks is matter for conjecture. Suddenly there is a scuffle and a burst of flame amongst them. A flying fragment of fire from the engine has ignited the coloured handkerchief in which ' Jonas ' enveloped his head before he went to sleep. We see the burning fabric flung o'er the side, and ' Jonas ' pulls his blanket round his head, and again disposes himself to slumber, not without blaming his ' fetish ' for his loss, were our ears but sharp enough to hear it.

This is an ever-present danger on this line. Sometimes one will see at a station a pile of half-burnt merchandise, taken from a truck which has been fired in this way. And it will probably continue until an adequate number of covered-in trucks are provided, or the promising Wankie coal-fields are opened out and coal fuel substituted for the logs of wood at present used.

And so the long weary night passes. With many a halt for wood and water, and more than one long wait in a siding for other trains to pass.

It is the breakfast hour.

Over the sides of the trucks hang the legs of the men.

Above are the rows of sun-burnt faces, innocent of a wash since the morning before. In one hand an enamelled mug of muddy-looking coffee. In the other a square of ship biscuit of stony hardness, thickly overlaid with Crosse and Blackwell's best strawberry jam. Swinging their feet in lazy content, the attention of the men is pretty equally divided between the biscuit and some of the grandest scenery in the East African hinterland, passing in panoramic review before them. We have climbed the range at last, and our coffee was made at Chimoio, at a height of 2,400 feet above the sea. We have passed the dangerous 'fly-belt,' for at Mandegas, guarded by stalwart Bushmen, are large paddocks of horses shipped through Beira.

I well remember a good story told by one of these men by the camp fire months afterwards and many hundred miles from where it happened. I chanced to say I had never seen an ox-team till I saw them in South Africa, and I think the Bushmen regarded me for a moment as something particularly green. For, as they said, oxen are largely used in Australia for the transport of timber and other heavy articles.

"But," said one, stirring the fire with his boot, and his eye glistened with innate fun as he said it, "*We* are perhaps as green in other ways. I remember some way back a mob of us were guarding horses at a place called Mandegas, amongst those Portuguese Johnnies. Lions were plentiful—attracted by the horses I suppose,—though we had seen none as yet. Only one of our crowd had ever seen a lion, and that was when Tim Wylie went to Sydney on a burst—and *he* saw it in a show. But we should all know them when we did come across them, for we had all read bags about them and their terrifying roar in books and other things.

"We were all tired that night. We had been running down buck with the horses most of the day, and some choice cuts from a fine steinbok were cooking at the huge fire in front of us, while the remainder of the carcase hung on a tree some way back. Suddenly, without a moment's warning, the air seemed split with the most terrifying noise I had ever heard. Echoing through the stillness, it seemed to fill the forest and ended in long-drawn shrieks and gasps.

"'I told you what that blarmed offal would do,' shouted Tim, as he rushed to the tent for his gun.

"Armed with our rifles, we preceded to stalk the disturber of our peace, for it struck us that a lion pelt would make a novel door-mat for the folks at home. Warily we turned the corner of the stockade, and in a patch of moonlight came upon the quarry. It wasn't a lion at all, but a full-blown ass. He looked mildly at us, and seemed to think his serenading had brought us out, and stretched out his neck to give us another lot. But we stopped that.

"But," went on the Bushman, "donkeys are very rarely seen in Australia. I could show you dozens of men here who have never seen one in their lives, much less heard his voice."

And he spoke truth.

I mentioned the ' fly-belt.' In South Africa the ' tse-tse ' fly is perhaps the insect most dreaded by the traveller who is dependent upon animal transport. It is a little more than half-an-inch long, and the body is marked with stripes of yellow and dark chestnut. It does not sting as does a wasp, but, like a mosquito, inserts its lance-shaped proboscis into the skin, and in the act ejects a poison which ultimately kills. To man and wild animals, and even to calves as long as they suck the cow, the bite is harmless. The mule, ass and goat are not much endangered. But to oxen, horses and dogs their bite is fatal. Fortunately the insect is limited to particular districts—called fly-belts,—frequently infesting one bank of a river whilst the other contains not a single specimen. The tse-tse fly will probably disappear from South Africa with the destruction of big game, especially the buffalo, which it seems to accompany.

The presence of one of these ' fly districts ' was the primary cause of the Beira-Umtali railway being constructed. The history of this line is probably unique in the railroad building of the world and deserves more than a passing mention. On the occupation of Beira at the mouth of the Pungwe by the Companhia de Mocambique, the harbour having been proved to be good, it was thought that Beira could be made a port for the north. The Pungwe River was navigable for boats of light draught as far as Fontesvilla, a village some 36 miles inland. From here merchandise had to be transported overland. But a difficulty arose. From Fontesvilla for many miles westward the forests were infested by the dreaded tse-tse fly, and transport by animals was impossible. To surmount this difficulty a narrow-guage rail (2-feet wide) was laid from Fontesvilla to a point some 40 miles farther on, from which it was considered safe for transport riders to work. It was found necessary, however, to continue the line to Chimoio, and then, river transport proving unsatisfactory, to prolong the line at the other end from Fontesvilla to Beira. Eventually the rails were laid to Umtali, 222 miles from the coast.

The difficulties connected with the building of the line have been altogether unprecedented, but chief amongst these is the inordinately large number of lives lost in its construction. These are estimated at no less than seven hundred. In 1896 the mortality was most heavy. In that year, of five hundred Indians imported to work on the line, two hundred had died within two months, and the remainder, frightened, had deserted the service.

Beyond Chimoio the rail descends to the lovely Revue River Valley. Down the magnificently wooded slopes we run, past the Vendusi and Lonodsi Rivers, and halting for water at Transrevue in the bend of the valley. From here we commence to climb the watershed which separates the Portuguese and British territories.

As we draw up at Macequece (pronounced *Massi-Kessi*) which stands in one of the richest gold-fields in South Africa, the time is passed in chaffing the Portuguese policeman, and in reading the only procurable copy of the local journal, which one of the enterprising Sharpshooters has secured. It is not much to look at, and dear at the shilling they charge for it. Eight pages, each 17 x 10½ exactly, half printed in *French*, and the remainder consisting of an English translation of the first half.

From its pages we learn that the bad season for malarial fever is over, and that this year is one of the most unhealthy ever experienced in Macequece. Moreover, five-sixths of the deaths which have taken place have occurred in the town itself, and only one-sixth amongst the miners in the surrounding woods and hills.

" Now when we consider," to quote the *Manica Mining*

Journal, " that those dwelling outside the town, prospectors and others, are generally obliged to live under very uncomfortable conditions, often the opposite to the mode of living recommended for tropical climates, having to come in contact with freshly turned-up soil, and numerous other disadvantages, we may well be astonished, and ask ourselves what must be the cause of this anomaly ? Why are there so many fatal cases of fever in the town, and so few, comparatively speaking, in the surrounding districts ? "

After exploding this enigmatic bombshell upon his readers, the writer naively suggests that the water as at present supplied to the inhabitants of Macequece, is the cause of much of the sickness.

For " this water supply runs right through the town in small shallow canals or sluits, which are never cleaned, notwithstanding the orders of the police, and which are used for washing and other purposes. So that it often happens that the drinking water is taken from a place in the canal above which dirty clothes or other things are being washed. When we consider that these streams flow close by the stables and the hospital, we surely are justified in assuming that the serious attacks of malarial fever in New Macequece, and so many deaths taking place, almost exclusively among people living in the town, are due to the supply of bad water."

And I should think so, too.

Malaria is not the only drawback to Macequece. For we read that a few days before the town was visited by four lions, which very inconsiderately killed five oxen belonging to a M. Ribiero, at a distance of only 600 metres from the town. Whereupon the Nimrods of Macequece turned out in force. The Portuguese method of lion-hunting is *magnifique mais ne c'est pas*—lion-hunting.

To quote the *M. M. Journal* : " Nearly every store in town was denuded of whiskey, gin, and other courage-revivers, and, as a night had to be passed in the field, a detachment of boys were loaded with bedsteads, mattresses, etc."

The hunters were not successful in their quest, for " the lions, not appreciating whiskey, did not put in an appearance, but the following morning, when our warriors had barely started for home, another of the unfortunate M. Ribiero's troop of cattle was killed." Which, considering that that gentleman had 'stood' the courage-revivers, and was moreover paying the expenses of the expedition, was rather hard upon M. Ribiero.

As we continue to climb, the character of the scenery changes. The trees become smaller in size, and bear evidence of the higher regions in which they grow. The gradients are steep and the railway makes great snake-like curves as it winds in and out between the hills. On the steep inclines our speed sometimes slackens to a man's walking pace, and more than once the brakes grind on the wheels and the train stops completely till more steam is gained. But on the down grades the driver lets it go and tries to make up for lost time—until another hill is reached, and the struggle recommences. The views are magnificent. The rail skirts the side of a hill, and as we sit with our legs over the sides of the truck, stretching away in front of us are miles upon miles of tree-clothed valley, where in the clear atmosphere the sharp shape of every stone and boulder can be seen at distances where, in mistier climes, they would be lost in haze. Bounded by the hills, which rise in heaving masses, their great clefts full of rolling mists and deep dark shadows; their summits lost in clouds.

Or, dipping into wood again, thick tree growths cut by narrow deep ravines, we flit by rock-strewn streams o'er rickety bridges seeming far too frail to bear our burden. Here, native girls, with graceful upright carriage, pause, calabash on head, with curious gaze, on their way to the kraal from the hidden spring below. And, on the beaten ground before the huts, their lords and husbands answer our salute with grave uplifted hand, as they squat with knees bent chin-wards and draw through the water in their curious pipes the smoke from the intoxicating 'dakra.'

The telegraph poles are very primitive affairs. Simply slender trunks of trees stuck in the ground, regardless of their shape or crookedness. There were two wires, and in some cases one pole would support them both, but at the next each wire would have a separate post, only to unite again at the third. These fragile supports seemed prone to accident, for occasionally one would see several feet of post and an insulator swinging from the wire, but where the lower part had gone, we could not say. The wire did not always follow the rails, for where a big curve was made, it would run away across the valley, to join us again some miles farther on. Sometimes a gang of blacks were passed, renewing broken or worn out posts under white supervision, and I should think their services would be constantly needed, for when one thinks of the bushfires sweeping round the posts, it is not difficult to imagine how the telegraphic communication in the South African interior is sometimes interrupted. Near Umtali, however, these rough and ready supports are superseded by the usual slender iron poles.

Higher yet, and we look back on views that can hardly be described. Selous says of this part,—" We rode over the mountain-chain which divides the valley of the Umtali river from the Revue. . . . . . This part of the country is without exception the most mountainous and broken and withal the most beautiful that I have yet seen in Africa. It is simply a mass of rugged hills, rising to a height of over six thousand feet above sea-level, among which there are many fine open valleys, watered by rushing streams of the clearest water, all of which are fed by the innumerable little burns that, rising amongst the summits of the mountains, have cut deep fissures for themselves down every hillside. Many of the ravines thus formed are clothed with banana-trees, especially on the southern slopes of the mountains. Lemons of excellent flavour also grow wild in these ravines, as they do on the eastern and northern slopes of Mashonaland."

We follow closely the track of the first narrow railway, which from Bamboo Creek*, has been replaced by the wider guage. Where the new line exactly follows the track of the old, the disused rails have been torn up in great lengths, and flung with iron sleepers attached in the long grass alongside, or rest upright on their edges like stretches of an iron fence. Where we diverge into a newer course, the narrow rails have not

---

* Since the above was written, the whole of the narrow guage as far as Beira has been replaced by the broad guage. The 60 miles to Bamboo Creek was laid in three days, a smart piece of work, of which Messrs. Pauling & Co. have reason to be proud. The first train on the new guage steamed into Beira on July 8, 1900.

been disturbed, but wind through the hills, partly hidden by the encroaching vegetation, rusting and unused. The road grows steeper as we near the border, and, in the last few weeks, accidents have been far from uncommon, caused by the hinder parts of trains breaking away and rushing back down the steep slope in mad career, either to be derailed at some sharp curve, or to crash, with deadly effect to horse and man, into some other train.

But the steepest part is passed at last, and, crossing the Frontier, we enter Rhodesia through its Eastern gate, Umtali.

CHAPTER VII.

The Goldfields Hospital—Umtali.

THE heavy feet of the orderly tramp slowly up the four rickety wooden steps of the 'annex,' and he opens the door with difficulty. It binds upon the floor.

"Six o'clock. Time to get up."

The sleepers growl and pull the blankets closer round them.

"Shut that door for Gawd's sake" for he has admitted a whiff of raw morning air, straight off the hills. "Can you get me a drink? I'm as thirsty as a fish."

"See what I can do," and down the steps again recede the heavy feet of the orderly.

So the day opens with the convalescents in the Goldfields Hospital at Umtali.

A restless tossing, but sleep has been broken and will not again be wooed. The voice of a Sister giving instructions to an orderly comes subdued from the courtyard. The soft chatter of Kaffirs mingled with the softer patter of naked feet passes the door. Then a pungent reek of wood smoke fills the room as the door is hesitatingly pushed open, and 'Bokus,' the ebony sweeper, stands on the threshold, brush in hand. His eyes glance furtively round on the look out for stray missiles, for he knows his dusty mission is no popular one with the patients.

Reassured, he settles down to work vigorously—that is, for a native. He softly strokes the floor with his brush, gravely and deliberately, for with luck, if he can escape the lynx-eyed orderly, this will constitute his morning's work. He sweeps the open space in the centre of the room, and looks under each bed. If he sees any dust particularly prominent, he pushes his brush under and fetches it out. If he doesn't he lets that part alone. Arrived at the door he gently sweeps the little heap of dust into the courtyard, all except that which is blown back into the room. And so softly closing the door, his early morning visit ends. Four times during the day will this take place, for Africa is a dusty land, and it is windy in the hill country of Umtali.

From the town some distance away steals crisply a continued tinkle, as of a school-bell.

"By Jove, its Wednesday. Want anything, you fellows?" and K——dresses hastily, for the market, or rather auction of vegetables is only held twice a-week at 6-45 a.m., and a green-grocer's shop is a thing unknown in Umtali.

Rather slowly, for he has not yet regained the strength sapped in the Beira paddocks, K—— climbs the hill to the town. There is no difficulty in finding the market, for the tinkling is still in full swing. It is made by a Kaffir, who sits with his knees serving as a prop for his chin in the usual Kaffir manner, and beats a ∩ shaped piece of iron suspended from a tripod for all he is worth.

The vegetable and farm produce is tied in small bundles or 'lots' and spread around the auctioneer.

I always thought an English auctioneer worked hard with his tongue, but he would stand in dumb amazement before this one. As the bidding goes on he has but one formula. He keeps up an unbroken two-two-two-two-two-three-three-three-three-four-four-four-four so rapidly as almost to resemble a man badly afflicted with stuttering. In the still morning air we can distinctly hear his monotonous cry in the hospital wards some two hundred yards away. When the bidding has reached its limit, he knocks the article down, asks the purchaser how many lots he will take, and before you have time to look round, is off on another spurt—three-three-three-three-four-four-four, &c., *ad. lib.*

By the time our marketer returns laden with radishes, tomatoes, and other garden produce, breakfast is brought round by the orderlies.

"Hm-m"—consulting his card—"two fulls and one low. Here you are. Sister B—— will bring your arrowroot directly"—to the unfortunate low-diet, who regards the viands with devouring eyes, but says nothing, knowing that it is useless.

A huge plate of porridge covered with sugar and swimming in milk—large slices of bread and jam (six if you like—they are great on jam here), and tea. Such is the first meal of the 'full' and 'middle' diets. As for the unfortunate 'low diets,' those from whose system they are starving the fever (though unfortunately they don't muzzle the appetite), I give their daily menu: 5 a.m.—arrowroot; 8 a.m.—cocoa; 11 a m.—soup; 1 p.m.—sago; 3.30—milk or arrowroot (sometimes both as a special treat); 5.30—cocoa; 8.0—milk or soup; 12.0—cocoa or hot milk. And this to a man who feels equal to eating a whole sheep.

"Well, how did prices go, K——. Did you get my eggs?"

"Yes, they were eleven shillings a dozen."

"WHAT! I gave you a bob."

"Yes. Well, here's your egg and a penny stamp."

L—— takes it gingerly, wondering if it isn't the 'golden egg' he has read about. But then L—— only came up from Beira yesterday, and isn't acclimatised to Rhodesian prices yet.

"Cauliflowers were eight shillings* each this morning," K—— goes on "Cabbages four-and-threepence; butter three-and-six a pat; potatoes elevenpence a pound. Fowls six-and-six. Strawberries——"

The entrance of the Sister to 'take the temperatures' cuts short the tale of vegetable extortion. The visit of the Sister is closely followed by the Doctor's rounds, and then the patients may follow the devices of their own sweet wills—within reason—until dinnertime.

The Goldfields Hospital was built as the Goldfields Hotel, but was taken by the military authorities before it was finished, when the inpouring of sick from the fever country below rendered the permanent hospital totally inadequate.

Its intended use is plainly shown in Ward 3, for there stands a large semi-circular mahogany bar. By the way, 'twas said that all the teetotal patients were put in here, as they wouldn't be so likely to rise from their beds and rap the counter in an absent-minded fit. But for the truth of this I can't vouch.

In the busiest times three doctors and four Sisters—trained Australian ladies who had volunteered their services for the Rhodesian Field Force, which was composed mainly of Colonials; one or two R.A.M.C. men and a few orderlies, lent by the

---

* These prices are facts.

different squadrons encamped here—completed the staff of the hospital.

And till dinnertime we hold a little ' at home' within the ward. Men from other corps saunter in to chat over our joint grievances—for soldiers always have a grievance. A New South Welshman returned from a stroll—a giant bearing a jaunty plume of black crow's feathers, the insignia of his corps. Another wears a soft brown emu plume. Or a Victorian in his loose-fitting light grey blouse. This peculiarly cut garment did not extend below the waist, where it was gathered in and fastened tightly by a broad band or strap. Very roomy to work in, no doubt, but the wearers always irresistibly reminded me of millers in helmets. Leisurely our visitors sauntered in, fragmentary was their talk, and deliberate their departure. For men do things slowly at the Goldfields Hospital. There is really no need for unseemly haste. A man has the whole day before him. He has nothing to do but to eat and grow well and strong. From the rush of the battling stream he has drifted for a time to the calm of the sheltered backwater. For a breathing space he is resting from the stress and strain of war.

"'*Deeshan Heral*', baas."

It is the news boy, bringing the only daily paper in Umtali. I have one before me as I write. A single pink sheet 17½ by 11, printed on one side only. The title of the paper takes up three inches. The remainder is divided into four columns of type. Three columns are advertisements. The fourth consists of two items—reports of the hospital bazaar and a polo match. And not a word about the war. Price 3d.

But the appearance of the orderlies with dinner disperses the patients to their wards.

From the door we can see the entrance to the main ward, by which usually leans a three-fold red baize screen. We suddenly notice that this is gone from its accustomed place, and our light talk is hushed, for we need no telling the dread significance of this.

An orderly passes the window.

" Yes, McC—— has just gone" and his tones are unusually softened."

" McC——, one of the few dangerous cases we had left, had

UMTALI—FROM THE HOSPITAL.

Photo *B.S.A. Company.*

dysentery and fever, and bad, too. For some time past, when the door across the yard was open, we had almost grown accustomed to the sounds of him, and the talk would slacken, and someone would say what we all knew—"That's poor McC—— again."

And now that was finished.

As we sit silent a young orderly comes up the steps, in one hand a bottle of tonic—a large sized wine bottle—in the other a glass. With puttee-bound legs, heavy boots and sleeves rolled above his elbow, he is the picture of rude strength. The sun catches his knotted arms and the half of his strong face—the other half is hidden by his felt sombrero—and he is a young giant of the Australian plains, of the Canadian backwoods, of anything other than a hospital orderly, whose gentle province it is to minister to the sick and ailing. The huge clasp knife hanging from his belt sways for a moment as he halts, and the dust he has raised begins to settle.

"Mc——'s just gone" we say, partly for the sake of saying something.

"Yes, didn't you see me put the screen round him. You ought to from here." The giant speaks nonchalantly, as though putting screens round men who have died was work to which he had long since grown accustomed. He holds up the glass and, tipping up the big bottle with a jerk, as another would hold a two-ounce medicine bottle, pours out the right dose at a gulp.

"See, K—— you're for tonic. And you G——, oh no, not you"—and he is gone, his broad shoulders blocking out for an instant the sun's rays from the doorway. And the laughter and the chatter of the Kaffirs goes on from the courtyard, and a sound of light furtive laughter comes from the front of the hospital. A lady friend has come to take Sister I—— for a drive. It is her afternoon off duty.

Outside the sun is shining brightly, and the patients are everywhere sunning themselves back to health. From here one looks down o'er the green strip of valley, past the rough hut and irrigated acre of the old Italian, who passes his time between growing tomatoes and other garden produce, and in fighting the periodical attacks of the fever fiend which first gripped him

F

years ago; past the sweet grass bordering the silver spruit; over the camp a mile away on the hill beyond; away to the sharp blue peaks of the mountains which gird about Umtali.

It is pleasant to sit here and dream. As my eye catches the camp I think of that journey weeks ago, though seeming ages, when, rolled in blankets and strapped on a stretcher, I was shouldered by four Kaffirs and brought across the valley through the darkness. How they chattered away as they trotted along the rough uneven ground. It was partly I think to keep up their courage, for they four were alone, save the burden on the stretcher. Until, just as they splashed through the creek, a dog barked somewhere near, and they became suddenly silent. And I recall how the stretcher swayed until the stars rocked from side to side, and my fear lest they should drop their burden and run, for if a Kaffir hates one thing more than another, it is a yelping cur round his bare defenceless ankles.

But these are recollections, and as the evening comes, we wend to our wards, to write or talk, until our drowsy eyes seek sleep.

And in the tent where he has been carried from the ward, Trooper McC——, of the Imperial Yeomanry, lies waiting silently for the morrow—for the creaking wagon, and the black team of patient oxen, which will jolt him to the cemetery beyond the camp. To be laid to rest to the ring of the farewell volleys and the sorrowful ' Last Post ' of the bugles.

I make no apology for transcribing a few pages from my diary. They were written from day to day, and better perhaps than a more ordered story, they may bring more clearly home the strange jumble of brightness and of pain in those days. When death obtruded daily on the living, and Tragedy and Comedy sat cheek by jowl.

June 1.—So many sick arriving from Bamboo Creek, that the doctors at their wits' end. So we with a number of the more convalescent patients were removed into tents some distance from the Hospital. Much colder in the tents and ground terribly hard. A decided change for the worse.

June 2.—Four extra men put in our tent; one, a little Irishman who suffers with spasms, and kept us awake half the night with his cries. Doctor comes to see us twice a-day. The prescription for those with malaria is quinine three times a-day and no food. Not very conducive to jollity.

June 3.—There is really very little to chronicle of these days in the hospital tents at Umtali. They pass away placidly in eating, or rather drinking, the sago, tea, arrowroot, and quinine, and in wondering how long it will be before they have starved the fever out, and begin to build you up again with something solid. . . Sick still arriving. This hospital was intended to accommodate fifty patients and to-day the orderly said they have a total of ninety-seven.

June 4.—To-day, to my surprise, the orderly brought me a large slice of bread and jam. I was sure he had made a mistake, as I was still on low diet, so when I had eaten the bread and jam I asked him. He then found it was for another man whose name much resembled mine, and made me promise not to say anything to the doctor. I said I wouldn't if he'd bring me some more to-morrow. . . . S—— died to-day.

June 6.—Was put on more generous diet to-day. . . . Managed to evade the orderlies, and with many rests by the way, reached the town. Paid a visit to first restaurant I saw. The proprietress, who was evidently of French extraction and spoke very broken English, seemed to pass the day in carrying on more or less mild flirtations with her customers, and selling Umtali-brewed soda water at a shilling a bottle. Brought some back with me lying *perdu* in the pockets of my great coat. . . . Woke myself several times during the night just to have the exquisite pleasure of a cool drink of soda water. . . . Two more men died to-day, one 71st and one 75th. . . . Dr. P——, one of the three doctors, is ill through overwork. So to save himself from a severe illness he has gone away for some days to obtain a complete rest.

June 7.—As some men have been discharged and others removed back into the wards, I slept to-night in the tent alone. In the next tent in the row, which is used as a mortuary, lay the bodies of the two men who died yesterday, awaiting burial. Rather creepy, if you let your thoughts dwell on it, but I am afraid what we have seen has made us callous to these things.

June 8.—Had a famous dinner with the orderlies to-day. They had served out to them a large piece of uncooked beef and a quantity of flour. So C——, who was apprenticed to a pastry cook when he was a boy but never finished his apprenticeship, and P——, who had once been a cook on a gentleman's yacht, volunteered to prepare the dinner. C—— said it was no use roasting the beef as we had no tools stronger than knives and forks, and moreover, we were only convalescents yet, and not strong enough for heavy fatigue work. So they made stew of it, with a quantity of potatoes which we all assisted to pare. And with the flour P—— made some dumplings.

The meat turned out much too tough to eat, and the dumplings were like glue, but the soup was really excellent, and so were the potatoes. When we congratulated our cooks, and assured them that the dinner had really turned out a partial success, P—— retaliated by telling us that a partial success was better than a total failure. And we couldn't refute his logic.

We gave what was left to the Kaffirs; but for some days afterwards we could never find a 'boy' when we wanted one about dinnertime. I think they were afraid we should present them with some more of our culinary ventures.

June 9.—Whilst walking out this morning met a man in khaki carrying the impediments of a half-plate stand camera. He is a New Zealand War Correspondent and is following the 4th Contingent N.Z.R.R. (New Zealand Rough Riders) through the campaign with camera and pen. I passed a most enjoyable morning with him. . . On my return learned that poor Brooker had just died. His death is the first break in the ranks of the 65th. . . . Many patients have been discharged during the last few days, so we were to-day moved from the tents back to the annex.

June 10.—Sir Frederick Carrington made a minute inspection of the Goldfields Hospital this morning. . . . Were kept awake for some time after we had retired to rest by a row in the next room, and the violent opening and shutting of the door. As the rooms of the annex are only divided by thin matchboard partitions, every word spoken in one room can be plainly heard in the next. C—— shouted to them 'to shut up and go to sleep.' Then the trouble came out.

A. said it was B. who would have the door wide open, and he was starved to death.

B. said he was obliged to have the door open for the sake of his health, as A. hadn't had his socks off since he left England.

And so on. The argument punctuated by the flinging open of the door by B., followed shortly by a loud bang which shook the floor, as it was forcibly shut by A. After some further altercation it finished by B. declaring he should make a complaint in the morning. Though whether the door was left open or closed I was too sleepy to remember.

June 11.—This morning B. of the next room carried out his threat, and the Sister tried to smooth matters over by gently advising A. to change his socks. The matter was eventually carried to a higher court, and when the Doctor made his rounds this morning we could hear him quoting cases by the score in which men had been obliged to keep their boots on for a month, and at last he managed to restore peace.

A. was shortly afterwards discharged from hospital, and there was no more strife, as the *casus belli* went with him.

June 12.—Four more men of the Yeomanry died to-day.

June 18.—Sister B—— had a narrow escape to-day. Some 150 yards from the hospital buildings a solitary bell-tent stands in the midst of a stretch of the usual sundried grass some three or four feet high. Here the Sister who had been on duty through the night may sleep in daytime free from noise and disturbance. By some means the grass caught fire to-day and swept over the tent, leaving the ground bare and black for many yards. The tent and its contents were burnt, but Sister B——, who was lying there, escaped just in time.

June 20.—I hear there is to be a Board of Inquiry ' sit on the tent ' which was burned two days ago. It was Government property, and therefore several officers will have to solemnly hold a kind of inquest on the tent before it can be ' struck off the strength.'

      *   *   *

I cannot leave ' Umtali ' without adding my small tribute to the single-hearted and unselfish kindness of its people towards the strangers within their gates.

To the Civil Commissioner who entertained them at the Residency when convalescent.

To Mrs. Myburgh and the ladies of Umtali, who loaded the hospital with gifts of eggs, fowls, milk, and fruit—those luxuries so valued by the sick.

To the Clubs which gave their literature.

To the ' people of Umtali,' who denied themselves of milk, that the sick in the hospitals might have the *whole* of the small supply which the district afforded.

And, lastly, to that devoted band of ladies who, from their homes in far off Australia, came as volunteers to nurse back to health, if such were possible, the stricken soldiers of the Rhodesian Field Force. To all who received their cheerful care and solicitude the sick bed was brightened, pain made more easy to bear: to their skilled and unwearying attention many a man owes his life.

CHAPTER VIII.

The Base Camp at Marandellas.

BEFORE the war Marandellas was known—if it was known at all—as a small station on the Beira-Salisbury line; the usual water-tank, hotel-store and half-a-dozen Kaffir huts, in no way differing from its fellows save from the soft romantic beauty of its name. To-day it is the busy scene of military activity, of the detraining of horses and guns, of munitions of war and of men, the site of piled up mountains of forage and of stores. In short it is the Base Camp of the Rhodesian Field Force.

Take three of the familiar 'lants' of a well-drained meadow at home. In the hollows between a narrow stream wide-bordered with treacherous bog. Cover the valleys with high rank grass and the higher parts with thin lichen-covered woods. Sprinkle here and there on hill and valley huge weather-split outcrops of granite boulders of the most curious shape and configuration. Now enlarge the whole until the central 'rise' is a mile or more in width and the remainder in proportion, and the topography of Marandellas roughly lies before you.

Away to the west of the railway along this central hill stretched the various parts of the base camp, covering several miles from the Headquarters at one end to the Hospital at the other.

Viewed from the centre of the far-reaching camp, the scene was one of the most intense interest, a picture of day-long movement and unrest, of ceaseless drill and warlike preparation. Rows upon rows of white bell-tents, with darker lines of horses sandwiched in between. In the middle lay the camps of the Yeomanry on ground beaten hard and bare as an English school-yard by the thousands of passing feet, and diapered with the ring-shaped marks of countless horses' hoofs.

East of these lay the Colonials—the Victorian Bushmen, the New Zealand Rough Riders and Tasmanians. Men of iron

TYPICAL RHODESIAN KOPJE.

Photo *B.S.A. Company.*

muscle and marvellous powers of endurance. Hard men of few wants, and with ability to supply them from the barest material. Skilled and immovable horsemen, who can shoot as well as they ride. Drawn from all ranks; squatters and owners of stations, overseers, drovers and boundary-riders, kangaroo hunters, rabbiters and shearers; they are the Duke's-son—cook's-son of the Antipodes, the pick of a Continent. Most of these lay in grass-green tents of thick texture, a great improvement on the British white ones. They are warmer at night and cooler under the hot rays of the sun. The green colour is much less conspicuous than the white, and the thickness of their texture renders an inside light practically invisible from a very short distance away. Possibly they would be heavier when packed than the regulation white bell-tent, but I think their many advantages more than outweigh this one drawback. The tilts of their wagons were of the same colour. Past these lay the Maitland Camp, the abiding place of the staff. Still farther east were the permanent police barracks—the small tin houses of the white troopers and the round mud huts of the ' Black Watch '—otherwise the Mashonaland Native Contingent. In these huts they live with their wives and little ' picanins,' and one could watch the ' umfaze ' or wife, with bare shaven head shining in the sun, making bread from the ' oofoo ' or native grain; or, after a swarm of these insects had passed over, spreading out locusts on mats to dry in the sun. Whilst her lord and master sat apart, and half stupified himself with his beloved ' dakra,' or plaited fine brass wire in intricate patterns round his knob-kerrie. The drill of these native police with the Martini is very smart, and the ' telling ' of hand and butt in the ' manual ' would delight the heart of a drill-sergeant; but, as will be seen in a subsequent chapter, they evidently rely upon their rifles more as a means of instilling fear into the heart of the enemy, than of putting lead into his body. Their serviceable uniform consists of dark blue tunic with black leather belts, brown corduroy knickers with black stripe, scarlet field service cap and bare legs and feet.

They are drawn principally from the Angonis, an offshoot of the warlike Zulu race. " Eighty years ago," says Selous, " some of the outlying Zulu clans broke away from the harsh and cruel rule of Chaka and migrated northwards, and wherever these ferocious warriors went their track was marked by the flight of the vultures which feasted upon the corpses of men, women and children they had slain, and the flames of the villages they had set fire to." Two of these tribes, the Abagaza and the Angoni, after devastating a great portion of what is now called Mashonaland, both settled near the head waters of the Sabi, where they soon came into collision with one another. A great battle was fought, lasting three days, and the Angoni were defeated and driven from their settlements. They retreated northwards, devastating the whole country through which they passed, and crossing the Zambesi to the east of Zumbo, made their way on to the high plateau which lies to the west of Lake Nyassa, where they are living at the present day. Though many of them have deteriorated by marriage with inferior tribes, the true Angoni are distinguished by a clean-cut lower jaw, stern naturally compressed mouth, bold eyes and a permanent and natural contraction of the eye-brows which gives a somewhat sinister expression to the countenance. Their limbs are splendidly developed, and their hands and feet small. They are worthy blood relatives of that Zulu race, which, even to-day, proudly style themselves the " black Englishmen of Africa,' implying that, as the British race stands first and foremost amongst the nations, so they stand superior to the black races of the African Continent.

From these Angonis the ' Black Watch ' are mainly recruited.

Near the police barracks is the post office, a square, mud-plastered hut, with several smaller huts apportioned to the sorting of the military mails. It was here that I first became acquainted with that *bête noir* of the Press man—the Press Censor.

The matter was really nothing. 'Twas my ignorance of things that made the import loom so largely. Wishful of sending home some horns I had bought or otherwise acquired, I packed them in an empty bully-beef box and despatched them by the rail to forwarding agents in Beira, intending to send by post the instructions and the charge for carriage home. So, returning by the post office I laid down my letter, and inquired the postage to the Portuguese port.

"Beira" said the clerk, "we can't forward this letter unless it is either passed by the Censor or sent open."

Here was a poser. As it contained money I could not send it open for obvious reasons. And the Press Censor. Well, I had never seen a Press Censor, and had only vague ideas of his personality and his power. I only knew that he was a military official, probably some Colonel or Lieutenant-General, whom age and gout had incapacitated for more active service, and whose mission it was to wade through all the letters that went from South Africa, cutting out—either with a big blue pencil or with shears, I wasn't sure—all matters relating to the progress of the war, and bringing to justice those unhappy wretches who offended by writing such. No, I daren't do it. So to disarm suspicion, I tried to look unconcerned, and said to the clerk,

"Oh, I didn't know that. I'd better go and see him then." And I made a bee-line for camp, diving into the wood, lest the clerk should come out to show me where the Press Censor lived, and find me going the other way.

And conscience troubled me. I knew it had appeared in orders that "all officers or men serving in South Africa, are forbidden to communicate either directly or indirectly with the Press." And for weeks I had been sending home letters divulging everything. The miseries of Bamboo Creek, our strength and numbers, our movements and the management or mismanagement of our affairs—I had told everything. And suppose all my letters had been opened and my name and number taken. Suppose when I presented myself before this Press Censor, he should refer to his ledgers, and—

"11991. Trooper —— h'm—— ah! you are the man who ——." No. I daren't risk it. Censor! The very name smacked of censure, reprimands and rows.

And so two days passed. But then—my box had gone by rail and no instructions sent. I must send somehow. Ah! happy thought. There had been no question asked about the contents of the box. The Censor only dealt with the post. Why not send my letter by rail.

So I procured a small box, and placing the epistle in the bottom, filled it up with hay, and making a neat parcel of it, wended my way to the railway.

The clerk took it up and weighed it in his hand.

" Why not send this by post ? It will go safer and quicker, and the cost will be less," and he handed it back.

" But I should like to send it by rail," I said.

" Why ? I tell you the better way for this will be the parcel post. I can't see——"

So I came away. He began to look suspicious.

Breaking up the box when out of sight, I extracted the letter, and resolved to try the post office again. Perhaps it would be some other clerk this time.

But it was the same one, and he stood outside at the door. I put on a bold face, and presented my letter.

" Beira. Get it passed by the Censor. He's in that hut there."

I was cornered. The hut was only a few yards away, and the clerk still stood outside, with his hands clasped behind him under his coat. It was neck or nothing. There wasn't even time to alter the name and number on the envelope. So I walked to the hut and pushed open the door—gently.

It was a rough mud-plastered hut with a small square opening cut for a window. With the window shut the hut would be in darkness, for the pane—there was only one—was made of corrugated zinc, like the door.

At a rough table sat a young man, a very young man, a lieutenant of something I could see by his single star. At his side were three unopened mail-bags, before him lay unheeded a small pile of letters, and he was smoking a pipe, and watching the smoke curl up to the roof. When I opened the door he slowly looked down.

" I—ah—I—came to see the Press Censor."

" Yes—I'm the Press Censor."

" Oh," wide-eyed, " I was thinking of sending a few horns—that is—a box of—a—things away, and I thought I had better let you know before—I mean the clerk told me——"

He looked at my hand, and seeing the letter between my fingers, the puzzled look left his face.

" You want that letter signed," dashing his initials across the corner, " there you are. Leave the door open."

And I was outside, and my interview with the Press Censor was over.

ANGONI POLICEMAN AT HOME—*p. 87.*

A NATIVE TELEPHONE— *p. 91.*

Photos by *P.S. Inskipp.*

I know now it was trouble thrown away, for from that day to this I have heard nothing more of either the horns or the letter. But, considering the congested and deranged state of the rails at that time, one can hardly wonder. Possibly my box has been sent to some outlying garrison under the delusion that it is a case of bully beef, and when they opened it the amazed recipients would think the canning company had by some error sent the wrong part of the cow.

Greater mistakes than that have been made in war time.

Between the post office and the station stood nothing but a store or two run by Poles and Jews, who were making a rich harvest out of the troops, as they do everywhere in South Africa. Then the station-yard with its countless heaps of stores, its forbidden hotel, and its gangs of busy Kaffirs. A favourite amusement of these children of nature was to shout to each other through the vacuum brake tubes with which the trains were fitted, and when they found several trucks coupled together their delight knew no end, and their respect for the white man and his inventions went up by leaps and bounds.

To the north of this stood a miscellaneous collection of transport wagons, oxen and Kaffir huts. And here, though it was not generally known, lived an old grey-bearded transport-rider who had pursued his wandering life from the Orange to the Zambesi, and farther, since 1839. His talk was a loadstone which drew me to his tent whene'er I'd time to spare, for he had hunted with Selous and trekked with Moffat, and he was never tired of telling how he had helped Mrs. Moffat when in difficulties with a broken wagon, by lending her his oxen, and of the welcome he ever afterwards received whene'er he passed their station, how they pressed on him gifts of prized vegetables till he could have carried them away in nothing less than an ox-cart. He travelled through the southern lands many years before the crossing of the Vaal by the Dutch on their way to found the Transvaal Republic, and before the natives of these parts had seen enough of the white man to know what money was. Once on the northern borders of the land afterwards called the Orange Free State, one of his most valued oxen died. But in the herds of a neighbouring chief was an ox much like the one he lost, and on which he set his heart. The black chief was however obdurate and would not sell his ox. Many tempting offers did the young transport-rider make but all in vain. At last, firm resolved to have the ox at whatever cost, he pulled out a handful of gold, four times what the animal was worth and spread it out before the native ruler. But he laughed in the face of the trader, saying " Nah ! hi ke eja se ? " (What use is that ? I can't *eat* that.)

Times have changed since then and the march of civilization has spread amongst the tribes. Now, even in Rhodesia, if you ask the price of anything a native owns, however small, he asks a " shilleen." He knows no lower coin. But if he enters a store to buy an overcoat, he at once opens the ball by offering the man behind the counter " seespence."

At the western end of the long camp lay whole streets of vast iron sheds and storehouses, and then the hospital, and the rows of huts built for the more convalescent when the influx of the sick rendered the hospital all too small.

Right through the camp ran a wide dusty road, and this was ever full of life and movement. Traction engines drawing huge loads of stores and forage, slow-moving wagons with their span of sixteen oxen, lighter wagons drawn by ten skittish mules, strings of horses going to and from the water-troughs—the clumsy-looking whalers of the Bushmen, the ewe-necked Texans and graceful Hungarians of the Yeomanry. And riding in and out, swift-moving orderlies on horse or cycle. The whole seen dim and indistinct through clouds of driving dust.

The water supply for all purposes was pumped from the creek in the valley by a small vertical engine, looked after by an Australian trooper, and fed with logs by two partially-clothed Mashonas, who wore fillets of coloured beads round their heads and home-made knives in curious wire-wrapt sheaths in their waistcloths. Part of the water fed the horse-troughs, where a thousand horses could be watered simultaneously ; and the remainder was pumped into a row of corrugated zinc cisterns standing by the road in the centre of the camp.

The fine ankle-deep dust of the road was a thing to be remembered. To obtain the full benefit of it, one had but to take four or five horses to water and ride through the dust raised by a hundred and fifty more before him. Either by good luck or good

THE BASE CAMP AT MARANDELLAS.

management, I held for some weeks the rather coveted post of cyclist orderly to the Headquarters Staff, and so had an unique opportunity of probing to the full the delights of this and other roads adjacent. The military machines—borrowed, I believe, from the B.S.A. Police—were perhaps 'things of beauty'—being painted a gorgeous vermilion—but I can certify that they were very far from being 'joys' for even the short time I used them. They were built very high, in order that the pedals should clear the various stones and projecting stumps which had to be negotiated, and they weighed just about as much as I could carry. One can imagine the keen pleasure to be derived from driving such a machine against a strong head wind, with the sand rippling through the wheel over the rims, and an uneasy conscience holding up to mental view the picture of a short-tempered staff-officer who had told you to 'use all despatch.'

But 'it's an ill wind, etc.,' and this plague of dust has saved more than one delinquent from the clutches of justice.

Posted near this road were several stalwart young men called military police, whose privileges were to escape all drills and fatigues and to carry a cane, and their duties to prevent an undue waste of the water in the tanks and to stop any equestrian, under the rank of an officer, from riding through the camp at a faster pace than a trot. But often when this guardian of the peace—or rather 'pace'—has strayed a short distance away, many a gallant trooper has enjoyed a surreptitious gallop, secure in the knowledge that, by reason of the dust he raises, his face and form are but faint and hazy to that excited figure, whose yells for 'name and number' grow fainter in the rapid-widening distance.

It was at Marandellas that the Yeomanry received their horses. They were principally Texans and Hungarians. The Hungarians were brought from the hilly tracts to the south of Hungary in the province of Dalmatia and the vicinity. Five transports filled with them came to Beira, carrying a total of 3,500 animals. It was thought that these Dalmatians would prove particularly suitable for South African warfare, as they have by generations of training acquired marvellous sure-footedness, being withal high-spirited, active, and lithe of body.

They are somewhat slender of build, with remarkably clean-cut limbs and have a very prepossessing exterior. They are small, averaging some 14.2, but are notwithstanding by no means poor weight-carriers, and have any amount of 'stay.' Besides their adaptability to rough country, they are not unused to extreme cold in their native mountains and vales, whilst they are no strangers to sultriness; so with this combination of qualities, the Hungarians were likely to prove themselves very useful animals for the work before them. Nor did they disappoint these sanguine expectations. They could not buck 'worth a cent'—to use an Americanism—but they could kick forwards, backwards, or in any direction. They were very fond of scratching their ear with their hind hoof, like a cat, and I have seen more than one throw himself down by putting his foot in his own stirrup while trying to do this.

In the earlier days of the Base Camp there was much sickness among the horses, and they were shot at the rate of fifteen and twenty a day. Their remains lay upon the veldt in a vast cordon some mile or more to the north of the camp. I was told over a thousand horses had been shot since the formation of the camp. Here one could see them lay in groups where they had been led out to be shot. In one place I counted nineteen lying together, in another fifteen. There, with the headstalls still hanging on their shrunken heads, they lay, whilst here a leg, there a tail, had been dragged a distance away by the jackals or other beasts of prey. But every horse was but a skin tight-shrunk on an empty skeleton. The vultures, jackals, crows and other carnivorous birds and beasts had seen to the rest. Even now one horse or more was shot each day, and from these one would disturb whole flocks of huge reddish-grey vultures, which rose heavily higher and higher, till they became mere motionless specks above. On one occasion I counted thirty-four of these unclean birds on one carcase, and the veldt around was strewn with the loose feathers from their plumage. The huge crows were most bold, and were of two distinct varieties. One with black plumage, save a large white ring of feathers round the neck. The other, a rather smaller bird, was parti-coloured, and had a pure white body with jet black head, wings, and tail.

THE BASE CAMP AT MARANDELLAS.

The smaller buck were plentiful, and were often shot round the camp. Once or twice some excitement was caused by a buck dashing across the camp, through the lines of men and horses. These occasions always caused much running and shouting by the men, but I never knew them to result in any dead buck.

Across the valley, on the farther hill, was the Remount Camp, where the unappropriated horses were kept. Here the country became more rugged, and on every hand were the peculiar heaps of granite boulders, which, but for their size, would seem piled up by the hands of man. Upon some were the remains of rough fortifications, and in the bloody rebellion of 1896 many of them were stubbornly held by the Mashonas. I explored one called 'Gatzi's Kraal.' It was of great height and most difficult to ascend. In and between the immense rounded boulders were crevices and caves, and dark holes which ran down far into the interior of the kopje. A well defined but narrow path wound round and round, climbing o'er the great smooth rocks, and again dipping into a crevice, but ever getting higher, and protected at each corner and open place by a breastwork of roughly placed stone.

It must truly have been a formidable place to storm, and the graveyard at Old Marandellas tells that it was not taken without the spilling of British blood. I carefully explored many of the caves, hoping to find some native weapon, but upon reaching the largest one near the summit I found I had been forestalled. For on the sides as far as hand could reach were the carved names of men in the Sharpshooters and other Yeomanry, and all I could find was a new cake of Pears' Transparent Soap.

This is not an advertisement, but a fact.

And on my way home lay a little graveyard, merely a levelled plot amongst the stones on the hillside, enclosed by rough posts and wire, and containing just sixteen graves in all. But on the head-stones one could read a blood-stained chapter in the sad history of but four years ago, when through the length of Mashonaland the natives rose and swept away practically the whole of the white settlers, indiscriminately slaying man, woman and child in their cruel lust for blood.

There are but three marble crosses—one erected by the officers of the Army Service Corps to

> Lieut. WILLIAM E. BAINES, Army Service Corps,
> Killed in action at Gadzi's Kraal, Marandellas,
> 10th August, 1896.

The second erected by the officers of the Mounted Infantry to

> Major FRANCIS STUDDERT EVANS,
> 1st Battn. Sherwood Foresters,
> Serving with the Mounted Infantry.
> Killed in action at Gatzi's Kraal,
> October 20th, 1896.

And the third stone tells its own tale of heroism and death—

> Sacred
> to the Memory of
> HERBERT J. MORRIS,
> Lieutenant Umtali Volunteers,
> Fatally wounded when rescuing a brother officer at CHIWARI'S KRAAL,
> October 2nd, 1896.
> " Greater love hath no man than this, that
> A man lay down his life for his friends."

All but these three are piled up heaps of stones, with roughly shaped wooden crosses at their heads, some with inscriptions rudely cut by knives. I can but spare space for one—

> In Memoriam of
> Mrs. C. M. HEINE and 3 children,
> Murdered by Mashonas. June, 1896.

And so day by day the organising and equipping of the Rhodesian Field Force went on. Each day train after train steamed in from the coast with military stores and with horses. The sound of the forge and the shoeing of horses—on fore feet only—was heard in the camps from morning till night. Several batteries of guns had come up in sections—15-pounders and pom-poms. These were manned by volunteers from the Yeomanry and the Australians. And on more than one occasion further south these batteries gave a good account of themselves.

Every few days a squadron of horsemen, fully equipped, with stores packed upon mule and ox-wagons, would parade for a final inspection and then file away along the roads that ran through the forest—some bound for Tuli, *via* Victoria, others for Buluwayo.

And those left behind eagerly looked for the day when they too would be ' ordered south ' away from the stagnation of the Base Camp, away to where the Great Game of War was being

DEAD HORSES ROUND CAMP—MARANDELLAS.—*p.94.*—Photo by *Surg.-Capt. H. Whyte.*
A BIT OF THE STATION-YARD—MARANDELLAS—*p. 91.*—Photo by *P. S. Inskipp.*

played in earnest, of which they had as yet received but rumours, vague and contradictory.

The climate of these Mashona uplands was a surprise to all. Though lying well within the tropics, one would never dream they were in tropical Africa, but rather in some wild moorland in Northern Europe. The temperate climate is due to the altitude above the sea level, and also to the fact that it is the highest land in South-Eastern Africa, and therefore catches directly the cold winds coming from the Indian Ocean. The nights are cool the whole year round—we rose nearly every morning to find the ground covered with white frost—and during the winter months bitterly cold, while the excessive heat of the sun during the spring and autumn is always tempered by the south-east breeze I have mentioned. Moreover, the dryness of the atmosphere prevents diseases of the lungs and chest.

The soil is generally speaking rich and fertile. When a water supply can be obtained—and the whole country is well watered —in addition to the maize, millet, rice and beans now cultivated by the natives, all the fruits and vegetables of Northern Europe can be produced. One feature of its pastures deserves notice. When the long summer grass is burnt off—usually in June or August—there springs up a short sweet herbage on which cattle and horses thrive. Thus, during the months of September and October, when Bechuanaland and the Transvaal are a scorched arid waste, and cattle poor and miserable, the Mashonaland valleys are everywhere green, streams run through every hollow, and stock are in splendid condition.

True, in the lower lying parts care must be taken during the season of the rains—from January to April—at which time the vegetation is rank and malaria prevalent, and anyone who is unduly exposed to cold and wet will be very likely to contract it ; but those not exposed to unhealthy conditions enjoy perfect health on the plateau. With a few reasonable precautions, such as avoiding the direct rays of the sun at noon-day, the boiling of all water for drinking purposes, the judicious use of quinine and other simple drugs, and a sparing use of intoxicants, especially in the form of spirits, a healthy person of either sex can dwell in Central Africa with almost the same comfort and safety as would be the case in Europe.

CHAPTER IX.

The Chastising of Mapondera.

NOW Mapondera, brother of Temaringa, in former times held high rank amongst the Indunas, and was the most influential of the Makori-kori chiefs. But his position had fallen from him and he had taken to ways which were sure sooner or later to bring him in closer touch with the white police whose eyes and ears were far reaching, and who kept peace amongst the tribes in the land of the Mashonas. Family quarrels had caused the fore-front of his offending, for he had commenced his evil ways with the killing of his father-in-law for no ostensible reason. Then came a series of minor raids on weaker tribes in the vicinity, followed by an elaborate system of commandeering for the wants of himself and his followers. And in the end a reign of terror came o'er the tribes, and the name of Mapondera made men's hearts as water and caused women to hide in the recesses of the kraals.

Likewise Zuni, a headman of Lomaghonda district had maltreated certain natives of the territory now ruled by the Portuguese, and, complaints having been made to Salisbury the capital, Captain Munroe, an officer of the police, had been despatched with a handful of the native contingent, which are called the 'Black Watch,' to effect his arrest. But chancing on his way northward to hear of the doings of Mapondera, he altered his plans, and leaving Zuni for a while, went after the greater rascal.

Mapondera was a sturdy rogue of some natural ability, and having elected to live the lawless life of a bandit, he had designed his residence to cope with any emergency which might arise from his mode of living. His stronghold, consisting of a few huts and caves, stood in an almost inaccessible basin formed by the natural arrangement of rocks on the hillside. The entrance

THE CHASTISING OF MAPONDERA.

to the stronghold was by way of a narrow pass. Through this Captain Munroe and his small patrol pushed their way. Mapondera and his men opened fire, and in the ensuing fight, Sergeant John, of the 'Black Watch,' was killed. Thereupon, Captain Munroe, perceiving the strength of the position held by the bandits, returned to Sinoia and telegraphed his reasons to Lieut. Col. Flint, Commandant of the Mashonaland Division of the British South African Police.

This officer at once realised the gravity of the position. The British rule over these savages is maintained much more by prestige than by force, and this prestige would be lowered materially by the small success of the refractory chief. Already other kraals were wavering. Tsingwaru's, Uzmajinjera's, Kapondi's, M'paraganda's, Kavvri's, and Tsefamba's were known to have accorded help to Mapondera with men and with grain. Also the struggle far southward 'twixt Briton and Boer had been watched with feverish interest by the black tribes of Rhodesia. Already distorted accounts of Boer successes had been disseminated, and news flies from hill to hill in these parts with the swiftness of the telegraph. The situation was a grave one, and it was of paramount importance that this chief should be crushed in his stronghold far north by the Dande River.

Therefore was an expedition hastily organised, consisting of the 3rd Division of the British South African Police, a body of the Mashonaland Native Police, and one squadron of the Imperial Yeomanry forming part of the Rhodesian Field Force. And there was joy and hasty preparation in the ranks of the 65th I.Y. the Leicesters, for they had been chosen for the work in hand.

Black were the reports of the country where the outlaw had made his home; of the malaria that ran rampant through its wooded valleys; of the trackless hill-ranges they would have to cross. But this did not damp the spirits of the squadron. For latterly there had grown a dull fear, born of their tardy progress, that they would go south just in time to be shipped home again without once having heard the singing of a bullet fired in anger. But here was the prospect of action, the chance of winning their spurs. Fever, forsooth! they had braved that already. The Zambesi valley could not be much worse than Bamboo Creek.

And so, on the 28th of June, a long train of boxes full of horses, and trucks heaped up with stores and men, steamed northward from the station of Marandellas. The railway would take them as far as Salisbury, and from there the punitive force would trek with horses and ox-wagons as far north as the rough roads allowed. And after that. Who cared?

* * * * *

'Tis fifteen days since the tents and civilization were left behind at Salisbury the capital. At the kraal of Sepulilo, a loyal headman, a camp is formed. For from here the path is impracticable for wagons or horses. From here everything must be carried on the bodies of the men or on the heads of the native carriers.

It has been fifteen days of hard roughing and vexing delays. A tale of weary trekking o'er bad roads—if roads they may be called. Of transport getting stuck in wide and rapid rivers. Of burning sun by day, and of nights passed in the bitter cold with no blankets, the wagons being miles in rear. Of watchful guards and huge fires through the night, necessary to protect the horses from the lions and other beasts of prey which prowled nightly round the camp. And lately, of rations going bad, and having to be eked out precariously with antelope shot by the way, and once by a dinner of wild ostrich. Sometimes in the narrow forest path, the oxen would swerve, running the wheel of a wagon round the wrong side of a tree. Then it was "out axes," for you can't manœuvre a transport wagon and sixteen ox-team like two mules in a Cape-cart. And the tree would have to fall before the column could proceed on its way—to the next obstruction.

And to all the villages had been sent runners, calling upon all men who were loyal to repair upon a certain day to the kraal of Sepulilo, to hold a great 'indaba' and to hear the words that the chief of the white soldiers had to say to them.

The scene was a strange one, a scene not likely to be forgotten by the men who were privileged to witness it.

In the centre of a vast clearing, beaten bare for the purposes of the camp, stood the tall figure of Colonel Flint. By his side Captain Gilson, of the Police, who repeated the words of the Colonel to Tom, the black interpreter, in Makalaka. These were then translated by Tom into the dialects of the tribes who had assembled. Twenty yards in front of the central group squatted the line of headmen of the villages, nearly all old men with grey heads and short grey beards, and eyes which shone keenly from lined furrowed faces. Outside these again the natives, each squatting on his haunches in the native fashion, in a vast half circle, four and five in depth. The whole framed by the Rhodesian bushland, by long grass and shrubs and tall mopani groves. Whilst forty miles northwards lay the mountain ranges in which Mapondera the outlaw lay hidden. Nightly from Sepulilo's kraal was the glow of his signal fires to be seen.

The air is filled with the low buzz of the natives, and over the great sickle of black men runs the ripple of movement, of shifting heads and limbs. Carelessly, but with infinite care, the white men are scattered around, and in the hands of every man an unobtrusive rifle.

The Colonel lifts his hand, and instant the buzz dies to silence like the dropping of the wind. And the sun lights up a great ring of ebon faces, from which shine eager five thousand eyes, fixed on the central figure.

"Tell the chiefs of Lomaghonda"—the clear ringing voice of the Colonel can be heard by the furthermost native—"I am pleased that so many have come at my bidding, sent to them by the runners who carried my message. But I am sorry that there are some who have not come. They are all subjects of the Great White Queen"—

The Colonel pauses, and his eye sweeps round the listening circle. And like a heaving wall the whole of the natives rise slowly to their full height, with arms uplifted and hands bent over forward; while from every lip breaks a sound—more like a loud long-drawn moan than anything I know. It is a sign of acquiescence, of loyalty, of allegiance. Back to the earth slowly sinks the living wall and the Colonel goes on.

"Under the rule of the white men, who are the servants of the Great White Queen, they have prospered, and have tilled their fields and gathered in their crops, without fear of raids from the warlike tribes as formerly. They have been governed by just laws, and their complaints have been listened to with patience.

And tell them, Tom, if they are loyal and keep the laws made for them by the Great White Queen, then will the Great White Queen give protection to them, who are her children, and peace and prosperity will dwell in their villages "—

" Wa-a-a-ugh ! " Like a black wave rises the thousands of figures—a wave from which breaks the sough of the gale. Silent it ebbs and the Colonel goes on.

" But "—and his voice rings stern in the stillness—" Tell them, Tom, that tales have come to my ears of evil-doing amongst the tribes, of bloodspilling which is forbid by the laws of the white man, and the Great White Queen has sent me her servant, and has sent her soldiers, with good guns, to punish the evil-doers, and to restore peace in the kraals. And if any of them carry falseness in their hearts, and disloyalty to the Great White Queen, let them beware. For the Great White Queen will send thousands of her soldiers, with good guns, and will kill them and burn their kraals. Tell them that, Tom."

" Wa-a-a-ugh ! " The cry has now the ring of fear, for the stern words of the Colonel mean grim visions for most. They have not forgotten the severe lessons of the rebellion of four years ago.

" Bring the prisoner."

Into the bare space in front, guarded by two privates of the ' Black Watch,' is brought a wily-featured sturdily built native. His neck and waist are hung with bones and teeth and other fetish. He is the ' Mandora ' or witch doctor of the district. Sullen he squats in the sight of all, on each side of him a stolid black levy, bayonet on rifle.

" Tell the people of the kraals that this man had great power with Mapondera, who was the paramount chief, and with the headmen. But he is a bad man. He has turned the hearts of the headmen against their mother, the Great White Queen. Therefore will he be punished. And it is the wish of the Great White Queen that Sepulilo be placed in the stead of Mapondera. Therefore is Sepulilo appointed paramount chief of the kraals, and the Great White Queen wishes her children to obey the rule of Sepulilo, their paramount chief, and so shall the heart of the Great White Queen be gladdened by the welfare of the tribes, her children. I have spoken."

WOMEN BRINGING IN NATIVE BEER AT A WAR-DANCE. Photo *B.S.A. Company.*

THE CHASTISING OF MAPONDERA. 103

"Wa-a-a-ugh!" And amidst it the witch doctor is led away —to his merited punishment.

Then came forward Sepulilo, and kissed the feet of the Colonel, and rising to his full height, he spoke. And as near as I could get them, these are the words he used.

"Ah! Murumbi! huru dishe ewuto!*

Sepulilo, the least of his servants,
Has heard the words of the White Chief—
The words sent to him by the Great White Queen.
Sepulilo is old, and his hair is white,
Yet (proudly) with age comes wisdom in Council.
And if as the White Chief has spoken,
It is the wish of the Great White Queen that he be chief of the headmen,
Then will he rule them with wisdom.
And his tongue shall be straight, and his heart shall be white in his dealings.
So the warriors of the White Chief may not visit the kraals in their anger.
When the young men took up the 'pfumo' and 'nobo' †
Led astray by the words of the 'madzwiti' ‡
And went with blood in their eyes through the country;
Then came the soldiers of the Great White Queen, with many guns, and the blood ran red in the rivers,
And there was sorrow in the land of Lomaghonda,
And in all the kraals there was mourning.

But under the rule of Sepulilo,
Peace shall dwell in the hearts of the headmen,
And the people shall gather in the harvests
Of the groundnuts, the pogo and mealies,
And their cattle shall again fill the valleys
As when Sepulilo was swiftest of foot of the young men.
And the White Chief shall carry to the Great White Queen
The words of her children
Spoken for them by their chief, Sepulilo,

---

* Oh! white man! great chief of warriors!
† The assegai and cowhide shield—referring to the rebellion of the Mashonas in 1896.
‡ Matabele. The Mashonas were incited to rebellion by the Matabele leaders through the instrumentality of the 'Mandoros' (lions) or witch-doctors.

And the heart of the Great White Queen shall be glad
For that peace and plentiful harvests
Shall again fill the land of the Makalakas.
Sepulilo has spoken."

* * * * *

It is dark night. Through the forest moves a phantom line of men. A thin three-mile line, in single file, winding in and out amongst the trees. It is the punitive column.

Several days ago they left on foot the kraal of Sepulilo, and to-morrow at dawn they will be within striking distance of the rebel chief. One troop is missing. They have made a wide detour and will prevent Mapondera from breaking away to the northward when the attack takes place. No voice is heard. All commands are passed in undertone from man to man; and ever and anon from the tall figure stalking on in front the inquiry runs quietly along the line "Are the carriers all right. Is the rearguard all right?" And back ripples the reply "The rearguard is all right, and close behind the column."

Thus, up hill, down dale, by Kaffir paths known only to the sable guides, until at two hours after midnight they arrive as near as it is judged prudent to go, and the column lays down till dawn. Every safeguard is taken against surprise, for more than once during the night march have distant beacon fires been seen in the hills, and it is more than probable that his spies have warned Mapondera of our approach. There are no fires, and one man in every four is constantly on guard, lest through the gloom of the forest aisles should steal the dark naked forms of the foe.

Two short hours rest and the column is again on the move. Round the hill spurs, through deep-cut ravines, wading up the uneven beds of mountain streams or sliding down places too steep for booted feet, hour follows hour and yet no bandit lair is reached. There is consultation with the guides. The hour fixed for the attack is past, and there is nothing to attack save untenanted rocks and empty crevices and caves. A miscalculation has been made by the guides, and the distance to the rebel stronghold has been woefully understated. On again along the tiring trail. Another hour and the distant sound of firing, loud echoing in the hills, is heard. The little column pushes on.

THE CHASTISING OF MAPONDERA.

But the troop sent out to flank the rebel chief and cut off his retreat. How have they fared?

This troop left the column at dawn on the preceding day. After the first three hours there was practically no path to be followed, and they were led by the native guides through thick cane-brakes, under an excessively hot sun, across an almost waterless country. Till, half dead with exhaustion—for they were in full marching order and carrying great coats—they gladly flung themselves down for a few hours rest and sleep. With the dawn came the precipitous descent to where, nearly two thousand feet below, the Dande lay in a series of large deep pools. The river made many turns, and round one of these bends they knew lay the stronghold of Mapondera. Here they waited for the opening attack by the main body. But the time went on and no shots woke the stillness.

Now it chanced that morn that one of the eight wives of Mapondera went to the river to fish, taking with her her youngest son, a naked little 'piccanin' of five or six. Some way up the stream was a deep pool she wot of, where the fish were larger and more easy to snare, and thither she wended her way. On ahead round the bends ran the boy. Suddenly she heard him scream, and dashing round a projecting rock, saw scrambling o'er the stones and splashing through the pools, a round score of the white demons she had been taught to dread. They knew they had been discovered, and were making a dash for the kraal. Scream after scream and frantic high-pitched warnings rang through the canon, as, fleet of foot, she sprang away towards the kraal, and easily outdistanced the more cumbrous Yeomen, who, over these slippery rocks were no match for the swift-footed native. They turned the last bend just in time to pour a volley into the bandits, who were making good their hasty retreat up the mountain side. Taking cover far up the hill, the blacks took 'pot shots' at their pursuers with their ancient flintlock family guns, curiously wrapped with wire, and loaded half way to the muzzle with scraps of iron and the legs of iron cooking-pots. Happily, their aim was not so good as their intentions, for had a man received the full charge of one of these pieces of ordnance there would have been very little of him left to bury.

And then, two hours late, the main body appeared, but the birds were on the outside of the net.

The two forces now joined, and spreading into extended order, drove the blacks from cover to cover until they could no longer be seen. Then descending to the kraal, some of Mapondera's goats were killed, and the hungry troops were soon in the middle of a sorely needed meal. It was now late afternoon, and they had been marching almost continuously since eleven o'clock on the evening before, through a nearly inaccessible country, in full marching order, and had eaten nothing but a few fragments of biscuit carried in their havresack.

But the longed-for meal was never finished. For the enemy crept back, and suddenly came the thunder of the family guns, and the fragments of rock were being chipped off all round them. There was hasty scattering for cover, and then once more the blacks were chased from rock to rock, and pursued far into the surrounding hills. They did not escape scatheless, for five bodies were eventually found. Also many women and children were captured, including several of Mapondera's wives, and the whole of his goats and caves filled with grain and groundnuts (the familiar monkey-nut) were left in our hands. And amongst the rocks was found the coat of the unfortunate Sergeant John, the stripes still on the sleeve. The captives were eventually taken to Salisbury, and the stores of grain and the kraal with its contents were burnt by the 'Black Watch,' a task which they seemed to carry out with savage delight.

I do not think these native police did much execution with their rifles, as they seldom brought them to their shoulders to take aim. They would load as fast as possible and fire from the hip, pointing the muzzle somewhere in the direction of the enemy. There is not the slightest doubt that they made a great deal of noise, for the reports of the Martinis and the big-mouthed family guns made in the narrow ravine a deafening uproar.

One had no difficulty in judging where the enemy lay concealed in the rocks, for they were covered as much by the thick smoke they made as by the boulders they lay behind. One

Photos by *Lieut. R. B. Muir.*
BIVOUAC OF THE NATIVE POLICE.
A BIT OF MASHONALAND.

of the 'Black Watch' fell, shot through the chest. Without a moment's hesitation, Captain Gilson's black boy—a non-combatant—sprang forward, and, without giving a thought to the poor fellow's wound, tore off his bandolier, and picking up the rifle said, with a deep sigh of content, "Ah! now I've got a gun," and immediately commenced to blaze away at the rocks.

After the caves had been thoroughly searched for stores of grain, and these had been destroyed, the little force withdrew from the valley, and encamped near the scene of the engagement. A patrol was sent out in pursuit of the routed outlaws, and others placed in ambush by the paths leading to the kraal, to catch any native whose curiosity might lead him to return. The patrol followed the foe till night, and, sleeping on the trail, again hotly pursued them with the dawn. They came up with a small party, and, in the skirmish that ensued, two more blacks were killed, and more women and children captured. But Mapondera and the broken remnant of his bandit band escaped across the border into Portuguese territory, where they could not be followed.

It was not known whether Mapondera was amongst the slain, so Colonel Flint sent out parties of the 'Black Watch' to search for and bring in any bodies they might find in the vicinity, that they might be identified by the captive women. Only one of these parties met with any success. After half a day's search they appeared before the Colonel, and to his disgust, opened out a cloth they were carrying, and emptied at his feet—two black heads. Of course they were punished, but in their mistaken ideas of war, they imagined, with some show of logic, that a man could be identified as easily by his head as by the whole of his body, and, in the hot sun, the heads were infinitely more easy to carry.

*   *   *   *

There is the throb of excitement restrained, and the unrest of constant coming and going in the kraal of Sepulilo, the paramount chief. For to-day have returned the victorious white men, with captives and many goats. And no longer will there be terror in the kraals. For the power of Mapondera has been broken, and his hunted followers have fled through the forests, over the Great River which flows far to the northwards.

And, when the darkness has fallen on the forests, then is a Great Feast to be given, and a Great Dance in honor of the victors, such as has not been seen for many seasons. And the people pour in from the villages, carrying shields and sticks—for the bringing of arms is forbidden—and attired in finery of beads, and the skins of the wild cat, and with necklaces of wondrous stones, charms 'gainst the unseen spirits.

The huge fire in the centre of the clearing crackles hungry 'midst the dry limbs, and glows redly on the shining skins of the circle half hid in the shadows. There is no sound but the spitting of the flames. A strained expectant silence holds the tribes. Then, from deep in the woods, comes faintly the single cry of a jackal, long-drawn, melancholy ; and it seems to break the spell.

From somewhere in the darkness breaks a human voice, shrill, piercing ; a native chant of victory, sung in the tongue of the tribes. In an unbroken stream it flows, chaining the ears of the listening natives, till one's breath quickens, and one falls to wondering, oddly, if this continued lung-strain is turning the reciter black in the face.

Sudden the chant is ceased and from the thousands of black throats breaks an excited song, one monotonous strain repeated times without number, to the music of beating tom-toms and the loud clapping of hands.

Then from the gloom, scarce reached by the fire-light, a row of savages advance in step. Held high o'erhead, their sticks and shields are clashed in time to their rhythmic movement. The tom-toms grow fast and furious, and as line after line of black figures rise and join in the dance, the very earth shakes with the simultaneous stamp of a thousand naked feet. The dust is beaten up in clouds, and soon the flames light up but a dazing mass of savage movement ; a thousand points of light from arm and ankle rings of brass, from pearly teeth and shining eyes, wild with excited eagerness, glinting through haze of ruddy-tinted dust.

Now the movement changes. The heaving line falls back, and, at the call of the chief, a lithe young savage shows his skill alone. With high excited leaps, he wards off the attacks of an imaginary foe, singing at utmost stretch the tale of his deeds, or what he'd like to do. Twenty more are eager for his place, but with giant leaps—into the verge of the flames, back to the shadows—his gyrations are continued till he falls exhausted, or, at the call of the chief, another takes his place. And through all runs the beat of the tom-toms and the ear-splitting clapping of hands, beating the tune of the chant

"Yamee—i—o ! Yamee—i—o ! O—oh—o—o."

Till with heads aching from the whirl and the babel of shrill sounds, and overpowered by the odour from the countless reeking bodies, many of us quietly withdraw ; and far into the night our dreams are mixed with the

"Yamee—i—o ! Yamee—i—o ! O—oh—o—c."

*   *   *   *

Again o'er the line, the laden train carries from Salisbury southwards the same burden as seven weeks before rode north.

With this exception.

With them rides the pick of the outlaw's herds—the pet of the squadron—' Mapondera ' the goat.

CHAPTER X.

Trekking across the Plains.

THIRTEEN days ago we returned from Salisbury and once more slept on the Marandellas plateau. Returned to find a part deserted camp. Three squadrons of Bushmen and ourselves are all that are left.

And since we came we have been torn by tales and rumours. A week ago an orderly was overheard to say that all mounted troops were going south at once, and we went singing round the camp. Two days later an officer's servant heard at mess that one squadron of Yeomanry would be left to garrison the camp, and as we were the only squadron of Yeomanry left behind, it didn't need much calculation—but why go on; our spirits sank to zero. Once we *should* have gone if the horses had been inoculated. Again we *were* going upon the arrival of a regiment of foot which had already landed at Beira. And so for thirteen days our hopes have been played puppet with, and have been led along Rumour's switchback at the sweet will of the gossips. But yesterday the order came, and at 4 p.m. to-day, having returned our tents and other impedimenta to stores, our little column moved out en route for Buluwayo, three hundred miles away. Our force—five officers and a hundred men or more; our artillery—two maxim guns and limbers; our transport— two light 'floats,' five mule wagons and three drawn by oxen. Our pace will be regulated by the pace of the oxen, and including halts for rest, will not exceed an average of ten miles a day.

This march through Rhodesia came nearer to the 'picnic' prognosticated by Hon. Cecil Rhodes than anything we saw before or since. Rising each day with or before the dawn, we rode through the keen morning air, till nine or ten in the morning. Then in some shady wood by a cool stream, if such conditions were at hand, we halted and turned out the horses to graze on the long dry grass that flourished everywhere. Another short march in the afternoon and the day's trekking would be done. It was ideal campaigning, though I am afraid we did not fully appreciate it till we had had some of the real kind with which to compare it.

Now our course lay through woods just donning their spring garments. One might easily mark the age of the foliage by its colour. Here is a tree clothed in tenderest leaves of vivid Indian red, glossy and half translucent. The red changes to red-brown. There the longer action of the light is seen and the brown is softly tinged with green. From greenish-brown to brownish-green they merge; then through every shade of tender green as the leaves gain age and size.

These trees of the Mashona uplands have a beauty all their own. Their height and girth is small, and heavy opaque masses of foliage would look but burdensome upon the light and tapering limbs. But Nature never errs in this respect, and their light feathery branches stretching out in horizontal cedar-like arms soften the ruggedness of the kopjes' outlines, whilst the tender reds and greens break and make beautiful the vast stretches of tall pale yellow grass. Here a tree is covered with small white blossoms like an English hawthorn at its best. There a monarch in size compared with its fellows, though devoid of leaves, is clothed from lowest branch to crown with long flower spikes of brightest crimson hue.

Or through groves of thorny trees covered with large orange-like fruit. The natives ate them, calling them 'Kaffir oranges,' so we quickly followed their example. The hard gourd-like shell is filled with large flat seeds embedded in dark brown muddy-coloured pulp. This pulp, which is eaten, tastes like decayed apples flavoured with cinnamon, but is refreshing when one is thirsty on the march.

Or for days across great undulating plains, here waving yellow grass, there blackened wastes through which the red soil showed—the track of the bush fires; and then again fresh with the vivid green of the young grass, on which the wild buck love to feed.

Often were passed traces of cultivated fields and razed huts marking where villages had stood. But the whole land seemed deserted and tenantless. The reason is not far to seek. First the Angoni and the Abagaza,* then the cruel Amandibili Zulus under their ruthless chief Umziligaas, have by raid and massacre made this unfortunate land a depopulated desert. Until a few years ago were these raids carried on from Buluwayo, the chief kraal of Umziligaas and Lobengula his son. Until the downfall of Lobengula brought peace to the harried tribes.

Our wagons only carry forage and stores for a third of our long journey, and passing through Charter, on September 3 we reached 'The Range' a large Government depôt where our stores were replenished. Half a mile from the camp ran the river, a branch of the Sabi, a beautiful wide stream; here a deep reach in which our swimmers spent half their time, there running over great slabs and boulders of granite rock, clear and limpid as crystal.

But apart from their beauty and their vegetation of unfamiliar shape, these far-reaching plains are steeped in romantic associations. A Romance so limitless and enthralling that as one learns, he is awed and feels as though he stood on next to holy ground. For there exists little, if any doubt that the gold producing region of Ophir was the 'red-land' of East Africa, now know as Mashonaland, where the Sabi River flows.

From here the Sabeans obtained there gold. From these rocks were crushed that hundred and twenty talents which their monarch, called Queen of Sheba, carried on her overland journey to the court of King Solomon. Away there to the south of us stand the ruins of temple and fortress, built in hewn stone without the aid of mortar and cement, by the mystic race who delved here for gold a thousand years before the Christian era. A race that has gone. Worshippers of Baal, for such the structure of their temple proves, but who have vanished so completely in the dimness of the ages, that the natives living around these erections in the present day can tell nothing of their origin or history beyond that they were built by the 'ancient people.'

Having taken up fresh stores we moved on to Enkeldoorn the same night. The trees in the woods around, though dwarfed in

---

* See page 88

A MASHONALAND STREAM—*p. 114.*—Photo by *P. S. Inskipp.*
THE SALISBURY-BULUWAYO COACH—*p. 114.*—Photo by *Lieut. H. T. Munn.*

TREKKING ACROSS THE PLAINS 113

size, were evidently of a great age. The trunks and limbs were silvery grey with lichen, and hoary moss of dull green colour hung in beard-like festoons along each branch and twig. Quantities of small doves flew about the road. They were extremely tame and seemed to court the company of the troops. Three years ago there was no such town as Enkeldoorn. At the end of 1897 three hundred Dutchmen from the Transvaal trekked north into Rhodesia, and formed a laager near this spot, the remains of which can still be seen. The locality pleased them and they decided to stay. So the Rhodesian Government bought a large farm and formed a township in the usual Rhodesian method, by laying out streets at right angles and selling by auction the 'stands' or lots between. Many of the Dutchmen took farms in the vicinity, and so Enkeldoorn was founded. During the present war several of the inhabitants have fought on the side of their adopted country, and have had farms granted to them for their loyalty. One at least was known to join the Boers, and his possessions have been confiscated. The English clergyman, from whom I gathered the above, and many other facts, said we had arrived at the worst time of the year to see Rhodesia—just before the Spring. Next month a few showers, and in a few days everywhere would be clothed in most vivid green, interspersed with masses of flowers of every hue. He incidentally mentioned that his parish was nearly as large as England and Wales.

Enkeldoorn of the present day—by the way, the name means 'Single Thorn'—is not a particularly interesting place. One long street bordered by very young trees in 'guards;' a few brick stores, some having a bar attached; a well-equipped hospital and red brick Dutch Church; a police camp on a neighbouring hill and a few mud farms dotted around. And a Post Office—I had nearly forgotten the Post Office—a plain one storied Post Office built of sun-dried bricks from which most of the mortar had long since crumbled away; and before the door the bleached skull of an immense 'hippo' shot by a local Nimrod and presented to the town, which had nowhere else to put it. The clerks lived at one side of the office, of which many of the windows had been broken. On the door an official proclamation announcing that on Saturday last (September 1), the South African Republic

H

had been formally annexed—and in the window a hand-printed card bearing the legend

> CLOSED BECAUSE
> WIND COME IN.

Such is Enkeldoorn, the Dutch settlement in Rhodesia.

Two days later, crossing the Sebakwe River, we passed from the land of the Mashonas into Matabeleland. Though near the end of the dry season the whole of our route was well-watered, and even in the smallest river beds lay pools at varying distances apart at which a plenteous supply of water could be obtained. In the rains the larger ones are rushing floods, and are crossed by a box or cradle drawn from bank to bank along a taut wire cable hanging in mid-air. Sometimes—as on the Sebakwe—a ferryboat, drawn across by a wheel which travelled along the cable, was substituted for the aerial car.

We were now upon the Salisbury-Buluwayo road, and were passed every other day by the Zeederberg coaches, which at present is the only method of passenger transport between the two capitals. Large lumbering vehicles of the familiar 'Deadwood' type, hung on leathern straps in place of springs, and painted red—some years ago. They are drawn at a fast trot by eight small grey mules, and complete the journey of 280 miles in three-and-a-half days. Piled up with passengers and baggage, they look far too clumsy and top heavy to negotiate some of the spruits we have had to cross. Every twelve miles or so the team is changed at the coaching stables placed at intervals along the route. These were not elaborate constructions; a description of one is typical of the whole. A rough wooden shed opening into a small brushwood corral, with a Kaffir hut or two alongside. Nothing more. The mules graze on the veldt until a coach is nearly due, when they are driven to the corral by the attendant blacks. They must prove a temptation to the transport drivers along the road, for nailed on every stable was a board setting forth the dire pains and penalties awaiting all delinquents. The Company had evidently left the boards to be nailed up by the 'boys,' whose educational advantages, it must be assumed, had been limited, for many of those we passed appeared thus:

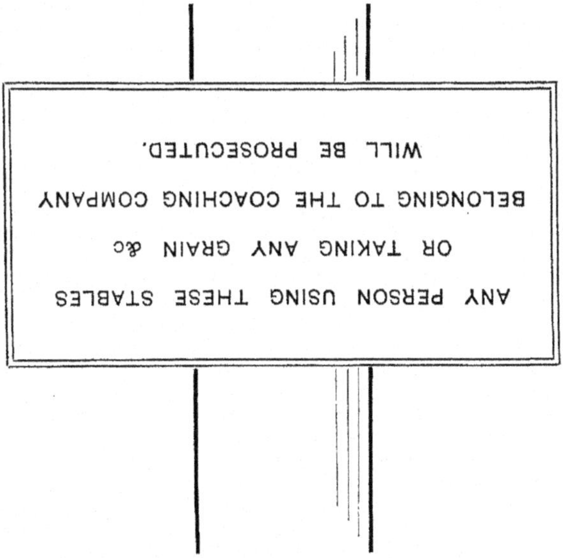
ANY PERSON USING THESE STABLES
OR TAKING ANY GRAIN &c
BELONGING TO THE COACHING COMPANY
WILL BE PROSECUTED.

a warning to all evil-doers.

The midday halt upon the day before reaching Gwelo was an ideal one, and typical of many along the route, We encamped in a wood at a short distance from the road. Plenty of dry wood for the fires, a beautiful stream not two hundred yards away, clear and sweet as an English spring, and good grazing for the horses quite close to the camp. More than this one could hardly wish for. We were in the midst of vast antheaps. The wood was studded with them. Here one over fifteen feet in height was overgrown with tall yellow grass, there another was topped by forest trees, decayed and broken with age. Everywhere over the plain huge convex boulders rose a few feet above the grass like gigantic granite mushrooms bursting through, some of them several acres in extent. These outcrops were entirely bare of vegetation, but were covered with patches of lichen-growth in every shade of yellow, and red, and brown, and green, and orange. Scattered about were the straggling 'M'quaan,' or monkey-fig bushes, bearing on each twig large blossoms, each flower a mass of feathery plumes of sheeny silken white.

During the after trek we came to a river whose perpendicular banks rose thirty feet in height. Through the banks on either side a sloping track was cut—so steeply that a man had perforce to go down it at a run. The stream was shallow but thickly sown with large and rounded rocks. I rode to the top of the overhanging bank and watched the scene below. The mule transport had arrived. One wagon at a time they crossed, the others waiting. A sharp crack from the driver's mighty whip—the stock twelve feet in length, the whip-lash nearer twenty—and the ten mules bound forward. Down the steep bank they come at a run, the heavy wagon lumbering after. Splash into the stream, the wheels bumping and leaping from rock to rock, excited men with flying whips, knee-deep in water, lashing them through. If the leathern traces but hold the wagon is bound to go. The water flies in showers as the mules stumble across the uneven ford; but they are out and now the hardest bit is faced. Up the steep bank, so wet and slippery from the feet of those who have gone before, they strain. The wagon will not move, for one wheel is behind a rounded rock as large as a sack of grain. The cruel lash whistles and curls o'er the team, cutting the mules on flank, on ear, on neck. There is a babel of hoarse cries from the leaders and drivers—haek ! hek ! *haek !* HA-A-EK ! ! Surely the force of the leaping plunging mules must start something—the wagon *must* move or the harness break. Look ! at length it moves. The wagon lurches as the wheel grinds slowly up the boulder, striking spark and smoke e'en from the wet stone. It surmounts the rock, and with a bump drops on the other side. Now for a pull together ; now for the cracking whips ! Up the hill foot by foot, every yard gained but by the incessant ply of whips of bullock hide, and the shrill strident urging of the drivers. A mule slips and stumbles, but is lashed to his feet ! Another is down and rolls on his side—they cannot find foothold on the slippery path. But never a pause of the plunging team. The cruel whips are round him and he is up almost before one has time to note his fall. And so

TREKKING ACROSS THE PLAINS. 117

at last the bank is won, and at an easy trot the team goes on its way quite unconcerned. For such is the daily life of a transport mule.

Gwelo. We here take up stores for the remaining third of our journey. Gwelo, at a distance, looks as if a huge shrapnel shell, loaded with tin buildings and brick shops, instead of bullets, had been exploded over the spot, and had scattered around its contents, which by some miraculous coincidence had all fallen right way up. The scattered appearance of the town is, however, easily explained. When, from the proximity of gold-bearing reefs or some other cause, a score or two of miners wish to form a settlement, they map out in streets and squares, in the usual large-check pattern, a city calculated to contain some 10,000 inhabitants. Then the 'stands' bordering the streets are sold by auction, and five or six of the miners will fix their habitations in the heart of the future city, whilst the others will buy suburban lots some half-mile away to the north, south, east or west as the fancy takes them. The town booms and in a few years some of the central streets get filled up, but one can readily imagine the sprinkled appearance of these towns in their earlier stages. And we must remember that ten years ago neither Salisbury nor Buluwayo existed, much less Gwelo.

The town stands in the centre of one of the richest gold districts in Rhodesia, and when once reached by the railway, which may be by the time this appears in print, Gwelo will advance by leaps and bounds. It has wide and well-metalled streets, bordered by the usual rain-gulleys and pepper trees. There are many General Stores and more Bottle Stores, a striking Post Office and Stock Exchange and some palatial hotels. In the older parts stand clumps of a peculiar dark-foliaged eucalyptus having a cypress habit of growth, and looking as though they had strayed from a neighbouring cemetery. New roads and streets, levelled and channel-bordered, run out some half-mile into the plain from each side of the town like the legs of some huge spider, ready for the inhabitants who have yet to come. High-cheeked black policemen, in white trousers and helmets, and khaki tunics ornamented with Austrian knots of drab braid, patrolled the streets, carrying knobkerries terminating in immense knobs. Sundry Kaffirs, whose apparel emphasized the fact that the world hadn't gone well with them, spread fresh metal on the roads. Tall thin sun-burnt men, in light-coloured clothing and B.P. hats, lounged at the front of the verandahed hotels talking business and smoking large cigars. Other white men and little white boys on bicycles dashed along the sidewalks or, crossing the intervening gullies with a bump, made short cuts across unbuilt-on stands. Near the Post Office a news-shop where all the English magazines and papers of a month before were displayed. Near by two chemists' shops with the usual coloured globes, and a small tin shanty from which, according to the sign, emanated *The Gwelo Times*. These, and a large well-equipped hospital, were, I think, the principal features of Gwelo.

Our camp lay in a grove of trees half-a-mile from the town, and was infested with white ants. Our girths and surcingles of webbing had to be carefully kept from the ground, or these pests would so eat into them in the night that they snapped through on saddling up in the morning. Though so fond of wood, the white ants have a great antipathy for wood ashes, and whenever we found any we gave them ample opportunity for showing it. Shiny blue-coated scorpions were numerous. I found two under my bedding, and more than a dozen were killed in the camp. Whilst returning from the town through the long grass in the dusk, a snake struck fiercely at my leg. The blows were delivered with some force, and I could distinctly feel them through the puttees, but these were luckily too thick for the fangs of the reptile to penetrate.

Sometimes we were all at once surrounded by locusts in vast swarms. They were of the red or more destructive variety. All around as far as the eye could reach the air was full of them. The thickness of the swarm exactly resembled a heavy snow-storm of black snow—one of those English storms when the flakes are very large. The lines of the landscape were blurred by their numbers. They alighted on every long blade of yellow grass and every leaf and twig, hanging on the branches like clusters of rosy fruit. Soon a small shower of half-gnawed leaves would begin to fall, mingled with the insects which had lost their hold. They are about three inches long, with bright crimson-shot bodies, heads and legs; and their wings are glistening and transparent, and scaleless save for a few transverse bars of brown. They covered everything, and each long grass stalk had its swinging burden. As the wind gently swayed the herbage and the trees and the sun caught the glistening wings, the whole country-side glittered as though encrusted with countless myriads of sparkling gems.

Hardly a day passed without these swarms. Often they were not so dense and flew over our heads, with their chequered shadows rippling o'er the ground like the reflection of trees in wind-stirred water. Or, as the dusk approached, they would come lower and lower, and alight on every tree or bush around us for the night.

Many of the camps were infested by the noisy 'cicadæ.' These are a dappled brown and grey insect like a large bee with a very broad head. They sit on the branches and so exactly resemble the bark in tint and marking that one may carefully search and fail to find them though they be within a few inches of his nose. They make a shrill noise which is extremely powerful considering their size. The sound completely fills the air for yards around and is so irritating in its intensity that one has to move away from their proximity; and this they keep up for hours at a time. The ancient Greeks, I believe, used the cicada as an article of food, and if they were driven to eating the insects as the only sure method of preventing them from making any more noise, I can quite enter into the feelings of the ancient Greeks.

I once had a chameleon. It happened in this way. As I was returning from water—we were encamped near the banks of the Chirume—the lance-corporal of the Maxims came running. There was something under the gun he had never seen before. It was clinging to a bent of grass and he couldn't tell me whether it was an insect, a reptile or a bird. The only thing he could swear to was that it wasn't a fish. So tying up my horses I went across to the little group who were watching the new discovery. It was a pale yellow chameleon, near the top of some reeds, bleached yellow by the sun. As they watched, it moved across to another reed, taking some three minutes in the operation. Slowly unclasping its two off-feet from the grass-stalk, it very deliberately, half-an-inch at a time, moved them across to the new stalk. Then, when quite certain that its hold was secure, it slowly unclasped the reed with its near feet and took them across to its new quarters at the same rate. Then pressing its yellow breast to the reed, it tightly curled up its tail into the semblance of a fossil ammonite, and gravely looked around, as though expecting applause.

" Kill it," said some one.

" No," I said, " this is mine. I'm going to tame it."

" Tame it. Will it follow you about ? " said one. And another said, chaffing, " You'll be an old man before you get to Buluwayo if you wait for it."

" I shall teach it to catch flies. It will sit on my shoulder when I am asleep and keep the flies from worrying me."

Then they laughed.

" Catch flies ! The fly would give it 99 yards out of 100 and romp home," said one.

" I'll put all the pay they owe me on the fly," said number two. But I said, " Wait."

And in time he came to know me and completely lost his fear. The most amusing things about him were his eyes. Eyes built on the principle of my chameleon's would, I am sure, be an incalculable boon to anyone afflicted with that unpleasant visitation commonly called a ' stiff neck.' For he could roll them in any direction and, without the slightest movement of his head, could look in front of him, or straight along his back, or any other way he wished. But more than this. Each eye moved independent of the other. As I stood before him he would fix me with his right eye, whilst his left was anxiously following a fly which had settled on his tail. These organs protruded so far from his head that there seemed very little eye-ball left in the socket to hold on by. And they were covered with a hard scaly skin, save for a small slit in the centre through which a keen watch was kept.

My strange pet had been partially forgotten by his detractors, though now and then one would fling across an enquiry after the welfare of the ' camelia,' for that was the nearest they ever got to his name. But, after some days, I invited them to an ' indaba,' and they all sat round in a circle whilst I brought out the chameleon.

He rested on my hand, which he much resembled in colour, and I held him near a fly, and said " Now watch him."

They watched him, but he didn't seem to notice the fly.

" He's not likely to see it," said one man in front of him, " he's watching me all the time."

" Watching you ! " the words came from the opposite side. " How can he be watching you when he's looking at me all the time ? "

" Well, strike me ! " cried number one, springing up disgusted, " if he hasn't got his eye on me all the time, I wish I may——"

" Don't quarrel," I said, " he's watching *both* of you. That's one of the tricks I've taught him. And you've frightened the fly away."

" Here's another," said they, for his first ' trick ' had made them interested.

The chameleon was about four inches long, and I held him some six or seven inches from the fly. Presently his roving eye saw it. A pause while he watched it, measuring the distance. His mouth slowly opened and, without any movement of head or eye, his long tongue shot across the intervening space and in a moment the fly was touched by the glutinous end of it and withdrawn into the mouth of the chameleon.

They fairly howled with delight.

" How does your back pay look ? " I said to the man who wanted to ' plunge ' on the chances of the fly.

But he evaded the subject and said, ' Let's see him catch another."

They sat and watched him catch flies till he was tired. At last he became so surfeited that he wouldn't look at a fly. Then they brought him a three-inch locust to see if a change of diet would tempt him.

I put him down in the shade under a blue coat.

" He's bad. Look at his skin," — for he had changed to a dark grey colour."

" No," I said, " that's another trick."

They put him on a leafy branch and his coat became green. On leaves of a darker green, and his skin took on the requisite shade. He changed through every shade, from dark slate, through the greens to the palest yellow. You couldn't tear the men away.

Then one man brought an empty bully beef tin, and wanted him to turn red white and blue all at once, to match the label.

So I closed the show.

His repute ran through the squadron. Men who hadn't seen him brought him flies from which they had carefully pulled the wings—" to give the camelia a chance "—they said. But when they had once seen him catch flies *au naturel*, they let him capture them after his own methods.

I was at first at a loss to know how to carry him on the march. I put him in an open box strapped before me on the saddle. But he climbed onto my shoulder, and, from that day, that was his favourite position, and there he rode some hundred miles or more.

But one day, after a gallop over some rough ground, I suddenly remembered the chameleon, and putting up my hand, found his place vacant.

He had fallen off, and I saw him no more.

Several times during this march a halt of half-a-day or more had to be made to wait for the ox-wagons. One may wonder that oxen were not superseded entirely by mule-transport, as their progress is so slow. But for every mule we have, there has to be carried 10 lbs. of oats per day. So for a ten days' journey each wagon—drawn by ten mules—must carry 1,000 lbs. of oats for the animals that draw it. Thus nearly half the loading space is lost. But an ox-wagon is not only larger than a mule-wagon, but the oxen get their own living off the veldt, and absolutely no forage is carried for them. Therefore, as the whole of the wagon is available for other stores, ox-transport is the more economical, if not so speedy.

More than once, between Gwelo and the capital, we crossed the made track of the Cape to Cairo railway. But only the levelled track. There are no rails as yet.

And on September 23, crossing Thabas Induna (Chief's Mountain) we encamped upon the banks of the Umguza River, twelve miles from Buluwayo. Here we waited until our horses had been inoculated for the detection of glanders amongst them, and here on the following day we were

TREKKING ACROSS THE PLAINS.

inspected by our General, Sir Frederick Carrington. As there existed at the time amongst the men many contradictory beliefs regarding the mallein inoculation, the following short note may prove of interest.

The mallein treatment is not a *cure* for glanders, but is an infallible agent for detecting its presence. The mallein is injected in the side of the horse's neck, and if the animal is healthy, or even suffering from any other complaint but glanders, no reaction will take place. But if the horse is affected with glanders in any stage, whether visible or not, or in however small a degree, it produces certain organic and thermal disturbance known generally as the glanders reaction ; and thus an infected horse can be at once destroyed. Mallein itself is simply an amber-coloured liquid obtained from the glanders germ *(bacillus mallei)*, and was first made and used by a Russian veterinary surgeon named Kalning, to whom its preparation was suggested by Koch's discovery of tuberculine.

On September 26 we marched into Buluwayo.

CHAPTER XI.

Buluwayo.

BULUWAYO is a town built on faith. It is a town of magnificent distances. Buluwayo may become a Chicago, though it is doubtful; yet it is evidently laid out with that end in view. There are miles of streets and sidewalks to be kept in repair, and one imagines it would be a great relief to the 'groaning ratepayers' if the town was squeezed into a third of its present size. But perhaps Rhodesian ratepayers don't groan.

The general plan of the town is not a complicated one. It is laid out in a large square, nearly two miles each way. This is divided into three strips running, roughly speaking, north and south, the centre one of which is park, and the outer ones streets and buildings—considerably more streets than buildings.

The western strip is the business portion of the town, and is cut longitudinally by ten Streets and crossed at right angles by fifteen Avenues. The Streets are named from men prominent in Rhodesian history—Lobengula, Jameson, Rhodes, Grey, Wilson and the like, whilst the Avenues bear consecutive numbers from north to south.

The eastern third is wholly residential, and is divided rectangularly in the same way. But here the Streets run east and west and are numbered First to Ninth, and the eight longer thoroughfares that intersect them are called Roads, and also perpetuate the memory of well-known men. There is one exception. The Seventh, or central Avenue traverses both business and residential quarters and on its way cuts the central portion into two—the North Park and the South Park.

Like the town, the Park is much too large for present needs. Therefore only part of it is laid out—and well laid out—in shady walks, and beds of flowers, and seats, and forms a most pleasant retreat for one weary of business and men and dust.

The rest is wisely left for Dame Nature to clothe with bushes of the 'M'oonga,' or Sweet Thorn, with a carpet of wild flowers and trailing plants between. Through the whole length of the Park winds the Matjesumshlope River, or perhaps I should say River-bed, for there was no water in it at the time that I saw it. The Matjesumshlope is not a large river—one can easily jump it without having the limbs of an athlete, but the mouth of a music-hall comic is absolutely necessary, I should say, in order to pronounce it.

It would seem impossible to get lost in a town built on such a delightfully simple plan, but this is a delusion and a snare. The far-reaching vistas of wide thoroughfare are so exactly alike. The stranger in Buluwayo should never forget to carry a compass, for when lost, this is an invaluable 'first aid' to getting found again. For, if the 'street' runs east and west, he knows he is in an 'Avenue'; but if, on the other hand, the needle points north and south, the weary wayfarer realizes that before him lies a straight mile-and-a-half or more of dusty 'Street,' and he either takes a Cape cart, or wishes from the bottom of his heart he was a cyclist.

And practically every Buluwayan is a cyclist. Every man, woman and child owns a bicycle. A business man could scarcely do without one, for his home is in the 'East End' and his office or store in the West. And for everyone the distances are so great, that that time-honoured method of progression—walking—is in danger of becoming antiquated and out-of-date. Even the 'boys' have taken to bikes, for on the outskirts, I saw a tall bare-footed Mashona riding a 'solid' in an undecided manner, clasping the pedal-rubbers with one dusty big toe, whilst the others spread away on each side, possibly as outriggers to save him from disaster in case of a fall.

But as we rode in from the Umgusa on that September morning, we were neither weary nor afoot. We had lived on biscuit and bully for a month, therefore were the large stores of more interest than the long streets, and 'vaults' were of more moment than vistas, for our eagle eyes had seen bar-maids and beer-pulls, and we knew where there were beer-pulls there was a great probability of finding draught beer. Buluwayo meant for us a release from bully beef, and did our General's promise of rest prove but true, then would we spend our back pay right royally and wax fat on civilization and square meals.

Riding through the streets, everywhere bordered with peppers,—practically the only tree which the white ant will not attack ; everywhere covered with telephone wires, numberless wires, these running from posts which everywhere supported also large electric globes for the lighting of the streets. The telephone seems a much appreciated boon. Every private house is connected ; to every little two-roomed tin cookshop—called into temporary existence by the presence of the troops—runs the wire. Even at one of the small churches—I cannot recollect to what denomination it belonged—the wire passed through a small round window near the roof.

Past the cafés, past the stores, past the hotels, over the railway and past the town itself. Then three miles through the thin thorn scrub to the long low white huts of the Hillside Barracks, which, for the next six weeks, was to be our home.

The barracks consisted of a double row of long huts round three sides of an immense square. Built of thin boards placed edge-wise some nine inches apart, and running diagonally from roof to floor. The interstices filled with mud. Whitewashed inside, plastered outside. Tin roofs and earthen floors. Infested with rats ; and in which an occasional snake or tarantula would be found. When the first rains came the outside plaster came off in flakes as large as a man could stretch across—*(See illus., p.* 128*)*,—and the workman who came to repair them said when the rains came in earnest, the huts would probably collapse and flow away in the form of soft mud, but fortunately we did not remain in them long enough to verify his gloomy forebodings.

At the back of the men's quarters were huts fitted with fireplaces and intended for cook-houses. So we appointed a squadron cook and gave him four Kaffirs to assist him. Our *chef* was a well-sinker before he came out, but he made an excellent cook, and we warmly congratulated ourselves on our choice. His assistants were not so good. Once X—— bought a quantity of lettuce from a Kaffir who came round with a cart ; and he told all the inmates of his hut to come sober for tea, as he had a treat in store for them. The men came. The tea was mashed and the bread and jam cut ready (we had no butter). And X—— shouted in important tones

"Leta lapa lo *lettuce*" (Bring in the lettuce). He didn't know the Kaffir for 'lettuce.'

In came Jim, the assistant-cook, and placed the dish upon the box which served for a table. But a yell went up from the guests, and a groan came from X——; for the Kaffir had *boiled the lettuce*.

L—— was constantly telling us how he could cook. He said his sister had taught him when he volunteered. So one Saturday we bought him half-a-stone of flour, and told him to use the ration jam and make us a jam roll for Sunday. We said it would be a pleasant change from the daily bread and jam, and more than that, would serve in a way to make Sunday different from the other days of the week, and he would therefore be really doing a good work by making this pudding. He at once consented, but wished we had given him something more difficult than a simple jam pudding. If we had said a Christmas pudding with brandy dip, or say a three-storey wedding cake, it would give him a chance to show his skill, but a simple jam pudding—however to please us he would soon knock that off.

And when he had made it, and wrapped it in one of his pocket-handkerchiefs with the corners pinned over in the orthodox way, it looked exactly like a genuine jam roll pudding. It looked so nice that on Saturday evening we held a kind of 'At Home' to the troop, to give them a chance of seeing it before it was cooked. We told them L—— had made it and the praise they lavished on him made him strut about and swell with big ideas. He told me confidentially he thought of going in for stripes when the next sergeant was reduced.

On Sunday morning we made him orderly, so that he should miss Church Parade and have plenty of time to cook the pudding.

After parade the trumpets sounded for 'water,' and as we rushed in for our bridles we just had time to see that L—— had been busy in the kitchen, for his face was scored with black finger marks, and he had ruined a new pair of drill slacks he was wearing.

Returning, we sat on our beds and fetched out our plates—or other substitutes.

" Pudding or meat first ? " asked L——, with a towel on his arm and an important look on his dirty face.

" Oh, trot in the pudding, we have trek-ox every day."

And L—— went out to the kitchen. But presently he returned.· He had lost the jaunty springiness of his step and his face was longer than the jam roll.

" There's something I can't understand about the pudding, you fellows. Come and look." he said apologetically.

So we went to the kitchen to investigate. It hadn't set as it should have done, but portions of the outer covering of the pudding had run out of the cloth and were swimming about in the water. And the jam was running out, too. We were all at a loss.

" Did you leave anything out—the salt, or the flour, or anything ? " we asked.

L—— assured us he had not.

" Perhaps you mixed it with too much water."

" How could I. The pudding was stiff enough before it was boiled."

So we gave it up and went back to the second course—the trek-ox.

But M——, who was a temporary hospital orderly, had a bright idea. He said he would ask the Sister when he went on duty in the afternoon.

At tea-time we said, " Did you ask Sister B—— what was the matter with the pudding ? "

He didn't reply to us, but looking at L—— said,

" Did you put it in hot water or cold ? "

" Cold," said L——.

" You bleeding ninny," said M——.

Though we had no drill, our days in the Hillside Barracks were fairly full. A horse-soldier never finds time hang heavy, for between feeding, watering, exercising and grooming we had little leisure time till after six o'clock. And the guards were numerous. We were the only squadron in Buluwayo—with the exception of a composite body of details from other squadrons—and had four guards to furnish in addition to our horse-piquets night and day. The guards were all for twenty-

SHOEING-SMITH BRAZIER AND 'MARMALADE'—*see part III.*—Photo by *H. Dunning.*
THE EFFECT OF THE FIRST RAINS—*p. 126.*—Photo by *S. H. Gilbert.*

four hours. In the early part of our stay there were only two, the Main Guard at the Barracks and one at the Agricultural Hall, a mile-and-a-half away. Then came a guard over a magazine half-a-mile away in the bush, called the Cordite Guard, and later still one at the Railway Station, for which we turned out in marching order, mounted.

Three days after the Cordite Guard was first furnished, I formed one of the party told off for this duty. We had a tent pitched close by the iron building, in which there were no windows and only one small padlocked door. Our instructions were very strict. We were to allow no fire of any kind anywhere near, and were forbidden to smoke or strike matches, or to permit anyone else to smoke within fifty yards of the building. And for the last three days and nights the most careful guard had been kept to prevent accidents.

The night passed without adventure, though about 1 a.m., on turning the corner of the building, I suddenly came upon four large light-yellow jackals, which were prowling round in the moonlight, but they didn't stay for a second look. But late in the afternoon of the next day a wagon drawn by eight mules came towards the building.

Of course they were halted and their business inquired into.

"We've brought the cordite," said the man in charge.

"What cordite? The cordite's in this shed. We're guarding it."

The man looked as though he thought we were pulling his leg.

"The cordite's on this wagon. It only came to the station to-day."

"Then what's in the shed?" we asked.

"Nothing. Here's the key, and it hasn't been out of my pocket since I swept the shed and locked the door four days ago."

And so it proved. For three days and three nights, the Cordite Guard had suffered in silence for lack of a pipe, and had been jealously guarding an empty shed.

We had almost given up the idea of seeing any fighting, as rumour constantly said that we should go home from Buluwayo. And we were satiated with grooming horses and sweeping up horse-lines. We came out to be soldiers, not stable-lads. And as the men wielded the brushes and the shovels, or passed the regulation hour at their horse's coat, they sang the 'Song of the 65th' set to the music of Dr. Duke's well-known Trinity hymn :

" Grooming, Grooming, Grooming,
Always blooming well grooming;
From Reveille to Lights Out
We're grooming all the day," &c., &c.

The Exercise was much more interesting work, for then we would take the horses—riding one and leading two—for a trot round the Buluwayo Racecourse, a well-made track of two miles. There was in addition a straight six furlongs, and a football ground occupied the centre of the oval track. Anyone coming down would suffer rather severely, as the course was thickly strewn with small sharp stones and chips of rock somewhat under an inch in size.

I have mentioned the three miles of thorn-bush which lay between the Barracks and the Town. But this was three miles 'by the road!' We had hardly settled down after our arrival before the 'details' were eager to show us the 'runs' of the place.

"Going to the town to-night? Splendid place, Buluwayo," and they launched into a vivid description of its virtues—and otherwise—which made our eyes open.

"But it's so far. I thought we should never get here to-day."

"Oh! there's a short cut. Come here. You simply follow that Kaffir path, and if it's dark, steer by the town lights. You can't go wrong."

So that evening Buluwayo saw an unprecedented influx of khaki-clad Yeomen, with polished spurs and large sombrero hats from which every speck of dust had been carefully brushed.

But though it had been easy enough to steer by the lights of Buluwayo, when we came to return we found our informant had forgotten to say that there were no barrack lights to guide us back. And so, to make a long story short, the absentee roll that night was a long one, and it was not till the light of morning enabled them to see the white huts in the distance that they straggled in by twos and threes, and went to look for the man who had volunteered to show them the short cut.

And during our stay the intricacy of this path was the *primâ facie* cause of much backsliding. For I hardly remember a case of 'absent from roll-call' where the delinquent hadn't lost his way in the bush. They knew it was the only excuse that would wash. Now and again the excuse took a more elaborate form. I recollect one morning I lay in the guard-room trying to sleep. It was six o'clock, and I had just come off two hours' sentry-go. One of our gallant troopers appeared in the doorway, coming from the direction of the bush. After looking round blinkingly for the Sergeant of the Guard he blandly offered his explanation :

"Beg par'n, s'ar'nt. M'besh r'sp'hks. Coon poshbly g'rome sooner. Losh m'way 'n fell over m'sphurs."

There was a canteen at the Barracks where Salisbury-brewed beer could be purchased at sixpence per glass. Also a dry canteen and an 'Australian Café' where 'steak and eggs' and other viands dear to the heart of a hungry man might be procured.

Near the guard-room lay the long stretches of hospital huts, for there was much sickness at Buluwayo—the usual soldier's foes—enteric, typhoid, malaria and dysentery. The convalescent huts were crowded, for when the squadrons which had preceded us here were sent on to Tuli, none but those of the most robust health were allowed to go. A further batch was sent down whilst we lay in the barracks. Rumour had painted the horrors of Tuli in blackest colours—though they were black enough in reality—and there were men who would rather face hostile cannon than the Tuli fever tract.

I one day had to attend sick parade. My horse had come down and rolled on me, and I was put 'off duty' for three days in consequence. Whilst waiting my turn I was amused by a six-foot man of the —th who preceded me. He did not look very ill. As we went in the doctor looked up inquiringly, softly rubbing his chin.

The man rubbed his stomach and said, "I feel very bad indeed, sir. Suffer from severe pains in the chest."

"That's not your chest, man. That's your bowels."

"Yes, sir; they haven't been right since I left the hospital."

"How long were you in hospital."

"Only three days, sir. I came out two days ago."

"Oh, I begin to remember your face. You were in for three days, and I couldn't detect what was the matter. Well, what's wrong with you now?"

"Well, the truth is, sir, they want to send me to Tuli, and I'm quite certain I'm not fit to go."

The doctor smiled sardonically.

"Oh, that's it," turning to the orderly, "castor oil and——" I couldn't catch the name of the other ingredient. I saw it was a yellow powder as the orderly mixed it.

"Here, drink this. Go outside and drink it," and against the man's name he dashed "Fit for duty."

The man took his medicine outside on the stoep, looking round with a frightened air as he gulped it down. Then he hurried away, looking much worse than he came.

The first batch of Southern Rhodesian Volunteers returned whilst we lay at Buluwayo. They had been all through with Plumer and received an enthusiastic reception from the town. Then they came into quarters at the Hillside Barracks till they were paid off. They were a rough lot but hard as nails. I don't think any of them slept in the barracks. Almost simultaneously with their disbandment a Company of 100 men for The Commander-in-Chief's Bodyguard was called for in Buluwayo and was raised from these returned Volunteers in several days. But I think that most of these men were totally misled by the name of the Corps, and did not realize that they were going South again to perform just the same work as they had come from, and probably none of them would ever see the Commander-in-Chief. After being re-equipped they were sent South again on November 2, having been at home just twelve days.

The days at Buluwayo were very hot, but curiously enough, though the most populous town and the commercial capital of Rhodesia, its inhabitants did not clothe themselves in black frock-coats and tall hats. Very far from it. No coat, no waistcoat, just the whitest of white shirts finished at the waist with a gaily-coloured sash, and the ends of a small kerchief hanging loose from the neck. Amongst business men,

BULUWAYO.

professional men, hotel keepers and shopkeepers the comfortable practice was in general use. At the restaurants, even in the theatres, you would see as many shirts as coats and one was as much *en regle* as the other. Sometimes the fine white linen was replaced by silken fabrics of cream or other tints, and the straw hat of various shape and size of brim was ubiquitous. But the Buluwayan always looked cool, and we in our tight tunics—for we were compelled to go into town " properly dressed "— envied them.

There are many magnificent buildings in Buluwayo. The Grand Hotel, with its vast stretch of tastefully tinted facade, its cool balconies, its palatial appointments and Oriental waiters is one of the finest structures of its kind in South Africa. One can scarcely realise that this electrically-lit city, replete with most of the latest devices of an up-to-date civilization, was but eight short years ago the site of the kraal, or collection of mud huts, of a blood-thirsty savage chief, whose ' impis ' roamed and laid waste the fair land of Rhodesia, revelling in the blood-thirsty havoc which accelerated the downfall of their nation, and the death of their king.

And as we stayed the seasons changed. The first of the rains came. Heralded by blinding duststorms, came storms of rain which were nothing but downward pouring floods, which peeled our huts of their rude plaster covering and turned our parade ground and the surrounding veldt into a vast series of shallow lakes. The outer streets of Buluwayo had become deep quagmires which it was almost impossible to cross on foot.

And in the midst of it we received sudden orders to move, and through a blinding storm which turned the horseman in front of you into a dim misty outline; which in a few minutes turned the dry land into a lake; which beat through thick cloaks as though they were paper, we marched through the scrub to the station, and waved goodbye to the cheering friends we had made —good bye to Buluwayo—goodbye to Rhodesia.

And argument waxed warm.

Men quarelled, each in defence of his pet Rumour.

And one said in fun—" Let the Goat decide."—And the idea caught on.

So Mapondera the Goat was brought, and he who had suggested it consulted the living oracle.

" Are we to see some fighting at last ? "

And the Goat said nothing.

" Or " taking him by the beard " Are we going Home? "

But Mapondera the Goat nearly butted him off the truck, and bleated in derision.

And all he said was—

" Baa."

PART II.

—AFTER.

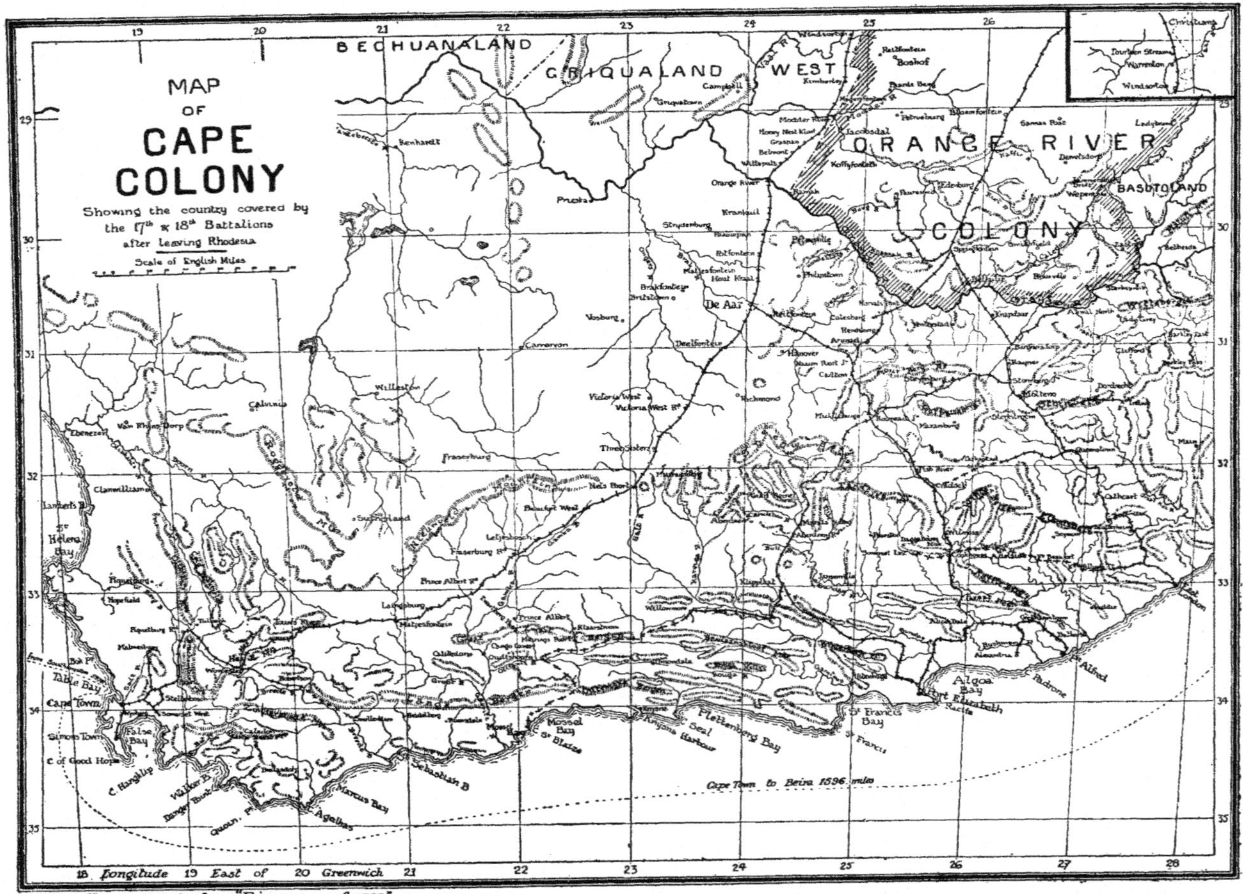

Specially prepared for "Rhodesia & After"

—AFTER.

CHAPTER I.

Watching the Orange Drifts.

'RATS' was a dog with some breed about him. One could see that with half an eye as he sat in the railway truck. He had been hanging round the camp trying to get himself adopted for the last two days—in fact, ever since we came down to De Aar.

The squadron had always been big dog fanciers. We had never been without a canine regimental pet since that big liver-coloured greyhound made a fuss of us on leaving Umtali, and had by mischance forgotten to alight until the train moved off, and it was too late. Rabbits were plentiful on the Marendellas upland, and here we expected the greyhound to pay something towards his board. But he was so well fed in the camp that he didn't see the fun in going after meat that ran away from him. So when we left we gave him to another squadron, just arrived, who wanted to do some coursing, they said.

Horse soldiers on the march exercise a wonderful fascination over dogs. I have noticed this repeatedly as we marched through the towns in the Colony. We had a kind of Pied-piper-of-Hamelin effect on them, and they would hardly be driven away. So it is not to be wondered at when we left Marandellas, two rough haired Irish terriers should follow us on our march to Buluwayo. One of these we gave to one of 'ours' who received a commission in the Sharpshooters, and he took it with him to Tuli. The other—Jim—accompanied the squadron when we entrained for De Aar. But doing a half-hour's halt at Palapye, Jim was missed, and it was not till we steamed away that we passed him some distance down the line, flirting with a low mongrel dog belonging to a Kaffir kraal. So Jim was struck off the strength. But the aching void he left in our hearts was filled by a stockily-built bull terrier who we called 'Palapye,' after the place he came from.

'Palapye' remained with the squadron for a long time. He completely gained the hearts of the men by once saving a Cossack post from surprise—by the officer of the day; and he was twice wounded during the chase of De Wet. And now 'Rats' had come to divide our affections. I don't know that his real name was 'Rats,' but we tried him with every dog name we could think of, and as that was the only word he was responsive to, 'Rats' he became. And, upon our sudden move north, what more fitting than that he should go too.

But it was not to be. Some Captain of Transport happened to see him sitting contented on a sack in the truck, and his actions became suspicious. He walked round in order to get a front view of him, and I heard him mutter something about 'Colonel's dog.' He went away but shortly returned with a private, evidently an officer's servant, and, pointing to the dog said: "Isn't that him?"

The servant said "Topsy. Topsy." It *was* him. Topsy pricked up his ears, and jumped out of the truck, wagging his tail. So Topsy-*alias*-Rats was lost to us for ever.

And so, taking with us two guns of "A" Battery, Royal Australian Artillery—the only battery of regular artillery in Australia—we went northwards, and detraining at Krankuil, marched to the village of Petrusville, forty miles inland from the rail. De Wet had brought us down country. It was known early in November that an invasion of Cape Colony was contemplated, and troops were hurriedly brought south to watch the drifts of the Orange River. At every ford from Colesburg westwards lay the white tents of a half company of Grenadiers, and at Petrusville, twelve miles from the river, but within striking distance of the whole length, were we stationed, ready to reinforce any point which might be threatened.

In our recollections of Petrusville two things will always stand out vividly from the rest—the patrols and the rain. The patrolling was incessant, almost as incessant as the rain. Fifty men with the guns, twenty men under an officer, ten men under a sergeant, three men under a corporal, one man by himself; hardly a day passed without a patrol. For half-a-day, a whole day, two days, three days—to every drift along the Orange and every farm between here and Houtkraal; until the men came to know the great triangle between the railway and the river almost as well as they knew the way to the cook-house.

And the heavy rains turned the roads into quagmires, and the spruits into roaring torrents. Often has a patrol been cut off from the camp by the sudden rising of the spruits, and had to sit on the wrong side for hours, waiting for the roaring tide to fall, and thinking of the mutton chops in camp. For we lay in the midst of the sheep farms, and to use our tinned rations except when on patrol was forbidden, an order which we had no wish to contravene.

Fierce howls the wind, and the rain sweeps in gusts upon the tents. Inside, the men lean on the elbows, and watch for 'drawing' tentpegs. And one near the door puts out his head to 'see the weather.'

"There's a man coming from the town with a lantern," he says, shaking the rain from his eyes,—" He's gone to the captain's tent."

"You needn't lace that tent up" says the pessimist. "There's another cursed patrol on the carpet. Orderlies don't come up in the middle of the night for nothing." And we under the blankets shiver in anticipation, as we listen to the beating rain.

"The squadron will turn out in full marching order in an hour's time to escort 'A' Battery R.A.A. on patrol to Rolfontein Drift." The pessimist was right.

A Grenadier has been sniped from the far bank. It may be by a wandering Boer, who saw his chance and took it. It may be by De Wet's advance guard. But one man or a thousand it is sufficient to turn out the guns and their escort into the night, and the wind, and the rain.

Across the spruit, through the dark shadows of the sleeping village, out to the plashy veldt. Dim cloaked shadows, showing in the darkness but as shapes of blackness more condensed. No sound but the squelch of the hoofs of the horses, the rattle of gunchains, the dull rumble of wheels.

Till the grey dawn, and on right and left the dim shapes of hills grow out of the darkness—giant forms of the backs of horses grazing, of rough-hewn heads, of alligators' backs, of whatever our rioting fancy may like them to.

And the guns swerve onto the sodden veldt to make way for a wagon—an unusual thing for the guns to do. A four-mule wagon with a Kaffir driver. Riding on it are three soldiers. Two swing their legs o'er the side as we pass, but the third lies still under a tarpaulin. On his medal his wife will read mistily, 'Belmont' and 'Modder River'—and he bled to death on the Orange, shot through the thigh by a sniper's filed bullet. The chance of a soldier.

Now the hills have closed in and become more precipitous. Before us stretches a long gentle hill, and over its crest lies the Orange. Leaving our horses we line this ridge on foot and the guns unlimber just behind the rise. The rain has ceased and from the yellow pom-pom blossoms of the acacia trees the softened wind blows faint perfume.

Below us stretches a long narrow valley beautifully green compared with the veldt we have crossed. Through its centre in a dark deep vein, meanders the thick belt of thorn trees which conceals the turbid stream. Half way across the nearer slope, and screened behind a low dark kopje-ridge, nestles the few white tents of the Guards picket. And towering on every side the grim silent hills, which rise tier on tier from the verge of the valley, boulder-strewn, bare, split by dark kloof and wooded ravine, affording a hundred concealments to a lurking foe.

Now the silence is rudely broken, and the guns search the bed of the stream and the hillsides beyond. Dammed by the heights, the pent scream of the shells have a most nerve-shaking sound. The boom of the gun is trivial, but as the great missile races on its quest, 'tis as though the very welkin was being rent and torn across and thrown back in shattered waves on the surrounding peaks. Then from around comes a strange sad after-tone, so diffused, so weird, as cannot be described. It is the echo of the outraged air. Though I have heard the sound of many shells—from the vicious one-pounder of the Pom-Pom, to the lordly 50-pound projectile of the 5in. Howitzer—yet never before or since have I heard anything quite the same as those Australian guns in the kloofs on the banks of the Orange.

But it draws no answering fire. Though the wooded course of the stream is thrashed by our rifle fire, and the little balloons of the shrapnel burst along every ridge, ours are the only arms that speak. And at length we limber up and ride away full in sight of the hills on the far side of the river. And at a farm two miles away we halt and off-saddle, hoping that the foe, believing us gone, will be tempted to reveal his presence. And there we wait till the evening falls, but he makes no sign. So through the dusk we ride home, with great lightning sheets lighting up the hills—home, just in time to evade the opening of another drenching night—home from another fruitless patrol.

The Grootverlangen road was not a popular one with the men. Perhaps this arose from the fact that, some fourteen miles out it crossed a spruit—rejoicing in the name of the Karbonaatjees Kraal River—which had a very nasty habit of rising to an impassable freshet at a very short notice and with very little provocation. More than once had patrols crossed dryshod in the morning, and returned six or eight hours later to find their passage barred by a strong current which, if crossed at all, could only be attempted with great risk. With all due deference to the Immortal Bard, the Karbonaatjees Kraal was one of those tides 'which, taken at the flood, lead to *mis*fortune.' Already one officer and three troopers had been nearly drowned, and a fourth held up to obloquy in squadron orders for 'losing his rifle whilst attempting to cross the river.' Moreover, a fifth now only used his baptismal name officially, being known on all other occasions as 'the wild duck' from his fondness for its waters. And they were never likely to forget the reception which awaited the gallant horseman who returned attired in a pink pyjama suit and carpet slippers (kindly lent to him by the officer in charge whilst his own things dried).

But this road led to the Grootverlangen Drift, and it was here that the 65th received their baptism of Boer fire. And thereby hangs a tale—the tale of a white shirt and of a daring deed.

It was an officer's patrol of twenty men who were sent to the drift to relieve the 21st (Cheshire) I.Y. As the Cheshires rode away they turned in their saddles, and told the patrol not to unduly expose themselves, for they had been sniped at nearly every day, and the Boers had got the range with a fair degree of accuracy. And the Leicesters laughed. This was just what they wanted. Practically all the Boers they had seen up to now were behind the barbed wire in the prison camp at De Aar.

As at most of these drifts, the road ran down a long slope to the edge of the river, which was on nearly every hand environed by hills, most of them inaccessible to horses and a very stiff climb for men. Halfway down the slope the road passed a low ridge, behind which the patrol fixed their quarters. During the day a watch was kept from stone sangars along its crest, and each night a piquet was placed on the edge of the river, near enough to hear the slightest splash or sound at the ford. Till the dawn, when the nearer bank, which was clothed with thick bush, was patrolled for a mile or more each way by one or two men. Then commenced the daytime watch again.

Nothing happened on the first day, and in the evening the officer in charge decided to water the horses at the river, instead of taking them some mile back to a spruit where the Cheshires had been in the habit of watering theirs. Every precaution was taken. Two horses were taken down by one of the men, watered, and well on their way back before the next two emerged from the cover of the ridge. And so the watering slowly proceeded, and the watching riflemen in the sangars saw the last pair return without drawing a single shot from the opposite rugged bank.

Yet somehow, they could hardly have told why, the little party felt that the whole operation had been watched.

The night passed without alarm, and at dawn the usual single patrols went out along the river bank. But on their return one man reported having seen men—he counted fifteen—creeping along the dongas and amongst the bushes on the far side of the river. The deduction was plain. The watering on the evening before had been watched, but for some unknown reason the enemy were unprepared, so a trap was being laid for the morning visit to the river. But the lieutenant frustrated their scheme by ordering the animals to be watered at the spruit instead. He himself had to ride to Reit Vlei, a farm some miles to the west, to procure forage for the horses, so left the watering in the hands of Sergeant Atkins, the senior N.C.O. of the patrol.

WATCHING THE ORANGE DRIFTS.

The way to the spruit lay for some distance up the slope, in full view of the opposite shore. The sergeant and two men crossed this ground in extended order first to see that all was clear. Then where the road entered a tiny kloof, they closed in, and finding all safe, he turned and waved for the waiting horses to come on.

Up the slope came the little troop, but the first two sections had barely emerged from the shelter of the ridge when a perfect hail of bullets rained upon them and the group above. Hastily waving back the horses, the three took what cover they could and opened an answering fire on the concealed foe. The Cheshires were right—the Boers had the range to a nicety, and the rocks around the little group were soon splashed with bullet marks on every side. The men in the sangars below now opened fire and the hills re-echoed with the sharp cracks of their rifles and the answering double reports from over the river.

When the firing commenced, several of the men were returning from the spruit with large kettles of water for the purposes of the cook. Thinking the scene of action was limited to the river banks and the sangars far below them, they increased their pace as well as the weighty kettles would allow, in order to get their rifles, and 'join in the fun.' But a bullet glanced from the foremost kettle with a sharp ' teeng ' and they found themselves in the thick of the ' fun ' before they were ready. A second well-aimed bullet settled the question, and, dropping the kettles, they made at a record pace for the nearest rocks. After the firing had ceased some time afterwards, one of these men counted nine bullet marks upon the small boulder behind which he lay prone, a sufficient testimony to the marksmanship of the Boers, who were firing from 1100 yards away.

And now comes the tale of the shirt.

Whenever we came to a standing camp near a town, a man's first desire—if he possessed any money—was to buy a shirt. And incidentally—socks. This in itself is a very laudable ambition, but when he buys a *white* shirt it borders upon foolishness. For he is not allowed to wear it on patrol, even in the heat of the day, without hiding it under a khaki jacket, which makes a man hot and uncomfortable. But, for some of our troopers the sight of a white shirt in a store possessed a fascination which they could not resist. And upon the next Sunday—how they knew it was Sunday was a wonder—they would have a shave, if they could borrow a razor, and blossom forth upon the camp in all the glory of the white shirt; and they really looked very nice and clean—until they had been to stables twice, or returned from watering the horses in a shower of rain.

Now one of the three men of whom I have spoken—he was a corporal, and a big one at that—was unfortunately wearing a white shirt when the attack took place. And this shirt, against the dark background of the rocks, was to the Boers as a red rag to a bull. The stone from behind which the gallant corporal was firing was hardly sufficient to cover his length of body, and every movement he made was the signal for a fresh storm of bullets upon that particular spot. After a considerable time the fire slackened, and once it ceased, and one by one the men above on the slope made successful dashes into comparative safety. But there was no such luck for the corporal. If, lulled into a false security by the slackening of the fire, he tried to ease his cramped body, the sequel always proved that the enemy had only been waiting for another view of his white shirt. And the corporal began to feel uncomfortable. But deliverance was at hand.

The officer of the patrol—Lieut. Challinor—had returned from Riet Vlei whilst the attack was in progress, and had ridden into the camp below. The rest of the men had by this time reached the shelter of the rocks, and he saw the difficulty in which the corporal was placed, far away up the slope. His horse stood near ready saddled. So without a second thought of the danger, he snatched up the khaki jacket the corporal had left behind in the camp, and jumping on his horse, galloped across the bullet-swept space, handed the tunic to the man, and returned as he had gone, untouched.

Deprived of the white shirt, the Boers seemed to lose their interest in the thing, and gradually the fire grew more intermittent, and then ceased—and they melted away as they had come.

Photos by *Lieut. C. E. Challiner*
FIRING ACROSS THE RIVER AT GROOTVERLANGEN—*p. 143.*
THE KARBONAATJES KRAAL IN FLOOD—*p. 141.*
THE ORANGE RIVER—FROM THE KOPJE—*p. 140.*

CHAPTER II.

A Stern Chase and a Long One.

"A--H!" We sighed with relief as we flung down our saddles, and flung ourselves after them onto the hard beaten earth round the horse pens at Houtkraal.

For we had been in the saddle since long before the dawn. Five-and-twenty miles in a straight line, to say nothing of the kopjes to be searched, the dongas to be crossed, the blind careful feeling of every inch of the way. But five days before had Hertzog and Brand, with twelve hundred Boers at their heels, crossed the Orange at an unguarded drift, and gone westward.

The scent was hot enough. Two miles of cut wires; iron railings laid low in stretches of half-a-hundred yards, the substantial iron posts snapped off short, as one would break brittle reeds. Also a few yards of broken railway, round which a busy break-down gang were working 'gainst time as we rode by; while, a little higher up, three or four ugly square boxes on wheels—called in modern war an armoured train—stood guarding. From the centre box came wisps of steam; from the outer ones peeped the muzzles of guns and of Maxims; round them sat dust-coloured soldiers in big helmets, smoking.

And we learned how the raiders had attempted to stop a northward bound train by tearing up the rails in front, and how the drivers—there were two engines—had dashed through the commando at full speed and escaped, their engines dented with bullets.

The prints of the enemy's coming had been plentiful and plain—they generally are when the trail crosses a railway. But of his further movements—— Well, that was our business to find out. But, thank goodness, not before to-morrow.

"See Marlow get in that donga?"

"Get in. Saw his horse put him in." And Hillson laughed as he lit his pipe from a 'red nob.' (Wood ember.)

Marlow muttered something about 'dongas,' and 'rotten banks,' and 'blarsted man-traps,' and pushed more burning wood under the camp-kettle. For Marlow was our cook.

"Should have seen the Irish Yeomanry if we'd been here yesterday. They went out early this morning on a big patrol. Took two wagons."

"The Seventeenth Battalion have been pretty well scattered. We've seen nothing of the others since Marandellas."

"The Dande River affair broke us away from them."

"An' the Captain wasn't particularly anxious to get back. Rather be on 'is own."

"Don't blame 'im. Another day like this'll give Blue Lightning a sore back." It may be explained that Blue Lightning was his horse, so called because it was a blue roan and the slowest 'trot' on the lines.

"Sore back! There won't be a horse fit to ride shortly. They ought to give us half-an-hour's stables now to make a good thing—— *Listen!*"

Faintly—sounds travel far in the darkness—came the beat of a horse—a horse at a gallop. We listened. Marlow, who was just about to put in the coffee, stood with the kettle-lid in his hand—to listen.

The hoof-beats grow more distinct. And now there are others, but farther away. Swiftly they approach. That is no ordinary gallop. *That* horse is being pushed to its utmost!

Then like a whirlwind came a dishevelled breathless rider. The foam dropped from the bit as he reined in for a moment.

"Where's the Colonel? *The Irish have been trapped and cut up.*" And he is gone into the heart of the camp.

Hertzog has taken no finding. He has found us.

"Saddle up everywhere. Sharp with it." The voices of the sergeant-majors ring through the squadrons.

And Marlow kicks over the kettle of boiling coffee with a savage curse.

As we form up a squadron of horsemen trot by. Closely followed by the two 15-pounders—our only guns—with a

A STERN CHASE AND A LONG ONE.

rumble and a business-like jangle of chains. Away to the west, where the darkness swallows the road.

" Tro—o—t."

The camp is behind and the road glimmers faintly in front of the horses, hardly to be told from the boulder-strewn veldt it runs through. But the steeds have caught the excitement. Gone from their limbs is the day's work they have done, and they pull at the bits as though fresh from a week's rest and a feed. The trot has long ago increased to a canter, we can hardly tell how. Swiftly the road flies under. Now a dip across the bed of a spruit, now a swerve onto the veldt as some ammunition train is passed—and one knows as the rocks are leaped or evaded that the safety of his neck hangs but on the sagacity of his horse. Back to the road, past the flanks of dark frowning kopjes, past straggling groups of nondescript horsemen—the remains of the Irish, all that are left of them—making their way back to camp.

Thus for six miles or more. Then a warning shout, and a turn to a tiny rocky kloof till morning light shall again let us take the trail. For to go on in the darkness is but to court the fate of the Irish squadrons.

But not to sleep. The saddles are kept on, and part holding the horses, part lining the rims of the basin, part snatching in turn an hour's sleep at a time, the bitter night is passed. Men's limbs seem frozen. To sleep, roused to consciousness and discomfort every few minutes by the cold, is a farce; and those with the horses pass their arms through the reins, and crouch in little huddled heaps on the rocks, to give the biting wind, perchance, a smaller body area to play upon.

And with the dawn begins the stern heart-breaking chase. Not the 'chase' of the Hotspurs and the Percys—the romantic dashing gallop o'er hill and dale after the Border cattle-lifters. That is the chase of olden times.

The modern chase begins at dawn and proceeds at three miles an hour till dark. Then, after a few hours' sleep—with every second or third night passed on watch 'gainst swift surprise—the chase again begins with another dawn. And so day by day, till the quarry is run to earth or your horse is killed. And the latter case is ten times more frequent than the first.

Next day we passed through the trap into which the Irish had fallen—the small hill-bordered horse-shoe valley, seamed with spruits like the vein of a leaf, all making for the one wide mid-rib of treacherous sand which ran 'twixt crumbling fifteen-feet banks from end to end of the valley. Our coming disturbed the great grey ' aasvogels ' which flew with slow wing and blood-dripping beaks from the horses slain in the fight.

Like a huge snake with octopus arms the column slowly wound its way, throwing out feelers before and to the sides of it; searching each donga, each kopje, each kloof.

But no Boers.

Yet another day's weary marching, and last night we encamped within eight miles of Britztown. It was the Eve of Christmas, and as we ate our fare of bully beef we wondered if the rules of the Geneva Convention provided for a rest on the morrow—for time to cook a meal, and eat it, and think on the fare and the good things they were having at home.

To-day the question has been answered. We have arrived at Britztown, but, since dawn, we have marched thirty-five miles to get there. We have been rounding up the commando which yesterday left the town—or trying to. To do this we forsook the beaten paths and took to bye-ways; to scouting over kopjes where the foot of man had never trod, and where the hoof of horse was never intended to. Our Christmas dinner consisted of two ship biscuits and a pound of bully beef between three men. Washed down by water from a ' vlei' shared with the mules—but unfortunately the mules got there first. And we got into Britztown just before dark, having for the last mile or two walked by our horses, to bring the poor tired brutes into camp—all save those we shot by the way.

And the Dutchmen of Britztown are indignant and fuming. For three days ago came their compatriots the Boers, 650 strong, and fraternized with them to the tune of £700 worth of goods looted from their stores. And when some complained, they had lavished upon them brotherly love and kindness—by means of a sjambok. Near the town lived Dr. Smartt, the Commissioner of Public Works. They had paid him a visit,

BRITZTOWN.

Photo by *Edgcome, Beaufort West.*

had " trampled to the earth 500 acres of ripe wheat, burned his wool stores and granaries, cut his fences and turned loose his ostriches." Moreover, they assured the people of Britztown they had come to stay with them for a while to rest their horses and eat up the good things around. But yesterday their plans underwent a considerable modification, for Col. Thorneycroft at the head of his Mounted Infantry, had appeared on the horizon. Britztown lies in a vast level plain, and one can see its chubby little church spire some six or seven miles away. Unfortunately anyone on that tower can also see the dust of a column for the same distance, so Hertzog and his guerillas got clear away.

Next day we joined our forces with the T.M.I., and now the chase commenced in earnest. Several times during the day did we of the rearguard have to dismount and sit awhile on the veldt to allow the convoy a little more start, for our horses could not walk slow enough, and if not checked would soon outpace the wagons we should be in rear of. Should we catch this guerilla great credit will be ours—the augmented credit of the heavily handicapped. For we have four miles of transport, of mule wagons and ambulance wagons, of Cape carts and Scotch carts and water carts. Whilst at a farm many miles back we passed the charred remains of the two wagons captured from the Irish. Hertzog did not carry the heavy wagons with him for long.

For Hertzog is no fool.

Six days' chase and no end in sight. Most of the morning was passed in getting the transport across a swamp. The whole of the narrow valley lay one vast sheet of glittering water. It was not two feet in depth, but hid beneath a sea of treacherous mud in which each wagon stuck in turn. Each load was fetched through by double teams; twenty plunging mules goaded to frenzy by the long cutting lashes. Seen from the crests of the bordering kopjes, 'twas a picture of dainty strings of mules and Liliputian horsemen splashing through a liquid glistening mirror, and breaking its surface into showers and cascades of sun-coloured spray.

Below 'twas what it was. A hell of waist-deep screaming

Kaffirs, of straining mules with piteous appealing eyes, of cracking whips, and long heavy wagons; the whole churning through a sea of semi-liquid mire—of evil-smelling, evil-looking, nauseating mire.

And to-day appeared a little day-light star, which twinkled to us from a hillside far ahead. It was the talking of the heliograph. De Lisle is acting with us miles away, and once we faintly heard his guns. Pray God he turns them back into our hands!

Seven days. And we rode into Vosburg—a half-looted village. Telegraph wires trailing across the streets; outside the granaries huge heaps of forage; the sidewalks littered with piles of clothing, with broken boxes of stores and barrels of ' dop' with the heads staved in. All hastily abandoned. For early this morning the guns of De Lisle had cleared them hurriedly out of the place ere their fell work was half complete.

Eight days. Through the same succession of never-ending valleys, kopje-bordered. Each day passing two, or mayhap three lonely farms with their dam, their one or two irrigated fields, their garden and their stolid Dutch inmates, not knowing the English tongue, though living in a British Colony, and subjects of a British Queen. Then across the veldt, mile upon mile of sand, thinly dotted with sun-dried colourless bush. The most barren part of the Karroo. Hour after hour with no change in scenery, no change in vegetation, no relief from the sand which burns the eyes with its glare, no shade from the scorch of the sun. Oh! for a change, a farm, a fall, an accident, anything; most of all, oh! for a fight.

Nine days. And once our spirits rose. For like a greyhound freed from the leash, a squadron breaks away from the column, and helter skelter, leaping gullies, half lost in a cloud of dust, whirls away to the flank of a tall kopje far to the right. Is it the enemy at last?

Whips flying, voices urging, and bump bump the guns are galloping for the rising ground a little distance away. They pull up in a heap. Back they come into shelter, but only the teams and the limbers. The guns and the little knots of attendant dust-coloured figures are left behind on the knoll. Is it the enemy at last?

Men open and wipe the breach of their rifle; one dismounts and tightens his girth, and the weary listlessness has gone from the column like mist smiled on by the sun. The long line of transport has halted, save for the rearmost lagging wagons, which are closing up at a trot.

And we wait, with eyes bent on that rapid lessening squadron now a mile away to the flank. They round the end of the kopje. Little specks detach themselves from the rest and go forward to search. Each little speck looks as though trying to escape from the little cloud of red-tinted dust which will cling round its heels. They are galloping for all they are worth.

We wait—with ears strained for the first 'tic-tac' of the Mausers.

But it doesn't come. From half-way up the kopje twinkle, twinkle, talks the helio.

A false alarm. Back come the guns. Back comes the squadron. They at anyrate have had an exciting race. And the column again goes forward at three miles an hour, one foot before the other, on the mechanical, monotonous march. To halt for the night at the farmhouse of a Colonist whose walls are enlivened with Kruger and Joubert with halos round their heads, flanked by gory battle scenes, printed in Holland, in which the 'rooibaatjes' are invariably getting very much the worst of it.

Ten days, and the horses are tired soon after they start in the morning. Poor brutes! they are on half rations as well as their riders. Fresh horses are taken from every farm where they are found. But Hertzog has been before us. Wherever there is a horse to be found, you may rest assured the T.M.I. will find it. In more than one part of the column may be seen a foal trotting at the side of its dam, ridden by some thin sun-dried trooper. For several days it will follow but not for longer. One day its pace will lag and its trot beside the mare become more heavy and laboured, and at last it will give up, and remain behind to die on the veldt where so many of its kindred have died before it. Many of these men were with their Colonel at Spion Kop, and grim tales they tell round the camp fires. And they swear by their Commander. Under him one need never fear disaster, for in action he never makes mistakes, say they. His virtues appeal to their tenderest feelings, for if there is food and forage in the land, he will get it for his men, or know the reason why.

Eleven days, and the horses want pushing, and at night the light of the camp fires shine red on blood-stained spurs. The shots at the rear of the column become more frequent during the day. Men ride in with the tail of the transport, an hour after their squadron has encamped; other men come in not riding at all. Their saddles are on the wagons, their horses lie miles behind, done to death on the veldt. It is the last day of the year, and we are within six miles of Carnarvon. Yesterday the Boers had approached the town, but our column was too close behind for safety, and they went southward. Unfortunately—or is it fair to blame 'fortune'?—the district had not been denuded of horses by the authorities and so Hertzog obtained a supply of remounts. Here those without horses were sent into Carnarvon for fresh ones, but they went on a fruitless quest. So they had to walk into Victoria West and the column went on, on its chase after the guerillas on their fresh horses.

Twelve days, and the sacrifice of the animals becomes piteous. Cruellist part of the war is the doing to death of the horses. The rider, whatever his hardships, can reason and look forward to brighter days to come—to the home-coming which must follow sooner or later. The horse has no hope, save in the kindness and thought of his rider. Generous and willing, though his ribs be all but sticking through his skin from insufficient food, he gives in his master's service all the strength that is his to give. And for him, and pitied by none but him, he gives his life, when he has no more to give—dumb and without complaining.

A dozen times a day the transport is pulled up with a jerk. A mule has dropped in its traces. In a moment the black drivers are down and the body is freed of its harness and dragged to the side of the road. If an odd mule is running alongside it is put in the place. If not the other one of the pair is taken away and runs by the side, the wagon proceeding with two less in the team. And the glazing eye of the abandoned mule takes its last look at the wagons and the white men who ride unconcernedly by, whom it has given its life to serve. A mule seldom requires the final bullet. It goes on and on with weakening sinews and breaking heart till it falls in a heap, dead in many cases before it reaches the ground.

And Hertzog is still a day in advance.

Thirteen days and the wagons are now drawn by teams of six in the place of the ten with which they started. By some Heaven-sent chance, we to-day unearthed a store of grain from a farm, and to-night the horses and mules received a four-pound feed of oats, the first they have tasted for four days. They have been existing on the bundles of oatstraw scraped from the district we passed through.

Fourteen days—and equine nature can keep it up no longer. The column encamped and an inspection of horses and mules took place. Perchance there might remain enough fit ones to mount several squadrons to continue the chase.

I can only speak on the veterinary's report on the troop to which I belonged, but it may be taken as fairly representative of the whole. We are twenty-one of the Leicesters, and we brought out twenty-one horses. We have lost three, obtained two remounts, and out of the twenty horses we brought into camp to-day, *four* were passed for further work.

On the fifteenth day we turned our heads for Victoria West— to refit.

* * * * *

The Cape papers said that during the chase we had accomplished the record march of the war—that with a four-mile transport train, we had covered 210 miles in 5 days.

This I know not.

But I know that on our track lay bleaching the bones of four hundred horses and mules.

And I know that we did not catch our hare.

CHAPTER III.

Guarding the Zwartberg Poorts.

WE topped the rise and the village of Prince Albert lay before us. The usual Colonial 'stad,'—a sprinkled cluster of white dwellings peeping from an ambush of green fruit-gardens. Its outline broken by the simple white spire of the church rising 'mongst the dark lance-points of cyprus and the bushier crests of blue gum. The whole backed by the sombre Zwartbergen (Black Mountains) whose fissured sides towered from the very outskirts of the place, rugged and grim, height above height, till lost in fleecy clouds.

But to what end. These villages we had seen before—outward smiling prettiness cloaking the black looks of a race-hatred too deep for words, and passive but from fear ; whitened sepulcres covering the blackness of treachery, rebellion, and other things akin, which an Englishman deems leprous, dishonest and unclean.

As we rode down the slope, our approach startled a flock of half-grown ostriches tended by a black boy, and from the doors of the scattered Kaffir dwellings came streams of 'picanins' to see the horsemen pass.

And then a strange thing happened.

A carriage came to meet us, filled with the ladies of Prince Albert ; the magistrate's wife, and the wife of the English clergyman, and the wives of the chief burghers whose names and station we did not know. They were in gala costume and carried flags at the end of sticks. And from the breast of the coloured coachman flowed a stream of ribbons. As our little column drew near, they turned and drove solemnly into the town before us.

"Blow me if we ain't a triumphant percession!" said a trooper.

And at the bridge stood the children and young girls in white and summer dresses, with flags and wide open eyes, big with the responsibility of forming part of the official reception of the first British troops into Prince Albert. No excitement, no waving of the flags, no cheering—for the Dutch are not given to these—but a quiet welcome, spontaneously given by the loyal few in a Dutch town in the centre of a disaffected colony.

It grew dusk as we off-saddled. All but twenty-eight of our little force—under a hundred strong—whose duty it was to watch o'er the safety of the rest. But these were not allowed to go out to their lonely night-watch on the bleak veldt without abundant fruit, and cakes, and steaming cups of such tea as we had not tasted for many a month.

Their hospitality did not end here. The days were short, and every evening the schoolroom of the English church was lighted up and placed at our disposal for the writing of home letters; and stamps and stationery were provided for those who lacked them. And from the schoolroom walls spoke the same kindly sentiments—"We School Children wish you Good Luck,"—and—"We Band of Hopers wish you God Speed." Trifles, you say. These things are far from trifles to men grown callously accustomed to cold looks and covert sneers daily met with from the people of a partial rebel colony.

And I am pleased to think that the people of this little 'stad' were not the losers by their loyalty. The day before each man had been made richer by an £8 instalment of his pay, and—with the exception of several known to be disaffected, whose stores were forbidden ground, with sentries at their doors—the traders of Prince Albert reaped a golden harvest during the week or more we stayed.

The 'peace' of the town was preserved by two troopers of the Cape Mounted Police, in whose district it lay, and by several black policemen who were also warders of the white-washed jail. These coloured constables could never forget their respect for the superior race, and although the *black* prisoners were put to the hardest and most menial tasks, the *white* convicts were invariably 'sirred' by their black warders and looked on more in the light of honoured guests than delinquents undergoing the penalty incurred by their law-breaking.

A narrow gorge running 'twixt sheer cliffs, deep fissured and emerald with weather stains. In the gorge a cold clear stream, threading through fallen rock fragments, carrying life and greenness and beauty to the village below. By the stream, through it, over it, making loops and eights with it, runs the track through the Zwartberg Poort. At first the pass is wider, and by the stream are stretches of green and clumps of thorn. But soon a seeming *cul-de-sac* is reached, and the path disappears round a huge rock, to enter a ravine where the footfall of horse and voice of man ring hollow as in a vault, and the path is part gouged from the side of the cliff to make room for the shallow rock-strewn stream.

Across the bold stretches of cliff-face run the strata of the rocks, here lengthwise, there dipping earthwards, and yet again buckled and bent in wavy curves. Bare of bush, save in the shelving clefts; mainly in ruddy tints as though scraped raw by a recent avalanche, they rise in dizzy ridge on ridge till they meet the blue strip overhead. Gradually the path is climbing; mile after mile hewn from the face of the cliff, whilst the stream sinks farther below. We are now in the heart of the hills. Here and there in little nooks stand the dismantled ruins of the stone huts used years ago by the convicts who constructed this masterpiece of road-making. By the path grow huge bushes of flower-covered geranium; and at the tail of the column come the mule wagons at two miles an hour.

Then the famous 'Zig-Zag' is reached. The road enters a ravine with jagged precipitous sides. In the clear African air the twigs on the far side can almost be counted, the width is but a seeming stones-throw. Our strongest throwers try their skill, and their missiles fall tired long before they reach even so far as the silver thread below us.

But the road. We look and marvel.

Along the face of the rock it runs ahead; till, at the end it turns on a stone-buttressed corner, and climbs the opposite side of the gorge. It mounts the heights above by a monstrous zigzag course—eight roads, each over the one below, hanging to the face of the almost vertical rock. Till, far above, like a faint pencil line ruled slanting, it gains the crest of the hill.

As we ride or lead our horses, the path is edged in places by a stone wall some two feet high, but in most is guarded but by large boulders placed with twelve feet intervals between. The top is gained, and we cross little valleys hidden amongst the summits where snow lies in the nooks sheltered from the sun; whilst rising above us to another thousand feet are peaks hidden in wreathing clouds.

And suddenly, the road runs into space. We have crossed the Zwartberg and are looking down a sheer six thousand feet to the valley below—a beautiful green valley, a picture of square fields and white houses and coppices and lines which must be hedges. Fed by perennial mountain streams, it is the famous Cango district, noted through the African markets for its tobacco, and the quality of its feathers. And those countless dark specks in every field must be ostriches. As the horses slip down the cliff-cut road, the downward journey is more nerve-trying than the ascent.

We called it the Valley of Aloes. I don't know that we owe any apology to its people for the liberty we took. When we asked they said its name was 'Voorbedagh.' Now in after years the name Voorbedagh would convey no meaning to us, if we remembered it at all; moreover, it is a name difficult for an Englishman, unless suffering acutely from tonsilitis, to pronounce as it should be pronounced. But when we looked upon the numberless upright agaves which covered its hills like battalions in skirmishing order, or edged its fields, close-set, like companies on parade, the 'Valley of Aloes' flew unbidden to our lips. It was Nature's own name, and the only name for us.

I think that wherever possible, the name of a place should be based upon some distinguishing trait which marks it; then the very name will conjure a mental picture of the place—memory will require no other aid. Even in England people do not always follow this. You will find a man letting into the front wall of his house a stone bearing the sculptured words "The Cedars," when he is unable to direct you to a single cedar tree any nearer than Lebanon. I knew a man who called his house "The Aloes." When he proudly conducted me round his little domain I looked in vain for the *raison d'etre* of the name, and managed to draw from him the confession that he had never seen an aloe in his life. He had once bought some from a shop, and recollected that it had a bitter taste. But why he should seek to perpetuate the remembrance by naming his house after it, goodness only knows. It is much like the theatre I once attended where the woodland scenery was represented by large green-painted boards, on which hung a card stating ' This is A FOREST' and—But this is digressing.

We could not stay long in this beautiful valley. Kritzinger was daily expected to attempt a passage through these hills, and our movements were rapid, and many times sudden, governed by those of the wily Boer we had to out-manœuvre. Back and forth we marched, often by night, along hill roads where a false step would have hurled us farther that we cared to think. Once a wagon went o'er the brink, and turning a double somersault, lay bottom upwards on a ledge below. But by dint of much labour and more shouting, it was hauled up again, reloaded and again on the way, without the head of the column halting at all. 'Twas an incident of African travel always to be reckoned with.

*   *   *   *

Twenty men at the mouth of the Meiring's Poort. Night has fallen, and in the bend of their saddles they sit smoking the final pipe before turning in. The tobacco is the dead leaves gathered from the tobacco plantations they have passed, and is no bad substitute for the manufactured article. They talk in security, for around, hidden by the night, are the sentries, and two miles in the pass, lays a Cossack Post with ready saddled horses and for companions the huge baboons which roam through these hills, descending at night for water, and whose cries re-echo from wall to wall of rock. These, and the little 'klipspringers'—the African chamois—which in the daytime spring at giddy heights from pinnacle to pinnacle, resting on ledges one would think would scarce accommodate a rat.

And the talk turns on the earlier days, and laughing tales are told of little trials then thought hardships, but now weighed by another scale.

" When the train came in, we were turned aht late to go dahn an' carry the bloomin' stores up to the gaud-'ouse."

GUARDING THE ZWARTBERG POORTS.

The speaker, who was evidently not reared in country parts, re-lights his pipe.

" An' I luks rahnd (puff) an' muzzles a borx as were morked ' Corndensed Milk ' (puff). I lahgs behind w'en we got aht o' the light o' the bloomin' lawmps; an' gort behind a bloomin' tree. O' corse it war dawk as 'ell, an' aw haccidentally (winking) cort my foot an' drorps the bloomin' borx. Orf comes the lid an' aht rolls the tins o' milk. They was neatly wrapped up in white piper, an' some'ow aw thort they seemed a curious shipe for Nestle's, but aw 'erd the sorgent 'urrying the blokes up, so I puts two in my pockets and turns rahnd—to see my pal, 'Arry 'Orcher a stahning there "——

But the story was cut short. For an orderly rode in with the news that Kritzinger had broken through the cordon that was said to surround him. And there was catching and saddling of horses in the dark, and hasty packing of blankets, and a silent ride through the shadows in the pass, through its seven miles of length to the post we were ordered to hold.

* * * *

At dawn the Boers on the hill-spurs rubbed their eyes and yawned. They were still tired, for they had ridden fast and far the day before. And they saddled up leisurely for the ride into Klaarstroom in the valley below. A congenial day was before them ; there were stores to be looted, bread and new clothes for them, and best of all, there were no Khakis within miles of the place. Had not their ' patroljes ' assured them of it.

And, as the light grew stronger, they rubbed their eyes again. For along the western road came horsemen, a scattered troop, riding at a trot. The advanced guard of a ' verdomde ' British column ?

" But Piet Uys and Jan and Tjaart were two miles out that way. Why had they not galloped in and reported the approach of the Khakis ? "

They waited and watched, in cover among the ridges. But no more troops came o'er the hill.

" Ah ! it was another of the British patrols, and coming straight into their hands. They knew now why Piet and the others had let them through and said nothing."

But they were wrong as it happened, for Piet and Jan and

Tjaart were prisoners in the hands of the approaching horsemen.

Right into the streets of Klaarstroom rode the little British troop. And from ridge to ridge crept the wily Boers, nearer to their prey. Then with a yell they burst at a gallop into the town, three ways at once. But the patrol didn't 'Hands up' as requested. They poured a volley into their assailants and then galloped back the way they had come.

"Aha! the 'verdomde' English are always ready to 'hardloop' when *they* come riding down from the hills. Never mind. The capture will be all the more exciting for a chase. *Ah!*"—— and they gallop for cover. The little band have dismounted, and are going to fire again.

They are off again. In wide extended order, galloping for life, with the expanding bullets cracking the rocks around their heels.

"This is fun. To chase the English. This is better than a grinding life as a bywoner on a farm."

So the running fight goes on. Five miles, ten miles are covered. See! the horses are tired. For the near sides of the stony slopes must be rushed at a gallop—there is no cover there from the singing bullets.

"Ah! there goes one. I shot him. No, it was my bullet. Leave him there now. We can go through him when we bring the others back. On, on, their horses are failing. Andries and five men gallop round that kopje. It will cut them off a mile farther on."

Another mile, and as the Boers gallop breathless up the ridge, a little bunch of Khaki stands dismounted on the opposite side.

"Good! their horses are done. They are ours."

But they make a little mistake. The little knot of chased horsemen who have carried out their task so well are under the shelter of a hill, breathing their panting steeds. And the other little group on the hill opens out and—every galloping Dutchman pulls his horse viciously onto its haunches—

For—*Boom*—and the air is split with the sound of a 50 lb. lyddite shell.

"A trap. It is not war—to draw men into traps and then cut them down with guns unawares." Every panic-stricken

THE MEIRINGS POORT.

Photo by *Edgcome, Beaufort West.*

Dutchman is getting the very best pace out of his shaggy pony in his mad race for cover. " Another ' verdomde ' English game."

But the hills are no cover 'gainst these guns. They are the 5-in. Howitzers, and they send their shells over the tops of the kopjes, and drop them into the hiding Boers. They ride for all they are worth with the sinking fear of the lyddite in their hearts. Where can they go? Five of them race for a ridge and get under its cover, but their hiding-place is marked.

Boom—a shell screams upwards and with a grand curve just clears the crest. There is a second report. Up from the ridge flies a great spurt of yellow flame, seen through the middle of a cloud of earth and smoke. Then the thin yellow-green after-smoke drifts aside, and from the cover hurtle two terror-stricken horsemen.

No one will ever find the other three.

It is the night after the fight. In the dry bed of a river (the Oliphants) lay the troops—the Yeomanry, Brabants, and the guns. The huge fires light up in strong effects the bearded faces telling of the fight. Some are still missing. But now and again one comes in from the surrounding blackness telling of wide detours amongst hills and spruits to evade the bodies of the routed foe. One relates how, after much wandering in the darkness, he luckily discovered the marching troops and joining them, rode on. It was not for some time he found that he had by mistake joined a body of Boers stealing silently away o'er the hills. Luckily he had not been recognised, but replying by a surly grunt when spoken to, he rode for a mile or two, his knee ever and anon bumping against the burly Boer beside him. Till he saw a chance to hang behind and make his escape.

A rough crowd are the 2nd Brabants, amongst them adventurers drawn from every quarter of the globe,—Poles, Jews, Texan cowboys, Mexicans, Norwegians and Swedes, and of course many Dutch. One night I lay for several hours an interested listener, though truth to tell, a none-the-wiser one, to a conversation in Spanish—the Spanish of Chili—between two bearded troopers. They were old comrades-in-arms, and had helped in the overthrow of more than one South American ruler. Here is the life-history of yet a third. Born in Belgium, when nine years old he emigrated to the United States with his parents. Drifting into Texas he, when old enough, became a cow-boy. But he was a true rolling-stone, and was to be found wherever the clash of arms was heard. He had taken part in *nine* South American revolutions. The Spanish-Cuban War proved irresistible, and he fought upon the Cuban side until the Americans landed, when he joined and fought with his old companions, the cow-boy ' Rough-riders,' until the conclusion of the war. Then came the South African War, and he and twenty more, taking their high peaked saddles, at once crossed the Atlantic and threw in their lot with Brabant's Horse, in whose ranks, having been once severely wounded, he was still enrolled. On his hat he wore one of those bone discs so popular in the States, and on it ran the ennobling legend :

" I don't want glory. I want oof."

The men are merry, and song follows song round the camp fires.

And under a mound of freshly-turned earth, in the deep shadows of a drooping ' wilge-boom,' sleep those who have fallen, surrounded as they would wish to be, by the rough bivouacs of their comrades.

The talk slackens, and the men smoke contentedly. A huge branch of dead thorn is dropped onto the fire, sending into the black night a thousand tiny glowing sparks.

" Finish your yarn of Twenty-three Mile Creek " suggests one, and the idea calls forth approving grunts.

" Where had I got to ? "

" Where you turned round and saw Harry Archer."

" Oh ! Well, when aw looked rahnd—

" ' What's them,' ses 'e.

" ' Cow-juice ' ses I, putting two more under cover.

" ' Strike me ' ses 'e, an' he collars 'awf-a-dozen tins an' does a vamoos inter the lorng graws. 'A thort a'd open one to see as they wer awl right, an' I undoes the piper—an' aht tumbles a lot of blorsted *prayer-books*.

"Well, bli' me, I was fair knorked back, I warn yer, an' I sees 'Arry a comin' through the graws, lookin' as silly as a blorsted sheep.

"'Wart abaht yer bloomin' cow-juice?' ses 'e.

"'A ses nothing, an' we packed 'em up in the borx, an' shoulders 'em acrors to the gaud.

"'Sorgent,' ses I, 'aw've 'ad an haccident. Cort my foot an' burst open a borx of stores.'

"'E looks at me 'awd for a minute, but I looks at him strite as a bloomin' tent-peg; an' he blarmed my eyes, an' so it parsed orf awl right."

The story was finished amidst a burst of laughter, and a man on the other side of the fire said,

"The books didn't fly open at 'Thou shalt not steal,' did they, Bill?"

"No. Why?" said Bill, not seeing the point.

CHAPTER IV.

In Scheepers' Hands.

TRUTH to tell we were in an ill humour that morning, as we filed out from the town of Aberdeen before the dawn. The patrol was late in turning out, for one thing, so we marched without our coffee, which was left half made upon the fire. And to start on a day's patrol in the raw morning air on an empty stomach is apt to disturb the amiability of the most even-minded man.

Yesterday the column to which we belonged detrained at Aberdeen Road. But before the last wagons were taken off the trucks—it was about mid-day—the sudden news had come that the Boers were attacking Aberdeen, twenty-two miles away. So there was hasty saddling of horses, and the guns and a strong escort were despatched to the relief. Ten miles out the guns had taken a needful rest, and three troops of horse were sent on as fast as they could push their steeds.

Arriving at a gallop, we found that in the early morning the Boers had succeeded in penetrating into the streets of the town, but had been driven out by a handful of Lancers and the 'Cape Boys' of the Town Guard, who had behaved with a daring worthy of the best white troops. But the Boers, on leaving, promised to return in superior strength at five o'clock, and sack the town. We rode in at half-past four, and prepared for them a little surprise, but something must have altered their plans, for they failed to appear.

And the people of Aberdeen seemed disposed to make much of the troopers who, by a narrow half-hour, had saved them from a second visit by the raiding Boers, and there were hints of hospitality upon the morrow.

But, for us, in place of petting, the morrow had brought a patrol, and we felt disgusted with ourselves and disposed to quarrel with our bosom friends.

EXERCISING HORSES IN THE DRY RIVER-BED.
Photo by *A. G. English*.
DUTCH GIRLS WATCHING THE ENTRY OF THE TROOPS.
Photo by *Captain R. B. Muir*.

IN SCHEEPERS' HANDS.

We were a triple patrol. Fifteen of the Leicesters in the centre, and upon left and right a like body of the 70th (Scottish) Sharpshooters, and the 6th (Inniskilling) Dragoons. A miniature ' Union Brigade.'

Each party was under the command of a lieutenant, and with each rode one of the Aberdeen Town Guard as a guide. Our courses lay parallel, and some mile or more apart, but though a connecting file rode between, the patrols soon lost sight of each other, owing to the nature of the ground.

And as we rode northwards the day-light came, showing the long plain in front, low-kopje studded, and bounded by the frowning masses of the Cambedoo Mountains. Our object was to ascertain if the Boer commando was still in the neighbouring hills. Little we dreamed that, high on those hill-spurs, Scheepers and Fouche, the Boer Commandants, sat watching us with powerful glasses as we rode over the plain; tracing our course, and making their dispositions for our capture or annihilation. Yet so we afterwards learned.

Two miles from the town a donkey-wagon bringing a load of wood to Aberdeen was stopped, and the two attendant Dutchmen closely questioned. But they reported the country clear of the enemy for miles, and we rode on. Later we knew they had lied, and had led us into a trap.

Across the plain, from east to west, lay the dry bed of a river, deep between crumbling banks, and fringed on either side with growth of thorns and prickly pear, so thick that from extended order we had perforce to close and cross where it was pierced by the road.

Beyond lay the long level plain, bounded near a mile away by a range of low ridges which hid from view the land beyond. Therefore, when half across, did our officer send two men, Forryan and I, to top the ridge and examine the country beyond before the troop came on. Forward we galloped, leaping the little sluits which everywhere seamed the veldt, until the foot of the ridge was reached. Then dismounting, I handed my horse to my companion, and scrambled to the crest, some fifty feet in height.

I had but time to take a sweep round with the glasses, when from behind broke a fierce crackle of rifle fire, and hastily turning, I saw the little troop, each horse in a ball of dust, making at top speed for the ridge, whilst around and amongst them the little spurts of sand plainly told their own tale. The Boers lay in ambush in the river-bed we had crossed, and had allowed us to get through unsuspecting before they opened fire, thus cutting off our retreat from the town and the column.

The horses were fresh, and they took the side of the kopje as though it was level ground ; and as the officer passed me he shouted,

"Take cover over the ridge."

I didn't need twice telling, but ran as fast as the rough stones allowed to the higher crest for which the others were making. My horse had been led up by the man who was holding it.

We found ourselves in a little hollow between two higher knolls. and the one near us was the highest in the whole chain.

Leaving several men in the hollow with the horses, we made for this ridge under a shower of bullets, but found very little cover was to be obtained on the top. We found the best we could and lay round the edge. The hill was much too large to be defended by so few men, but, two or three laying along each side, we kept the enemy back with our rifle fire, for we could do no more. From east and west the firing came, and at long range from the north, in which direction we were overlooked by the hills of the Cambedoo.

I was lying—the only one—on the south side of the hill-crest, and for some time found little use for my rifle. But presently I saw moving dust arising from behind the vegetable screen which stretched from side to side between us and the town. But the men who raised it were hidden by the mimosas and the pears. I knew then we were surrounded ; that our investment was complete.

All this time a very hot fire was going on. One could distinguish the different sounds made by the bullets. If too high they screamed over like distant swallows. If very high, they sang through the air with a sweet long-drawn note, which is impossible to describe on paper, but which all of us who were there can imitate to a nicety.

These we didn't mind so much. It was when they went by

with a short sharp 'zip' that you knew they had missed you by a few inches; or with an angry impatient 'pht' they struck up the earth by your body or face. We are told that in action a man forgets all about the bullets. In the excitement of a charge, or when rushing a kopje, this is true to a great extent. But when a man is lying with very little cover to be shot at from half-a-dozen directions; when if he moves a foot or raises his body an inch it is the signal for a volley at that particular spot; when he is six times within an inch of death in less than as many minutes, if to think then about the bullets is cowardly, then I must confess to being a coward.

To make things worse, there is no smoke to betray the whereabouts of your invisible assailant, and you may be aiming at him, or he may be ten yards from that spot. Many of us know, from being actual eye-witnesses of it afterwards, that when behind a ridge, a Boer will fire one or two shots from one spot, and then, getting down behind the crest, will run for twenty yards or more, and open fire from another point, whilst the fire of his assailant is still poured upon the spot he has vacated.

After some hour-and-a-half, the enemy grew bolder, and would ride in small parties from one cover to a nearer one. They did not always do this with impunity. Once or twice we saw the saddles emptied by our fire. It is surprising how easily one is deceived in the distances in this bright clear atmosphere. Once during the morning, four men rode at an easy canter across my front—three in a group and the fourth some way behind. I hastily put my sight to 700 yards, as I was sure they could not be a yard farther away than that. But my bullet sent up a spit of sand nearly 300 yards short. I raised my sight to 1,000 yards, and my second shot was also short. They were nearing a cleft in the kopjes, so hastily raising my sight another 100 yards I carefully took aim—and missed again. But this time I had the range, as the ball struck the earth just behind one of the horses. The three men were now under cover, and I had just time to get in a shot at the single horseman behind. Of course after the first shot they had put their horses to their hardest pace. To my disgust I missed again, for the sand spurted up under the horse's nose, making him spring upward. But we didn't get many such opportunities as these; most of our fire was directed upon nothing more tangible than the crests of ridges and lines of dark bushes.

I soon had cause to think that the four men I had fired upon had been sent out as a decoy to draw our fire from that side, for it soon became evident they had marked the fire coming from my stone. From behind me, where I had no cover, came volley after volley from four or five rifles, all directed at that particular spot. They chipped around and over with little angry screams and thuds. Every volley came nearer. At last I could stand it no longer, so inch by inch, moving like a snake, I moved round to the other side of the stone. But I had forgotten the river-bed. My movement had brought me partly over the crest, and I was now plainly in view of those lying in the river.

'Pht' came a single bullet into the earth, not a foot away to the right. Then a pause. 'Zhip,' the next was just over me. Then another pause. I realised all at once that they were taking careful pot-shots and that the result would only be a question of time. Even at home at the targets one is pretty sure of scoring a 'bull' sooner or later. 'Pht' came the third shot, and a little spurt of sand sprinkled my hand. So I wormed myself back again and took my chance of the volleys.

I have only described my own experience during our investment. I could see none of the rest from where I lay, but each one was undergoing a similar, if not worse, ordeal. How a man escaped under those three hours' cross-fire is more than I can say.

The enemy were gradually creeping nearer under cover of the succession of ridges and our position was becoming untenable. They had also gained a point from which they could enfilade the little hollow in which our horses stood, and four of these were shot. The arm of one man was also broken by a bullet. Every ten minutes now, the officer would call to me (I was the only one in a position to see) " Are any troops coming from the camp or town ? " and every time I was obliged to answer,

" There are no signs of any."

I had still about thirty rounds left, but I could hear men on the other sides calling to one another for ' a few more rounds.'

They had been firing more heavily and the ammunition was fast giving out. It was but a question of time.

Then, though we were all quite willing to keep it up whilst a round was left, our officer judged it was not his duty to let us be slain in a further resistance from which no good could come, so with heavy hearts we heard the order ' Cease fire.'

A handkerchief was put on a rifle, but the whitest one amongst us was nearly khaki, and it was not seen by the enemy, who still poured in their fire. Then it was remembered that one man had a white shirt under his tunic ; but it was not until he received a direct order that he would tear off half of it. He would not hoist it but flung it behind him. I could hear one say, " It's more to your left ; no, move your foot another inch," and I knew they were groping for the piece of rag, for to rise to one's feet was suicide.

Then above the herbage I saw the upper end of a rifle, with the pitiful white rag fluttering from the piling-swivel, and I knew all was over.

It was some seconds before it was seen ; then the firing fell off and ceased ; and we waited.

But not idly. My thirty rounds I pushed far under the stone, and pulling out my bolt, I flung it far down the hill-side amongst a clump of bushes. Some of the men also rendered their rifles useless.

Then above the crest appeared a head, followed by a second, and we could see others coming from all directions at a gallop. Bodies followed the heads, dark-clothed bodies, each with a rifle and two crossed bandoliers. The rifles were covering us, and several rode to each man, shouting peremptorily ' Hands up ! hands up ! ' It was a scene one will never forget—and never wish to see again.

Scheepers, the Boer Commandant. was one of the first on the hill, and to this I ascribe the lenient way we were treated. They of course seized our horses, rifles, bandoliers, and stripped us of water-bottles, spurs, and other articles of our equipment. But they did not touch our persons or our pockets ; and they allowed us to take our greatcoats from our saddles and retain them. They were so busy stripping us and securing their loot, that when I gave up my rifle, barrel downwards, the man who took it did not notice that it was without a bolt. I immediately mixed with another group in the hope that, if he found out the discrepancy, he would forget from whom he had it. But I heard nothing more of it, and they afterwards smashed those rifles which were thus rendered useless. Scheepers himself was a far superior man to the rest. He was quite gentlemanly in any intercourse he had with us; and indeed, many of his men, in asking us to hand over articles of our equipment, added the word 'please' to their request, which sounded rather comical, situated as we were. Scheepers was dressed in a neat navy blue suit with puttee leggings, and carried two bandoliers crossed over his body, as did all his men. He was a youthful looking man, but looked older than his actual age, which we afterwards learned was 26 years; had a light moustache, but clean shaven chin, and wore a dark grey sombrero, fastened up with a gold ornament. At one time he carried a rifle, at another a large sjambok. Nearly all the Boers spoke English, and were Cape rebels, though they told us they were Transvaal Boers and had been in the field sixteen months. In the bandoliers of some were soft-nosed bullets, and they seemed rather ashamed when we pointed this out.

Each of the three patrols had been attacked, almost simultaneously. The Dragoons managed to extricate themselves, having their Lieutenant and four men severely wounded, and the Scottish Sharpshooters, by making a wide detour, worked round the enemy's flank, andreached the camp, leaving one man a prisoner in the hands of the enemy. The two 65th men forming a connecting link with them, ran into a party of twelve Boers and were captured, stripped, their pockets emptied, and then turned loose to find their way back to camp on foot—the enemy, when a short distance away, firing several shots at them to expedite their pace.

Now came a crackle of firing from the south, and Scheepers and his men rode off in that direction, leaving some twenty men to guard us until their return. We were taken a little distance down the hill, and the Boers dismounted and talked together in groups, whilst we sat on the ground in the middle, and gloomily thought over the situation.

IN SCHEEPERS' HANDS.

I learned the same night the sad meaning of the firing we heard. We were captured at half-past nine in the morning, having been under their fire for just three hours, and it was near ten o'clock when a force was sent out to our relief.

The Boers numbered between 250 and 300—there were two commandoes, Scheepers', who wore yellow puggarees, and Fouche's, who wore white ones—and the force sent out to our relief was composed of a Lieutenant and twenty men of the 75th Sharpshooters, under the command of a Captain of Dragoons.

This party, riding at a gallop nearly the whole way, tried to outflank the Boers who were cutting us off from the town by making westward, but were headed back by a volley from a number of the enemy concealed in the bush. Again they were headed from the other side by the hot fire and the Captain eventually found himself upon the northern slope of a kopje, under a heavy fire from a ridge but two hundred yards to the north of him, and two cross-fires from the bush on his right and left flanks. But with him were only the Lieutenant and six men. The pace at which they had ridden had thinned them down to that. The other men fought their way back to camp. Hastily dismounting, the little band of eight threw their reins over a bush or stone or whatever offered and took what scant cover they could find. And there they lay under the withering fire until one by one their rifles became silent, and after a time but one man was left—wounds or death had stilled the other seven.*

This man—Trooper Legg—seeing that he was but drawing the fire upon his wounded comrades, ceased firing, and waited. Soon their fire ceased, they thought their fell work was done. On foot from all sides they came to the hill. From where he lay this shelved away for fifty yards, then the descent became steeper, so that the Boers were hidden from his view until this shelf was reached.

Legg waited until the first man's head appeared above the ledge, then, carefully covering him, he shot him dead with his last cartridge.

The next minute he was surrounded by excited Boers, who,

---

* For more detailed account see " Story of the Sharpshooters " Part III.

calling him 'Murderer,' levelled their rifles to shoot him. He pointed to the seven men round and said,

" If that's murder, what is this ? "

Nothing would have saved his life, but at that moment Commandant Scheepers came up and ordered them to lower their weapons.

Legg asked for and received permission to attend to the wounded Lieutenant. He was shot in both ankles, and Scheepers assisted in the work of mercy, pulling from his pocket a small pair of scissors to cut away the cloth from the wound. Legg was then sent in to the camp for an ambulance, taking the white silk kerchief Scheepers was wearing to safeguard him through the Boers.

Under a promise that it should come back, Legg was allowed to take the Lieutenant's horse, a fine grey, but before this promise could be fulfilled, fortune's wheel had turned, and the Boer commandoes were hurrying northwards to bury themselves in the fastnesses of the Cambedoo, out of reach of the British guns.

CHAPTER V.

The Escape.

SURROUNDED by our guards, we sat listening to the distant crackle of rifles. Suddenly a loud boom came from the south. We all knew what it meant. Our guns were in action, and were following up the Boers. Immediately after the report came the crash of the shell, but far away to our left rear. They were the Howitzers, and fired 50 lb. lyddite shells.

I watched the faces of our guards. I could see that that one sound had scared them more than a thousand rifle shots. They hastily mounted and hurried us northwards down the ridge. Truth to tell we were now as anxious to get under cover as were they, for we knew those shells would respect neither friend nor foe should they drop in our midst, and we had seen their effect before, but from the other end of the gun. They sounded very different now.

Another gun and the bursting shell was nearer, but we could see nothing, as we were buried amongst a succession of ridges. We had donned our overcoats for facility in carrying, but we now stripped them off, so that perchance, should the gunners come in sight of us, our khaki would be seen. Onward we stumbled on foot over stones and rough ground, our guards riding behind and around us, and leading our horses. If a man lagged behind it was—" Hurry, khaki ! "—or—" Get on, khaki ! "—and we needed no second bidding.

For some time the guns had been silent. We well knew what that meant. After seaching one ridge with their fire, they had limbered up and were galloping forward to a nearer position; so they would take ridge after ridge in succession. Would the next be ours?

Anxiously, and almost holding our breath as we were hurried on, we awaited the next shot. It came, and almost with it came the crash of the bursting shell, on the very ridge we were crossing, but some two hundred yards to our left. A huge flash of flame, an immense cloud of dust, stones, and pieces of shell as it ploughed up a great hole in the ground where it burst; then the yellow fumes of the lyddite, which became greenish as they floated higher and thinner. We felt the concussion of the air where we were standing. Our guards at once turned at right angles to their former course, and went eastward, away from the track of the shell fire, and hidden from view by the rise of the ridge we were skirting. Another shell, and nearer than the one before, but behind the ridge. This was the last that came near to us.

Crossing a dry river bed with steep perpendicular banks, we had to separate, for there were only a few places where horses could get through the thorny barrier. As I jumped into the deep nullah the thought of escape first crossed my mind, and I stood in the shadow of a big bush hoping they would not miss me. But one horseman looking back, saw me there, and galloped up handling his rifle and shouting—

"Hurry up there, khaki!"

Needless to say I obeyed.

Crossing this valley we mounted a further ridge and then turned eastwards through thick growth of big mimosa thorns. After some time we came to a beaten path or goat-track, and following this for several miles a small dam was reached, on the farther side of which stood a small Dutch farmhouse of not very prosperous appearance. We were now some eight or ten miles from the kopje where we were taken. Running round the edge of the dam—where the Boers watered their horses—the road then turned northwards, striking into the recesses of the Cambedoo Mountains.

Many of the Boers rode up to the farmhouse, and were evidently welcomed by the family, who were all grouped round the door. We were not allowed to go near the house but some of our captors hurried us down the road, which was now a wide one, and ran in a straight line for half-a-mile, the whole way in full view from the front of the farmhouse.

Some distance down, the road was crossed by a small spruit or stream of water, and some of the prisoners on foot turned a little to one side to where the stream was narrower, and they could spring across dry-shod. And here my opportunity came at last.

The side of the road was sparsely bordered by thorn bushes, and by this stream grew one large bush round which ran a little trodden footpath, joining the road again on the farther side of the bush. It was some three or four feet to the right of where the other prisoners had crossed, and this path I took. I disappeared for an instant behind the bush, and was just going to step in the road again, when I saw a slender chance of escape open. It was all done in an instant; a moment before I was not thinking of escape at all.

I stood behind the bush until the few Boers who were with us were occupied in splashing through the spruit, then sprang behind a second larger bush, and stood still, breathless.

I had not been seen, and as soon as the three or four remaining Boers had passed (there were still a number at the farmhouse), I made two or three big springs across a little open clearing and diving into another clump of thorns, threw myself amongst the undergrowth, and lay listening. I heard the rough talk and laughter of our guards grow fainter down the road, but expected every moment to hear them come clattering back in search of me.

And now I had a chance to think on what I had done. I knew, but had partly forgotten it before, that an escaping prisoner is shot without furthur ceremony on recapture, and my ruminations as I lay there were not pleasant ones by any means.

Soon more of the Boers came clattering down the road, and as I heard each two or three splash through the spruit, I felt as though it some fresh danger passed. How many had remained behind at the farm I knew not, so dared not move for a long time. The voices had all died away down the road, and the ring of hoofs on the stones could no longer be distinguished, and I was just preparing for my next move, when I heard the shouts coming back, and could distinctly hear the Boers crashing through the thorns and shrubs. They had missed me, and were coming back searching both sides of the road.

My recapture was now certain. Nearer they came; they

were not a hundred yards away, and with a dull sinking feeling I prepared to rise to my feet as soon as they saw me, and not be shot like a dog in a hole.

But, hark!—surely that was the sound of a big gun—and in the direction of their retreat, too. They checked their horses, and now the boom of the gun was mixed with the crackle of rifles. Some excited shouting took place amongst them, and fearing their retreat would be cut off, they turned their horses heads and went at a mad gallop after their companions. I was again safe and could do nothing for a while but lay down and try to take it in.

I then made my way to the edge of the road, and peering through the bushes, saw that all the Boers had left the farm, but the family were still round the door. Here was a difficulty. I had to cross this road, and if they saw me, they might bring about my recapture. I knew they were in sympathy with the Boers, and I was unarmed. But it had to be chanced, so arranging my blue overcoat, which I still had with me, so that my khaki uniform would show as little as possible, I stepped out into the road, and safely reached the bushes on the other side without the farm people making any sign. I was some thirteen or fourteen miles from Aberdeen, and had still to get through the remainder of the enemy who had continued fighting when we were led away. These had been broken up by the British guns, and I saw several small bodies making their escape through the ravines and along the narrow valleys. But I always saw them at a distance, and lay low until they were out of sight.

It was now late afternoon and I was parched with thirst and my uniform was partly in rags from the thick mimosa thickets I had traversed. Then I saw a sight which sent me forward at a run. It was the sun's western rays gleaming red on the surface of a little lake. It was but a small artificial dam, met with near every farm. Just the water from last season's rains collected in a natural depression in the soil, and retained by a bank of earth and stones built across the lower end. But for me it meant new life, it was as delicious as an English spring. Clambering over the bank, I stumbled down the rough stones and throwing myself flat by its edge, I drank—again and again.

Then, having at last quenched my thirst I raised my eyes,—

and saw two mounted Boers, each with a spare horse, watering their steeds at the opposite side of the dam, and the horses stood knee-deep in the water, drinking. There was not an atom of cover where I lay stretched on the bare earth, and the dam was not sixty yards in width. The Boers were facing me, and were talking together as they sat in the saddle, with their rifles slung over their backs. With heart beating much faster than usual, I could only lay perfectly still, and watch them under the brim of my hat, hoping the khaki colour of my clothing would save me from discovery. It seemed an age before the horses finished drinking, and one of them began to paw the water, as they will do, splashing the other man. He cursed the animal (I could distinctly hear his voice where I lay), and pulling up their horses' heads, the two men made for the bank, and rode on without having seen me. They were hardly out of sight before I was quickly over the bank, and in a thorn thicket before any more Boers could come into view.

Once again my luck stood by me. I was carefully feeling my way along the road, which turned to the right some thirty yards before me. Suddenly—it seemed to come all at once—I heard the sound of galloping hoofs coming down the road, just round the bend, but out of sight by reason of the bushes. The horseman must have been riding on soft earth or herbage, for I heard nothing of him before. I was then crossing a strip where there were no bushes or cover of any kind. In another moment the horseman would be round the bend. For a moment I was bewildered. Then I did the only thing possible, which was to fling myself flat on the earth and lie still.

Again my khaki saved me. The Boer—for it was an armed enemy—galloped by, passing within ten yards of me as I lay on the bare earth by the road side. But he had also a spare horse, and his attention being somewhat taken up with this as he passed, he did not once cast his eyes in my direction or he could not have failed to see me.

After this I had to abandon my greatcoat, for it was too much of an encumbrance, and taking to the thickets, worked my way by the sun, southwards, and at last, nearly exhausted, I came out upon the line of ridges where our capture had taken place.

Far away to the right, I saw the kopje where we had fought,

and, having a curiosity to know if my cartridges were still under the stone, I made my way towards it.

Once or twice as I walked along I heard a low booming sound coming from somewhere around, but took little heed of it. Just after eluding the Boers I had taken the cork from my waterbottle, and wrapped it round and round the strap, because the chain to which it was attached rattled as I walked, and I thought this half heard sound was the wind humming in the bottle. But chancing to turn, I saw about ten yards behind me an immense male ostrich, eight feet in height if he was an inch, who was gravely stalking me, and working himself into a fury with his booming war-cry.

It seemed so comical, after giving the slip to three hundred Boers, to be attacked by a mere ostrich that I laughed; though I fully realised the danger, for I was unarmed, even with a stick, and one forward kick of his great foot would tear a man open, or break his limbs.

My hilarity seemed to offend him, for kneeling down—if I may use the term, for his knees bent backward instead of forward as in a human being,—he spread out his wings until every beautiful feather stood out alone, and commenced to rock himself violently from side to side, uttering at the same time, his deep booming cry. Even then his head was higher than mine, and he looked nothing but a great black and white fluffy mass of viciousness and an ugly customer to boot.

A short distance away stood a prickly pear-bush, and I walked warily over to this, keeping one eye continually on the movements of the ostrich.

Immediately I moved away, he rose, and followed me, and for some time we two walked round and round the prickly pear, but I took care to keep him always on the opposite side.

This continued for a considerable time, and I was just elaborating a fresh plan of campaign, when the ostrich grew tired, and shaking his wings, stalked slowly away without a single backward glance at his vanquished foe, and disappeared over a ridge. And I continued my way, and in a few minutes the episode had been almost forgotten.

I was now in full sight of 'our' kopje, and made a

THE ESCAPE.

considerable detour to make sure that none of the enemy were lurking in its vicinity.

There was no one to be seen, so I made straight for the crest. Suddenly from behind came the quick sound of scraping feet in the sand. Quickly turning I saw my friend the ostrich coming for me at top speed with flying feet and outstretched wings, whilst the sand and stones rose in a little cloud behind him, flung up by his powerful feet.

When I turned he pulled up suddenly, but the impetus of his pace brought him to within six yards or less of where I stood. Down he went upon his knees and re-commenced the swaying of his body and the booming of his war-song.

But I was now in a better position for defence. Not many yards away grew a big bush of mimosa-thorn, and walking slowly towards it, I tore off a large branch, and advanced to the attack, holding into his eyes a huge bushy top, thickly covered with sturdy eight-inch thorns. He didn't like it. He tried to run round the branch, but I made a sudden dash at him and brushed his face with the thorns.

The day was won. He didn't wait to be captured, but hoisting the white flag of his beautiful wings, he fled o'er the hill, and I saw him no more.

The crest of the hill was a scene of confusion. Lying about were the bayonets of our men, belts and scabbards in one place, the blades flung elsewhere; for the Boers set no value on these. Cartridge cases, old blankets, nose-bags with the day's corn still in them, and many other articles of discarded loot, lay around. I found my cartridges intact under the stone, and quickly stowed them away. Lying amongst the bushes were also several broken rifles left by the Boers; Lee-Enfields with the wood-work cut away as far as the lower band to make them lighter, and one or two, the stocks of which had been roughly repaired by pieces of wire. All these they had carefully broken and rendered useless before discarding. But by some oversight, one they had forgotten to break. It stood against a bush some distance from the others. It was a Martini-Enfield (it hangs before me as I write), in perfect order, its barrel worn bright with constant use and handling. Of course my Enfield cartridges could be used with this, and, to my joy, once more I was armed. Had my late assailant the ostrich but put in a third appearance, his booming war-note would have been his death song.

Laden with this, and eight of the bayonets, I slowly made my way southwards, and piercing the bushy screen from which we had first been ambushed, saw a human figure coming towards me o'er the plain. But he was dressed in khaki, and when still a distance off, I could distinguish a certain something which told me he was a British officer.

It was Dr. Whyte, who, with his orderlies, were searching the plain for any wounded man, Briton or Boer, who might perchance be in need of their assistance. He gave me a much needed stimulating drink, and as the darkness first began to fall, I reached the British camp.

CHAPTER VI.

The Defence of the Jail.

IT was but an everyday occurrence—the everyday work of the little bodies of troops watching the Orange.

Three men, on the third day of a three days patrol. Riding loosely across the veldt—but keenly watchful. For that morning they had learned from a grey-bearded farmer of shots heard far towards Hamelfontein, and of the offal of many sheep found on the farms. Pregnant signs.

And when, a little later, they rode up to the Venter Vallei farm, and the farmer Du Toit pressed them to off-saddle and partake of his fare, the Corporal in charge reflected—and declined. The persistency of Du Toit seemed more than suspicious. The presence of Boers in the neighbourhood could be hardly unknown to him, for these things fly apace from farm to farm.

But the farmer was gone so long for the pass required by the Corporal that the men dismounted to ease the backs of their horses. At length he appeared, and handing over his pass for inspection, apologised for the delay, saying he had mislaid it.

Then following swift upon him, came his daughter, with hasty excited cries,

" Di Boere ! Di Boere ! hulle kom o'er di Kopje ! Hardloop! Hardloop ! " (The Boers ! they are coming over the kopje ! Fly !). And round the corner of the house a Kaffir boy came running with the same cry " Di Boere ! Di Boere ! "

They were but three. There was only one course.

" Get up ! We must gallop for it," said the Corporal.

As they left the shelter of the house the Mausers spoke, and their double reports seemed to say " Come back. Come back." And the bullets spit in the sand, or sang with little drawn-out screams o'erhead. Their road lay along the foot of a very stoney ridge, which it gradually neared until, a mile and a half away, it was crossed by a small stream, and then ran through a narrow nek through which a wagon might just pass. Beyond the nek was open plain, and three-and-twenty miles away lay Philipstown—and safety. And on the near slope of this ridge were the Boers. To ride away from the ridge was impossible, for the road was bordered on the other side by long stretches of stone wall, enclosing kraals, and gardens, and cultivated fields.

The horses needed no spurring. They knew—as horses do which have heard the sing of the bullets. They understood the message that had come through the knees of their riders, and the light-limbed Hungarians lay down to the road like coursing greyhounds. And the low-aimed volleys chipped the wall as they passed with little futile angry cracks.

Would they be headed and cut off at the nek? It must be chanced.

Before lies the gulley, a long scar in the earth cut deep by the rains. Gathering themselves for the leap, they are over almost abreast, and away at racing pace into the pass.

Now the ridge on which lay the Boers was far too rough for rapid progress, so some thirty of them, who knew the land, had hastily disappeared over the crest. On the far side, as far as the outlet of the pass, lay good galloping ground, and they strained their utmost to cut off the little patrol.

With panting steeds the Boers reached the pass—but just too late. For, three hundred yards away they saw three horsemen scudding o'er the plain, every stride taking them nearer to safety. Hastily dismounting, they flung themselves down, and took careful shots at the flying horsemen. But in vain. The bullets came close—to right, to left, singing ahead, or cutting the sand round the hoofs of the horses. But never a horse or man was hit.

And in such wise was brought to Philipstown the news of the coming of De Wet.

The only troops in the village of Philipstown—one of the most disloyal between Cape Town and the Orange—was a lieutenant and 25 men of the 65th I.Y. Making the village their headquarters their instructions were to patrol the surrounding district, visiting the farms and clearing the country of horses. It was one of these little patrols that was chased from the Venters Vallei farm.

On the western edge of the village, upon a little rising ground, stood the jail, and here Lieut. Munn, with an eye to possible contingencies, had fixed their quarters. The horses were picketed some hundred yards from the jail, and with them slept the men. And in a stone kraal fifty yards away were the few horses brought in from the farms.

It is early morning—the darkest hour before the dawn—and the Corporal of the outpost a mile out on the Petrusville road is uneasy; for more than once he could have vowed he heard the sound of horses. And——

"Halt, who goes there?" The Sentry has challenged sharply, as one almost caught napping.

It is a Kaffir who steals in from the darkness—a black scout placed farther out upon the road. He also has heard the sounds, and the Corporal goes with him to a rising knoll two hundred yards away, and lying down they listen.

There is no doubt left in his mind now. Across the veldt comes the soft thud of horses trotting through sand. And they are no loose horses, for there is just to be heard a faint silvery undertone of the rattle of bridles and the champing of bits. Hastily making his way back, he is met by a trooper, who has galloped out from the jail to recall the outpost, and who brings the startling news that the village is surrounded by Boers.

As the outpost came in the little garrison were already busily preparing for resistance. The Philipstown jail consisted of several flat-roofed buildings built round an enclosed yard; and upon the roof of these several men were stationed, whilst the remainder brought into the precincts of the jail the forage, saddles and the horses.

It was known that somewhere on the road to De Aar there should be a strong Australian patrol, and three men were at once sent out to attempt a passage through the enemy, and then to find this patrol and acquaint them with the state of affairs in the town.

Day was just breaking, and from the roof one could see small patches of dust, shimmering lighter through the half-light of the dawn; and the metallic clink of iron shoes on stoney ground could be heard. Time was pressing. So pressing that several unbroken horses in the kraal had to be left, as they dashed from side to side, and would not be caught. And as the last few men doubled across the open space to the jail, they were speeded by a scattering of leaden messengers from the approaching Boers.

As the light broadened, it was found that the enemy were practically on every side. They could be seen dashing at a gallop from one cover to another, but ever drawing nearer. From every rise, from every donga, a hot never-ceasing fire is concentrated on the jail. Now they are in the town. They soon learn from the people the insignificant numbers of the defending force. Twenty-three English Yeomen and four black warders against four hundred Dutchmen. Sixteen to one. They laugh and gloat o'er an easy capture. But they take care to gloat at a safe distance away. For they cannot get through that spitting leaden ring which hurtles round every head and limb they show. Now they climb the roofs of the houses which command the jail, and the odds are growing against the beleaguered few. Pray God their messengers got safely through !

The roof of the jail is protected by a solid parapet just twelve inches high, but over this a man must show his head to fire. An attempt is made to build it up a little higher, with rough loopholes between; but has to be abandoned by reason of the fire from the surrounding roofs. And now is seen the wisdom of choosing the jail for defence; for, standing a little higher than the rest it cannot be overlooked. Else were their plight a pitiable one indeed.

Standing nearer than the other buildings of the town is a square white-washed place called the 'Old Jail' and from this a particularly galling fire is kept up. This very much annoys Jacob, the black head-warder, and as one well-aimed bullet after another chips the parapet near by, he mutters grim threats, and allows his fire to slacken—for he is watching.

Round the edge of this building slowly steals the flap of a sombrero hat, under it a few inches of dark beard, and under that the sun glints for a moment on the barrel of a fore-shortened rifle. Jacob doesn't wait to see any more, for his face is spattered with dust, as the bullet strikes the ledge and sings waspily as it 'ricco's' away towards the distant kopjes. But he has seen all he wanted. He shows his teeth and says to the men around —" Next time me have that Dutchman."

On the wall just where the head appeared is a little patch of plaster of a darker tint, and on this Jacob trains his sights, and holds them there. A few seconds and the flap of the hat is again showing round the edge. It is slowly followed by the beard. The rifle should come next, but it hasn't time. For Jacob's foresight has gently worked along the darker spot towards the sharp upright corner of the wall. It reaches it, just misses it, and——

Jacob half rises from his cover, and showing all the teeth he is possessed of, says exultant—" Me said next time——" and then a hail of bullets round his exposed head quickly brings him under cover again.

And the men laugh. For at high tension men laugh at little things. But Jacob spoke the truth, for the Dutchman was found afterwards, and in the centre of his forehead was a little hole.

The movements of the Boers are peculiar. On the far side of the town parties can be seen galloping from point to point. Is help approaching? Then a large body leaves and at an easy pace rides away across the veldt. The little garrison was puzzled. But not for long. A swerve round a river bend and the course is shaped straight for a long kopje some mile to the southward. Then with an inward sinking the meaning of the move is grasped. That kopje commands the road from De Aar. Along that road must come the aid they have sent for, if it comes at all. With the enemy in possession of that hill, and they are cut off indeed.

But—— far away on the De Aar road comes a patch of dust, a little cloud no bigger than a man's hand.

The three men sent from the jail succeeded in getting through the Boers, though in doing so they had to run the gauntlet of a heavy fire. Nine miles out they found Captain Tivey and a patrol of sixty Bushmen just saddling up, preparatory to moving. But the tale of the men altered their plans, and they turned their horses and rode towards Philipstown.

The little patch grows rapidly. The Bushmen have heard the firing, and are pushing their horses, for they smell a fight. The value of the long kopje is seen afar off, and they turn in that direction, innocent of the Boers riding towards it from the other side; who, in their turn, know nothing about the approaching Bushmen. Who will win the crest? On the answer hangs the fate of the garrison in the bullet-spattered jail.

It is soon decided. The Boers reach the hill. They quicken their pace to take its rough uneven sides. They gain a third of the way up——to be hurled backwards in broken confusion by a volley from its crest, for the Bushmen have won by a neck. Galloping back to cover, the Boers again and again make frantic efforts to gain the hill, but vainly. Tivey and his Bushmen have come to stay.

Those in the jail watch the hill eagerly. What will they do? What *can* they do? They are but sixty strong. But soon it is seen that some attempt is to be made from the hill. A party commence to make their way to the relief across the plain westward of the town. But this is madness. From the jail it can be seen that that side is seamed with dongas bristling with Boers, but evidently unknown to the Australian Captain. If they come that way they will be cut off to a man.

There, but a short mile away, the men who have come to save them are riding to annihilation, all unwitting. And those upon the walls are forced to watch them, hand-tied, helpless. There seems no means. To ride through that zone of fire is suicide—is courting instant death; even was there the man to attempt it. But such a man is found.

Trooper William Sopp volunteers to make the attempt, and the offer is accepted.

No time is lost. Descending to the yard, Lieut. Munn's own horse is saddled, with every ounce of useless weight discarded. Then—a cheery word or two, the gate flung wide, and urging his horse with voice and heel, Sopp takes Death by the hand, and makes his dash.

For several moments the men above draw their breath, expecting instantly to see the fall of horse and rider. And the Boers themselves seem paralysed by his audacity, for twenty yards is gained before they fire. But not for long. Scores of rifles are swifty emptied on horse and man. For many hundred yards they ride through showers of lead. The fire on the jail perceptibly slackens, for every rifle seems turned on that flying horseman, who moment by moment grows less as the distance widens. He leaves the road and striking across the veldt, shapes a bee-line for the Bushmen's hill.

A horse with outstretched head and straining limbs, the rider sitting tight but still, riding to win. A horse and rider, faint seen through rising dust. A little dark patch scudding o'er an ocean of veldt. On, smaller, till a speck crawling up the far rise, and then——

"Hurrah! he's got through,"—broke from the men. And with a better heart, into the baffled Boers they pour their hail of lead, for they know the Bushmen are saved.

And shortly from the hill a black speck comes, and reaching the plain, makes townwards. It is a horseman riding easily, for he has not yet been noticed by the Boers. What is it?—men ask Surely no one man is so mad——

Ah! the Boers have seen him and he is riding under fire, for there is now no lagging in his pace. Nearer, till through the glasses he takes shape, and one says with a gasp—

"'Tis Sopp coming back!"

Nearer the flying horseman. This is a different task. To ride *into* the fire of a hundred rifles is not the same as flying from them.

"Pour in your fire! Draw their attention!" shouts Lieut. Munn. And the men strive their best. Nearer the horseman. In the still moments 'tween the firing the beat of the hoofs can be heard.

"Keep up the fire into that donga. There's where the mischief lies." And for the next few seconds the donga becomes a warm corner indeed for its sheltering occupants.

Three hundred yards away, and the horse still on its feet. The crackle of shots is like fresh thorns on a fierce camp fire.

"To the gate!" 'Tis the last order given.

Two hundred yards,—one hundred, and from the road fly little spurts of sand, thick as the first coming of big raindrops on still water. Back fly the gates. There is a sound of splintering glass, as every unbroken pain in the windows of the jail falls shivered by the storm of bullets. And with a clatter and a cheer from the men, Trooper Sopp gallops into the yard—without a scratch on horse or man.

'Trooper' for that day only. For from that date henceforward he is 'Corporal' Sopp—promoted by the Commander-in-Chief for his deed.

And, recommended by the Australian Captain, his name appears in 'orders,' which state in bald official terms that—

> "The Medal for Distinguished Conduct in the Field is awarded to 12040 Trooper (now Corporal) W. Sopp, who in the Boer attack upon Philipstown, Feb. 12th, 1901, galloped back to Captain Tivey, under heavy fire. . . After reaching him he volunteered to return and arrived safely under fire from 600 to 60 yards."

But with the repeated failure of their attacks, the enemy seem to lose heart. Though the firing goes on through the day, they make no more determined efforts to take the little garrison, and at half-past four the twelve hours strain is lifted, for from the west comes a British Column, and the Boers are driven from the town. One after another, single horsemen are seen making a dash from cover, and they make wide detours in twos and threes till, far out on the plains, they gather in larger groups and ride out of sight round the kopjes.

"Such"—to quote Edgar Wallace—"was the battle of Philipstown—nothing very great as battles go, but sufficient to hold De Wet's main body for at least six hours, and turn him back on the pursuing columns. It was his first check south, and it was fitting that the men from the Colonies . . . . and the Yeomen of England should have been the men who gave De Wet his first check."

CHAPTER VII.

The Chase of De Wet.

"THERE they go!—two, five, seven, eight, nine, ten—there! from that farm in the hollow."

And the men reined in their horses and watched them go. Ten black specks riding from the white farm-house—ten mounted Boers hustling over the plain for that kopje, half-a-mile away.

No more horsemen appearing, the Yeomanry patrol rode carefully on towards the great kopje which ended the chain of hills and, like some beetling cape, jutted out into the ocean of veldt—westward, towards the railway.

But the 'pointer' of the patrol rode back with the startling report that the far side of the hill was alive with Boers. They were the broken columns of De Wet, pushing westward from Plumer's hot pursuit.

And as the trooper spoke, the sky-line of the kopje was broken along its length by numberless figures of men on foot and of horsemen. Instant they were seen, and then the patrol were riding at full pace through a hail of bullets—southward, for Houtkraal, twelve miles away.

But the veldt was a muddy morass from heavy rain, and the horses could make no pace over the viscid road, o'er fetlock deep in mud. And as this road had approached the kopje at an angle, they were riding across the front of the spitting Mauser muzzles. One is down, with two bullets—a Martini and a Mauser—through his thigh. Soon he is surrounded and stripped by a dozen ragged Dutchmen, and his horse gallops riderless after the others. The Lieutenant reels from the shock of a ball which smashes his field-glasses and flattens itself against a handful of loose cartridges in his pocket, but he himself is sound and keeps his seat. Then they divide, and the officer

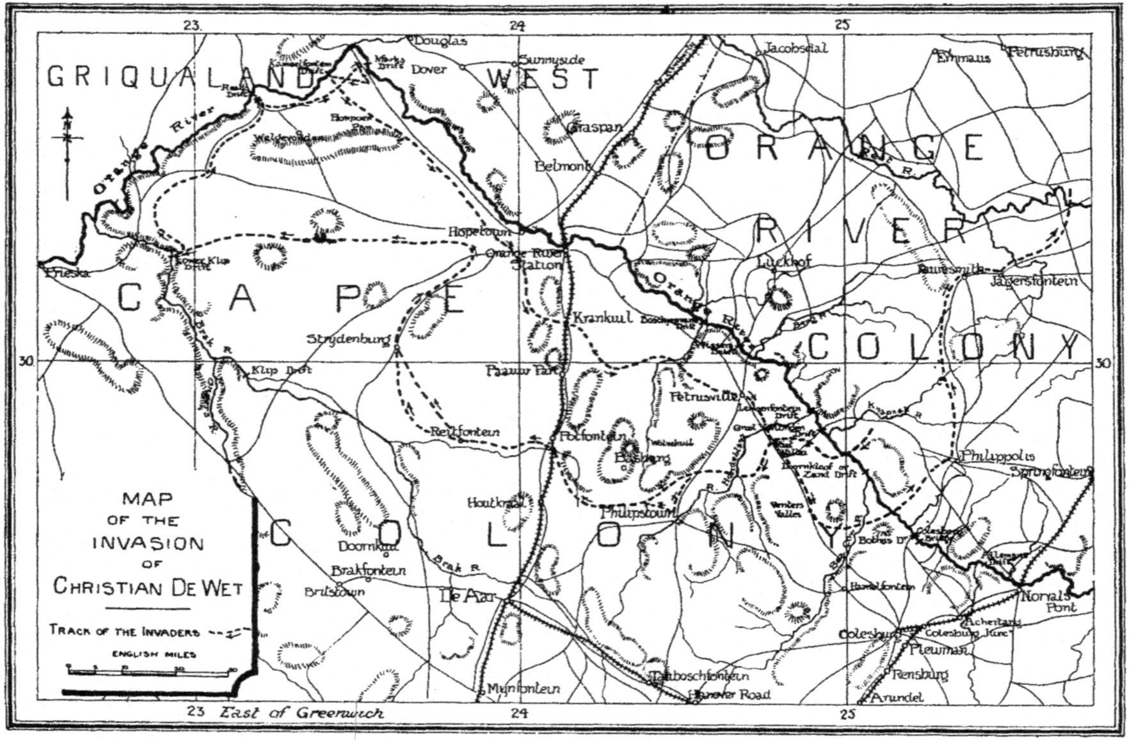

Prepared specially for 'Rhodesia—and After.'

and several of the men leave the road, and striking across the veldt to higher ground, gain upon and at length out-distance their pursuers.

But those who kept the road. They are cut off from the south by scores of shouting Boers. Another comes down with a shot wound in his foot and a badly wounded horse. They are out-numbered and surrounded, and one by one are captured.

And in the Boer laager a great surprise awaited them. For there lay a score more of their squadron, of whose capture two days before, they had known nothing.

That night the sentries in the camp at Houtkraal were puzzled by a dull sound from far to the north, a heavy booming sound which came twice between the driving rain-gusts. De Wet and a picked band of eighty men had pushed to the rail in the darkness, and at Baartmann's Siding, 'twixt Potfontein and Paauwpan, had blown up the line.

Four days before, De Wet, slipping between the columns north of the river, had crossed the Orange near Zand Drift, where he surprised and captured seventeen of the Prince of Wales's Light Horse. The river was so low at the time that a crossing could be made anywhere near the Drift for a distance of four miles.

And after him came hot-foot Bruce Hamilton and Knox, but too late. The Boer commandoes—2,500 men and 4 guns, with near 100 wheeled transport—had taken three days in the crossing, and as the British columns entered Philippolis, De Wet's rearguard had left but a few hours before.

The crossing of the Orange by General Knox was described to me by a Sergeant of Yeomanry who was there, and is of interest inasmuch as it gives a faint idea of what the invaders had to face when they were driven back across the river more than a fortnight later.

For the last mile, the rocky road zig-zagged down from the hills, rough-cut and very difficult for transport. Down below, and in sight the whole way, ran the Orange between thick-foliaged banks. But not the Orange that De Wet had crossed. Heavy rains had fallen since then, and it was now a tumbling yellow flood, running with vicious hiss between banks three hundred yards apart.

First came the advance guard of mounted men, and as they crossed, shaping a diagonal course down stream, in order to resist the current-as little as might be, the waters washed over the horses' quarters, and the lighter animals had to swim. Many men stripped, and rode across with their clothes in a bundle fastened on their shoulders. As the guns followed, the creaming current rolled completely over their great breeches, and the big heavy horses all but hid themselves in spray as they slashed through the foaming waters. Then, sixteen horses to a gun, they strain and plunge under the urging voice of their drivers, till the heavy burden is torn through the soft yielding sand to the crest of the opposite bank.

Then comes the hardest task of all—the heavy-laden wagons, each drawn by ten trembling mules.

As each wagon reaches the middle of the river, the effect of the strong current begins to be felt. Gradually, foot by foot, the team is deflected from its course by the rushing water and the mules begin to lose their heads in panic. But it will not do to let them stop, for every moment's halt means a deeper settling of the wheels into the treacherous sand of the river bed. Naked horsemen ride out to the head of each mule, and by voice and whip urge them to greater effort. There a wagon sticks ! A strong rope is at once passed round the rear of it, and at each end twenty men or more, with the tide washing under their armpits, strain to save it from sinking too deep for extrication.

But now and again the stream is too strong, the feet of the mules are washed from under them, and the poor brutes, as they feel themselves going, plunge and climb upon each other's backs, and becoming entangled in the harness, one or more are slowly drowned. When this occurs the men try to save the harness, but more than once the whole of the ten are drowned, and then they are swiftly cut away ; and as another team is attached, the old one goes down stream, harness and all, rolling over and over till lost to sight round a bend in the river.

One man—there are always some more clever than the rest on every column—thought he could cross more easily where the stream was narrower, and stripping off his clothes, essayed the passage. But he hadn't reached half-way, before the cruel current washed the feet of his steed from under it, and the river carried downwards the drowning body of a saddled horse, whilst the rider, who luckily could swim, gained the far bank a shivering figure *sans* horse, *sans* clothes, *sans* everything—but life.

To add to the difficulties of the task, with the afternoon came a thick dust storm which swept o'er the river; and from the bank, one could see through the driving clouds of sand nothing but a confused mass of struggling animals and wagons, carts and men.

The column commenced to cross at 8 a.m., and with the close of daylight all were on the southern bank—all but a few wagons firmly embedded in the soft sand in the centre of the stream. There they were left, and there they may be to this day.

Two days after his passage of the river, De Wet passed to the north of Philipstown and detached a strong body to occupy the place—with what success has been related in a previous chapter.

It was on the following day—February 13—that a patrol of the Leicesters, consisting of Lieutenant Muir and twenty men, had off-saddled at the farm of Wolvekuil. That morning they had ridden from Houtkraal thirty miles away, and now, after a couple of hours' rest and a feed for their horses, were preparing to saddle up—when a solitary armed Boer rode up to the house all unsuspectingly. Words cannot describe his astonishment when, instead of the farmer he expected to see, the door opened and he was confronted by a rifle in the hands of a British officer. Of course he was promptly relieved of his horse and his arms, and then questioned as to the number of his companions. The wily Dutchman, resigning himself to the inevitable, reluctantly admitted that there were fourteen more coming over the hill, and Lieutenant Muir decided to wait for them.

Shortly they came, but he saw at a glance there was at least thirty instead of fourteen. Waiting until they came within 800 yards range, the patrol gave them a volley which quickly scattered them back to the hillside, from which they kept up a galling fire upon the farm. And now surprises grew apace. Forty or fifty more came over the hill, followed by another body of at least a hundred horsemen. And still they came. It was De Wet's whole army they were fighting.

Gradually the Boers worked round the hills—which in some places approached to within several hundred yards of the farm, and the bullets commenced to fall amongst the horses. So an attempt was made to remove them to a more sheltered kraal some distance away, but four or five were shot during the transit. As the last man galloped across, he rode through a family of barn-door fowls which flew clucking in consternation in all directions as he thundered by. One old hen however, though she escaped the hoofs, was not sufficiently nimble to evade the bullets, and the horse swerved as she was blown to pieces by an expanding bullet under its very nose. At the same instant, another bullet glanced from the wall of an out-building close by, and striking the man above his eye, brought him senseless to the ground, whilst his horse galloped away and joined the others.

Then each man taking the best available cover in the garden near by, they kept up a hot fire on the advancing Boers. The men did their best, and Lieutenant Muir seemed absolutely contemptuous of danger, coolly walking across the open several times from one little group to another, the better to direct their fire. But with odds of a hundred to one there could be but one result. The Boers crept up to the walls and actually into the garden itself, and the men were captured by twos and threes. Though the game was a deadly earnest one, the situation towards the end was not without its humour. The men themselves have laughed as they related to me how the heads of six or seven Boers would suddenly appear over a wall close to where two or three of them were lying, and, with pointed rifles shout peremptorily " Hands oop ! " ; only to duck again, as the reply came from another part of the garden in the form of a little storm of bullets. But at last the overwhelming numbers told, the fire of the patrol was stilled, and De Wet had taken twenty-one more British soldiers to join those already in his hands.

THE CHASE OF DE WET.

And this explains the presence of the men, which so surprised the scouts whose capture is related at the commencement of this chapter.

The 15th of February was an evil day for De Wet. For two days had his commandoes been harried by the relentless Plumer —indeed, only the day before he had barely escaped annihilation or capture by the timely advent of a driving hail-storm, under cover of which he slipped away from the pursuing troops.

And when at day-break the railway was reached, his jaded men threw themselves down to wait for the lagging convoy. For over four hours that morning had they struggled through the darkness, across a veldt which was everywhere one deep muddy morass from recent rain; and though their progress had not been rapid, it was much too fast for the tired mules in the wagons, and the worn-out oxen dragging the heavy guns.

Pitiable had been the lot of the British prisoners during these two days. Forced to march on foot over ground where, in places, the wagons sunk axle-deep, and the mules were ploughing through mud which reached their bellies, they were urged on by whips and cruel threats from their captors, who were rendered desperate by those khaki guns and horsemen which clung so tenaciously to their flanks and rear.

And as the weary Dutchmen lay, glad of the short respite, a sound—faint at first, but swiftly growing—came from the north, where the thin line of rails grew dim amongst the kopjes. And looking, they saw a dark speck upon the rails.

A train.

Larger it grew, and now it approached more slowly till near two miles away it stopped. And from its black sides broke a sharp coughing roar, and a shell came screaming over the veldt.

An ARMOURED TRAIN!

In a few moments the scene of confusion almost baffled description. Yet a distance away were the labouring transport, plunging across the soft veldt, almost a swamp. Men galloped back to urge on the wearied animals, cutting them cruelly with the whips they carried. And transport and guns, surrounded by a cloud of shouting horsemen, went forward at a lumbering gallop, making desperate efforts to cross the rail, out of reach of that black shapeless monster which barked havoc and death into their disordered ranks.

Shell after shell fell amongst them—but suddenly the gun was silent. One of the bolts which held it to the iron truck had broken, and the Boers, though they knew not the cause of the respite, began to breathe again.

But not for long. For from the south came two more armoured trains; and along the veldt, keeping pace with them, came the Australian 15-pounders at a gallop, in the midst of a screen of racing horsemen—the 65th and 71st I.Y. and Thorneycroft's M.I.

For five weeks had the column of Lieut.-Colonel Crabbe remained at Houtkraal, constantly sweeping the surrounding country with patrols; and in consequence of the information brought in by the remnant of the party whose patrol had ended so disastrously, a reconnaissance on a larger scale had been ordered for the morrow. And so, long before daylight, the column moved out northwards, parallel to the rail. Two miles out they found the two armoured trains, and together they advanced, the horsemen searching the ground on either side. Till the sound of guns to the northward sent them eager forward.

They come within range—instant the guns are swung round into position, and the first shell screams through a Cape cart from front to back, and striking the bearded Dutch driver full in the chest, hurls his shattered fragments through both sides of the cart—but the mules escape without a scratch.

Another and another, and the Boers in despair give up all hope of saving their transport. A few carts are already across, but the greater part is abandoned. The rearguard leave the wagons to their fate, and in a mad demoralized flight the broken army of De Wet gallop in confused heaps of horsemen and Cape carts across the line to the westward; leaving in our hands a Maxim gun, most of his wagons and carts, 6000 Pom-Pom and a quantity of 15-pounder shells, and 100,000 rounds of small arm ammunition.

Now in a thin skirmishing line, the T.M.I. gallop up to within short rifle range. The Yeomanry are escort to the guns, and

THE ARMOURED TRAIN THAT PLAYED HAVOC WITH DE WET.

Photo by Edgcome, Beaufort West.

must never leave their charge. But standing dismounted by their horses, they watch the fight through their glasses.

And truly it was a sight worth going far to see. Far away to the left front the ground rose steeply from the level of the plain to a plateau, which stretched away to the northward. In front of this several low ridges stood like outposts pushed out from a main position. And—now in the open, now hidden by a ridge, till they reached the plateau and rode or ran, for many were horseless—along the sky-line, streamed the whole of De Wet's broken army, in batches of ten or twenty or fifty or more. There was no dust to hide them—the veldt was too sodden for that. But through the glasses every figure stood out sharply distinct, a tiny black hurrying Boer—a literal 'flying Dutchman.'

Now they are harassed by the spitting fire of the T.M.I., who daringly ride to within ranges dangerously short, and pick them off as they pass. But the Boers, stung to exasperation, return the fire, and one or two of the foremost of the T.M.I. roll from their saddles. Then through the glasses those with the guns see several Boers come down on foot from the ridge, and having stripped the fallen troopers, walk coolly back again.

So they pass over the plateau in a never-ending stream. And now from a distant kopje on the right comes the twinkle-twinkle of the heliograph. It is General Plumer, who flashes that " *he* is pushing them on." Since the invaders crossed the Orange eight days ago has he chased them, and though his horses are dying and his men are worn out with fatigue, Plumer the Untiring is still at their heels.

The last mob have gone over the hills, and the guns limber up and give chase. Mile after mile on the littered trail of the flying commandoes till night falls, and the column halts to rest horses and men for the stern chase on the morrow.

And at Houtkraal lay the tents and the blankets of the Leicesters, in charge of the one sick man left in camp when the squadron turned out on their 'one day's patrol.' It will be many a long day, and they will have covered many hundreds of weary miles, before they again return for their bedding. And then not all of them.

Next day the column was astir at half-past three and again

wended silently westward on that grim chase which was never to relax until the invaders were captured or again driven across the Orange. Though a hot sun shone throughout the day, the veldt was still a half-dried swamp, and the 'going' was heavy and terribly fatiguing for horses and men. Midday came, and the column halted near a farm for needful food and rest. But on a sudden there was a clutching of arms, for out from a sheep-kraal on the hillside could be seen coming a stream of men. But when the glasses were levelled it was seen they were without arms and on foot, and one was waving a cloth in signal. They drew nearer and then came a glad re-union, for they were the haggard wearied prisoners released by De Wet. The pursuit by the British columns had been too close; he could no longer carry with him men who had to be driven on foot. And so they were left in his wake to shift for themselves.

Now Plumer and Crabbe were joined by Henniker, who had hastened up as fast as his wagons could move to take part in the chase; and next day the three columns moved out abreast—Plumer in the centre, with Crabbe and Henniker to the right and left respectively. The centre column furnished the advance guard whilst the outer ones were responsible for the flanks.

It was some time after midday—Feb. 17—when the advance guard arrived on the edge of a great valley, and there below them, but far away in front, the quarry was sighted again. Plumer's guns at once opened fire on the long sinuous dust-line ahead, and Henniker's Victorians and 17th Lancers pushed on, and getting on the flank of the Boer column, succeeded in turning them to the right. Shell after shell dropped amongst the flying commandoes as they passed the front of Plumer's column, but unfortunately Crabbe on the right could not get forward in time to turn them back onto the other columns, and they streamed round a large kopje and once more got clean away. Darkness was falling and the columns halted near Pienaar Pan.

Three days later, and the three pursuing columns lay at Zoutpansfontein, waiting for supplies which were on the road to them. The rest was much needed, for in the pursuit neither men nor horses had been spared. General Lyttelton, who had supreme command, and had been directing the movements of the many columns closing around the guerilla chief, sent a despatch to General Plumer " congratulating the troops of the columns on their splendid marching, which he hoped would be crowned with success."

But though the columns halted for a time, a strong patrol was sent out to ascertain the enemy's movements—a risky patrol composed of 15 of the Leicesters, 15 of the 71st I.Y., 50 of the T.M.I., and 120 Bushmen from Colonel Henniker's column, the whole under the command of Major Vialls, of the Australians. They were to return in three days, and carried neither food for the men nor forage for the horses, their instructions being to " live on the country they passed through."

During these three days, the men were extremely short of food. The country had already been cleared by De Wet's troops, and all they were able to procure was an occasional sheep, which they roasted over the coals and ate without salt or bread.

Upon the second day, at a farm visited in the early morning, the carcass of a whole sheep was found roasting over a fire near the house, and as the owner of the farm could not give a satisfactory explanation of the big meal he was preparing for his small family, he had perforce to accompany the patrol. From some cause or other, six men of the 71st remained behind at this farm for half-an-hour or more after the little column had proceeded on its way. As the men saddled up they saw two armed Boers riding leisurely down to the farm from a kopje near by. As soon as they came up, they received the inevitable invitation to " Hands up," and were made prisoners almost before they realized that they had been much too premature in thinking the ' khakis ' had all gone from the farm.

At midday the patrol was passing through a long valley, the ground on either side rising to some 50 feet and then stretching away in wide plateaux. Along these ridges the flankers rode scouting. Suddenly the Bushmen on the left flank commenced to fire, and reported the presence of the enemy on the flat, but in no great numbers. Then almost immediately came the crackle of rifles from the right plateau, and a trooper brought the startling news that the ridge on that flank was literally alive with Boers. And from a farm not 500 yards ahead a galling fire was opened on their advance guard.

Things looked serious. The patrol was but two hundred strong, and they were surrounded by De Wet's whole army. Night was coming on, and their only chance of safety lay in the darkness. The Yeomanry were sent out to the left flank, and quickly drove the enemy from that quarter ; and by this time the daylight had gone, and the little party prepared to secure themselves for the night. Major Vialls retired them to a little rising plain some four square miles in extent, which lay a short distance away. The men were distributed over the ground in little groups, and each group built a fire ; till at last, half the plain was dotted with their camp-fires, and to all appearance the whole of the three pursuing columns lay there encamped instead of the little body of two hundred men. A swift rider was also sent back to Col. Henniker to acquaint him with their position, as they fully expected to find themselves surrounded by De Wet's commandoes at daybreak.

The dawn came and anxiously they looked around. But there was not a Boer to be seen. A number of small parties were sent out in every direction to feel for the enemy. A mile-and-a-half away westward lay the Brak River in flood, and in a hollow near its banks they found the smouldering fires, half-eaten forage and scattered scraps of clothing of De Wet's abandoned camp. Their ruse had succeeded beyond their fondest hopes. De Wet, believing the three columns were upon his heels, had left during the night, and after trying vainly to cross the swollen river at the Lower Klip Drift, had turned northwards towards the Orange.

A despatch now came from General Plumer to recall them to the column, and they returned, having admirably succeeded in their object—keeping De Wet upon the move and gaining valuable knowledge of his movements.

On their way back they learned that small parties of the Boers had been enquiring at the farms after the British columns. De Wet, when too late, had discovered his mistake, and was now seeking the whereabouts of the pursuers he had for a time lost sight of Their escape was a narrow one indeed, for in the camp by the river De Wet had over two thousand men and two guns, and they learned from prisoners afterwards captured from him, that had not the Boer leader been totally deceived by their numerous camp-fires, he would have overwhelmed them with his numbers.

It may be worth noting that, upon their return, the officers of the patrol were invited to lunch with General Plumer, and the fare placed before them was the same upon which the General himself was living—bully beef and biscuits. And, after their three days' short commons, they did ample justice to it.

The dawn is breaking—the dawn of the 23rd of February—and the combined columns are again on a hot trail. For information has been brought in that De Wet lies laagered near Kameel Drift, twenty-two miles away, and the rested columns are eager for battle. Moreover, the Leicesters have one of their comrades to avenge, shot through the heart from behind at Elsie Vlaakte farm, two days ago.*

Meanwhile De Wet has had no rest. Fast as one column dropped out, killed by the cruel strain on horse and man, another rested one was ready for its place. Turning northwards from the Brak, he tried the Orange Drifts; but the constant rains still kept the river in a deep flood which it was impossible to cross. Read's Drift, Mark's Drift, Kameelfontein Drift, he tried them all in turn, but every ford was buried deep beneath the waters. Sixteen feet of rushing current barred his front. In rear came the grim determined columns.

Crabbe's column leads, with the T.M.I. for advance guard and the 65th and 71st I.Y. in support; followed by the Australian guns and their escort.

After them—Henniker in support, and Plumer forming flank guards and reserve.

Upon a long ridge at Pampoen's Pan the Boers are found, and the Yeomanry and Mounted Infantry of Col. Crabbe's column, supported by Henniker's Victorians, are ordered to clear the ridge. Under a heavy fire they advance at a gallop.

---

* See ' Story of the 65th Squadron.' Part III.

Sudden from another part of the ridge breaks a well-known sound—pom-pom-pom-pom—and a stream of vicious little shells lend an added excitement to the gallop, though they burst wide of the mark they are aimed at. De Wet's gunners, in their white German-shaped caps—the only attempt at a uniform in his whole bedraggled army—have got something to learn in the science of gunnery before they stop the advance of the Yeomanry and the Bushmen. But the Pom-Pom is soon silenced by the deeper cough of the Australian 15-pounders, and the rifle fire alone remains unslackened.

Side by side the troops breast the hill, and the men of the Yeomanry laugh as they see Bushmen leading spare horses, Bushmen leading pack-horses, every Bushman in the squadron, all taking part in the charge on the Boer position. They reach the crest, but De Wet's rearguard—for it is only the rearguard thrown back so check the advance of the columns—breaks and flies, a demoralized mob, after the rest of the commandoes.

The broken Boers fled in a panic-stricken stream in the direction of Hopetown, followed hotly by the Yeomanry and the Australians. Everything that would lighten their flight was cast away, and for eight or ten miles the veldt was strewn with blankets, clothing, arms and ammunition. Even the saddles were stripped off, and they rode bare-back to lessen the weight on their horses. Here, as the British gained upon them, men would jump from their horses and dive into the bush on foot, leaving horse and rifle a prize for the pursuers. There, as the troopers thundered o'er the veldt, panic-stricken Boers would pop up out of the bush before their horses' heads, crying " Don't shoot, Khaki ! don't shoot ! " And the bolts would be taken from their rifles, and they would be roughly told to get to the rear and give themselves up; for the advance guard had no time to waste in taking prisoners. Then they would sit in little groups by the roadside, smoking their pipes, and calmly watching the pursuit of their comrades as though they were not at all interested parties—glad, on the face of it, that they at least were safe—and captured. Till they were picked up by the main body of the column.

THE CHASE OF DE WET.

So utterly demoralized had the Boers become, that when a Sergeant of the Leicesters—Sergeant Diggle—came across six of them hiding in a donga, they at once gave up their arms ; and he brought them in to the column single-handed, his horse laden with rifles and bandoliers.

Surely never was witnessed such a strange scene as the chase of De Wet's rearguard from Pampoen's Pan to Disselfontein.

So till noon, when Col. Crabbe's column was ordered to hold a position upon a ridge until Plumer came up with the Reserves ; and Col. Henniker's column dashed on in advance in pursuit of the flying Boers. Then, aided by Plumer's horsemen, the pursuit continued the whole of that afternoon till, between eight and nine o'clock as it grew dark, De Wet's two guns—a 15-pounder and a Pom-Pom—were seen far in front, the jaded animals being urged on by their desperate drivers. And farther still beyond lay the Boer laager.

Without a moment's hesitation the Victorians, led by Capt. Marker, of the 2nd Battn. Coldstream Guards, made straight for the guns. The Boers saw them coming. In a few moments the larger gun was unlimbered and a shell rammed home. But the Bushmen never faltered, and before the gun could be fired, the horsemen were amongst the gunners, and they fled for their lives, leaving the two guns in the hands of the Australians. But so hot had been the pace, that when the guns were reached, Captain Marker had but three men at his back—and one of these was leading a spare horse.

And De Wet fled southwards, leaving in our hands his guns, his camp, his transport, and a number of his men—retaining little beyond an earnest wish to get back across the Orange.

Over forty miles did the Leicesters ride that day, with no food for horses or men until the following morn, when a convoy was met—belonging to Major Paris at Hopetown—and their pressing need was relieved.

Resting a day at Hopetown (Plumer had entrained for Orange River Station), Henniker and Crabbe again took up the chase of the Boer leader who, destroying the line on his way, recrossed the railway at Krankuil Station. Where—did he but note the unconscious sarcasm—there confronted him one of the three-language notice boards found at every crossing on the Cape Government Railway :—

NOTICE.
Trespassers will be prosecuted.
By Order.

KENNISGEVING.
Overtreders zal vervolgt worden.
Op Last.

ISAZISO.
Aboni bonka bakohlwaywa.
Ngokomteto.

Thorneycroft had been hurried north by rail as soon as it was known that the Boers had recrossed the line. On the 24th he joined hands with the pursuing columns of Henniker and Crabbe, and together they pressed on the chase. Petrusville was entered on the 25th and a rearguard action fought with the Boer forces.

Only twelve miles away lay the Orange, but the rains, which still continued to fall, mainly during the night—though they rendered the lot of the columns, without blankets, and half-starved for want of food, a most wretched one—still made the river impassable. Therefore De Wet continued a south-easterly course in his flight, making towards Colesberg.

Still they pressed on, and as night was falling, after a march of thirty-four miles, the wearied troops again were in touch with the enemy opposite to Zand Drift.

The columns were closing in upon their quarry. To the left of him rolled the impassible river. Behind and to the right were the British troops—Crabbe, Henniker, Thorneycroft and Hickman, who had marched from Philipstown—each column in touch with the one before it. Other columns were hurrying up but were farther away. There was but one road open—up the river ; and Major Byng was rapidly advancing from the

CHRISTIAN DE WET.—Photo *Glassberg, Worcester, C.C.*

THE CHASE OF DE WET.

direction of Colesberg to cut him off there. The heart-breaking work of the columns seemed at last to be nearing fruition—the capture of the famous Boer leader seemed well within sight.

On the 27th Colonel Byng's patrols came in touch with part of the Boer force, and he flashed the news to De Aar, from which place General Lyttelton was directing the movements of the columns, in order that he might communicate the exact whereabouts of the enemy to the other leaders.

But—somebody blundered.

The message was incorrectly given, either in its transit or return; for back came an order directing him to move southwards—an entirely opposite direction to that in which the Boers were known to be.

The traditions of the British Army say—

" Theirs not to make reply,
Theirs not to reason why,"—

and in this case blind obedience to a mistaken order lost us De Wet.

Colonel Byng turned southwards, and the Boers hurried through the loop-hole left by his column to Lilliefontein Drift, where the river was very wide, and therefore the current not so strong. And in despair, losing many men and horses by drowning in the attempt, he swam the remnants of his shattered army back across the Orange.

CHAPTER VIII.

Under Orders for Home.

IT was Sunday—Sunday at Somerset East. And as I lay writing home by the last rays of daylight, the men strolled into camp from the town by twos and threes.

A beautiful town is Somerset East. Vistas of white houses shrinking coyly at the sides of tree-bordered streets, folded in the cool windings of the Little Fish River, and guarded by the frowning black masses of the Boschberg, which rise sheer to 2500 feet from the very outskirts of the town. And of hospitality unwearying are its people.

And we—Colonel Henniker's column—were racked with the usual uncertainty. Some said we were moving; others knew we were not. But it grew dark and no orders had come, so men spread out their blankets under the stars, and disposed themselves for sleep. And we growled as we saw an orderly make his way to the officers' tent; for here we knew were the expected orders to move.

But we couldn't make it out. Shortly the sergeant-major was sent for to the officers' tent; then coming back to his own, he called the sergeants. And from the tent we lying by the horse-lines heard a cheer, suppressed and faint.

And a man rushed across to me from near the tent, and clutched me by the shoulders till I drew back from the pain of his grip. He looked white and excited, and he gasped rather than said—

"*It's come. We're going home!*"

My breath caught and seemed to stop, but I asked him quietly what he meant.

"We're ordered home!"—he said huskily—"I heard the sergeants say 'It's come at last'—and you heard them cheer." Could it be true? There seemed little doubt of it, and soon there was none. For we heard the sergt.-major shout " Fall in for orders." And not a man was absent.

" Telegram from Col. Haig. Dated May 3.
1. The enemy have been tracked further north.
2. The 65th I.Y. will be reorganized, and time-expired men will be sent to Capetown."

So it ran. And then the scene became beyond description. There were cheers and yells and cat-calls. Men caught each other and began to waltz and schottische and sing. One couple polka-d into the horse-lines and were nearly brained for their pains. A Kaffir boy was caught and so severely mauled in very joy that he nearly cried. The men yelled at him,

" We're going *lapa*—to England."

And the boy kept on saying " Yah! yah! baas," but didn't seem to like his treatment.

Soon the excitement spread to the other camps, and from the darkness where the Bushmen lay we could hear them shout "The Leicesters are going home," and they yelled and cheered for sympathy.

At last comparative quiet came. But sleep was out of the question. Men stood about in groups and discussed the glad news. And some stood apart, with a smile on their bronzed faces, and a soft far-away look in their eyes. They could hardly grasp it yet, that the weary trekking was over, that the cold and the wet nights on the sodden veldt were at last coming to an end. More than all, that they were going home.

And we eagerly planned it all out. The order could not have come at a better time. Scarce eighteen miles away was the railway by which we could reach the Cape. To-morrow we could give in our horses—the other troops wanted remounts sorely enough ; and after spending a few days in the town—the officers would be sure to want that—we should march to Cookhouse—we could easily do it on foot, and—

But we reckoned without our host.

" The Column will move at 9 p.m."

So we saddled up and left behind the deep-shadowed streets of the town ; out on a good road across the veldt towards Cookhouse and the railway. It was bright moonlight, and the pale beams played on the sparkling white ground, for everywhere was covered with frost. We were escort to the wagons, and as horses walk much faster at night than in the day, we out-distanced the convoy from time to time, and had to halt and dismount for them to come up. Once a halt of half-an-hour had to be made. The cold was piercing. We lay down by the roadside with the reins over one arm, and tried to snatch a few minutes sleep. But we should wake up nearly frozen, and have to walk and lead our horses as the only means of restoring the circulation in our numbed limbs.

Once we laughed. During a halt one of the Bushmen lay down, and in a moment was fast asleep. His horse, taking in the situation, lay down too, and stretching his head along the ground close by the body of his master, was soon also in the land of dreams. There they lay side by side, dead to the world and the war, until, when we again moved on, we had to wake them both.

Convoy escort is slow work, and it was 4.30 a.m. before we flung ourselves down by the station at Cookhouse, and snatched what sleep remained to us before the morn.

Nearly a week has gone since we left Somerset East and we are still with the column. We have had a brush with the enemy—at Daggabours Nek—and driven them hot-foot into the arms of Colonel Gorringe, who accounted for many; though on our side 'tis said seven Tasmanians fell in the fight.

Two days ago we again reached the railway at Witmoss, where, by-the-way, the name of a late acquaintance and host confronted us—in the manner shown on the opposite page —from every official wall.

This morning, after two nights in the rain, we again left the station; and no man dare now mention 'home,' unless he be desirous of bringing the whole squadron upon him. For in our eyes we have suffered a cruel wrong. When some distance on our way from the station a telegram had followed, giving instructions for ' all time-expired Yeomanry to leave the columns and proceed to Worcester to mobilize.' This the Colonel did not tell us until it was too late to send us back, for ' he cannot yet spare the squadron.'

£250 REWARD.

ARREST OF
Daniel Scheepers.

A reward of **TWO HUNDRED & FIFTY POUNDS** Sterling will be paid to anyone arresting **DANIEL SCHEEPERS**, lately of Upsaal, in the Division of Somerset East, charged with the Crime of Murder, committed on the 24th day of March, 1901, at **Dwingfontein** in this District.

LANCELOT HARISON,
Resident Magistrate.

Resident Magistrate's Office,
Cradock, 28th March, 1901.

DESCRIPTION,

Dutchman, of about 26 years of age, stout and strongly built, about 5 feet 7 inches, thick neck, fair hair and moustache. Speaks English, was a pupil of Gill College, Somerset East, son of Gert Scheepers of Upsaal, District of Somerset East.

So we ride forth once more to the veldt, and our dreams
of release grow fainter as the miles are covered. The
hillsides are gay with the scarlet flowers of the aloe, which
spring in huge clustered fingers from the top of every tall plant.
But to us the landscape is coloured by our thoughts, and all is
gloom.

Now we pierce a narrow kloof, just wide enough for a house
or two to nestle between the road and the cliffs. Long narrow
gardens adjoin them, and extend to the very rocks which rise
perpendicular on either hand.

Great euphorbias with candelabra-shaped branches grow
around, and these and the other South African plants retain
their usual green appearance; but in the gardens pear and peach
and other fruit-trees have been planted, and these are covered
with a thin coat of yellow autumn leaves, or stand stark and
bare, with a carpet of dead leaves about their base. We had
hardly realized that it was autumn till then, and the men
pointed them out with delighted eyes, saying it was just like
England. But it wasn't all English, for amongst them stood
large orange-trees, thickly studded with ripe golden-coloured
fruit.

As we rode through the pass, splashing through the stream
which wound across the road from time to time, monkeys
could be heard chattering in the trees, and now and again the
hoarse cry of a baboon far up amongst the rocks.

We had been constantly climbing, and our march at last
brought us over the hill range, and far below us we saw the
road winding away through the valley, till in the distance it was
lost amongst the thorn groves.

It was some hour or more later, when winding under the
shade of giant mimosas in the valley below, a sudden noise
came from far ahead. Some said it was a big gun of another
column. I thought it more like a volley of rifle fire, but if so
it was a very good volley. Again it was repeated, and a third
time, but as no one seemed to notice it, we thought we had been
mistaken. We were riding in front of the guns, and Colonel
Henniker was behind us. But no orderlies came in from the
front, so we soon forgot the noise we had heard. But five
minutes after, a Bushman cantered past from the front—the

Australians were advance guard—and then came a shout from behind,

"Divide the road."

Pulling our horses aside, the Colonel and staff clattered past. We wondered for a moment, but a large farm-house lay in front, and as no more firing came—if it had been firing—we thought the Colonel had gone forward to choose a site for the camp.

Walking up to the house, we formed up in line, preparatory to dismounting and off-saddling. But as we stood, came the sound of firing from a long ridge running at the bottom of the farm garden. We then knew the enemy were about, and understood that our men were on the kopje, firing into them. And we wondered what part we should take.

"Double files right, walk march," and troop by troop we rode through the garden towards the kopje. Evidently going to support the men on the crest.

Soon we broke into a slow trot along the garden path. But 'pht, pht' several bullets sang by, and what we had not noticed before, there were several double reports amongst the firing.

Then we at once knew—for the first time—that the men on the crest were Boers, not friends, and we were crossing the garden under their fire. For a moment we had a strong desire to break into a faster pace, and men unconsciously touched their horses with their spurs.

But no. Our officer—who came to the war as a trooper, and was now a Lieutenant with a medal for gallantry waiting when he got home—would not let us increase the pace an inch. He rode at the head, and, though some cheeks were rather paler than usual, and inwardly we were not calm by any means, the slow pace steadied us, and we tightened our reins and rode for the kopje, every man in his place in the ranks.

A thud, and a Corporal said—" My horse is hit!"—but it still carried him on. A few more yards, and a horse came down with a crash, struck by four bullets, and the rider came over his head. But at last we reached the foot of the hill, where there was shelter for the horses. Then dismounting, we extended and taking advantage of every cover started up the kopje, keeping a hot fire upon the crest. There were 150

Dutchmen on the ridge, and the climb was an exciting one—rushes from cover to cover, but ever higher, and our barrels getting hotter with firing. Then a gun spoke from the valley below, and over us screamed a shell, followed by another, and yet another, bursting beautifully and raking the crest with shrapnel.

The effect on the Boer fire was instant. It slackened, and with a cheer, we crossed the remaining space at a run, arriving breathless to find the scared Boers mounting at the foot, and riding o'er the plain beyond as though their lives lay on it. Which indeed they did.

Again it was Sunday, and the day after our encounter with the Boer commando. Our camp lay in a narrow valley, hid away in the hills. Though the wind was rather strong the weather was fine, and as we rolled ourselves in our blankets by our saddles, many of us took off boots and coats, little dreaming what the night would bring.

Somewhere about midnight I was awakened by the rain, which was coming down in a heavy storm, driven by the wind, which had increased greatly. But we had slept through many a wet night before, and I knew from experience the best thing to do was to lie still and let it rain. So I pushed my head farther into the saddle out of the wind and slept again.

An hour or more, and I again awoke. This time I found the water running under me in a stream—we were lying on a gentle slope. I was wet through and a tremendous storm was howling over my head. This was too much, so I stood up, but had no sooner left the shelter of my saddle, than the hurricane of wind and rain literally fetched me off my feet. The veldt all round was one big marsh, with the higher bits rising like islands all round. Unfortunately my boots were off, and as I stumbled from the force of the wind I stepped into a pool of water. I hastily slipped on my boots, only to find that they were full of water too. It was too dark to see anything a foot away, a darkness one could almost feel; and the rain, which had changed to an icy sleet, cut across in horizontal sheets which it was almost impossible to face. To stay where I was was clearly impossible, so I wrapped my sodden greatcoat round me, and started in search of anything better than this, leaving my soaked blankets and saddlery to their fate. After going a short distance, feeling in the darkness for the islands to step on, I fetched up by the shivering body of a horse, and found I had strayed into the horse-lines. At last I reached our wagon, and crouching down under its shelter amongst a group of other unfortunates, spent the remainder of one of the most wretched Sunday nights I ever wish to see.

At last morning broke, and we turned out to feed the poor horses. They looked pictures of misery, with their backs to the storm, and standing over fetlock-deep in a lake of soft watery mud. And their flanks were all a-tremble with cold as the cutting wind swept round them. The sky was one dull leaden sheet, and soon the rain and sleet turned to a thick driving storm of snow. Everywhere was white, save where the water lay in pools, or where the horses stood in the miry horse-lines. Under the poor shelter of the thorns we stood, and stamped our feet alternately to keep up an apology for circulation in them.

All the early morning the snow came down, but at last it ceased, and when the sun came through it shone on a circle of white ridges and peaks, dazzling in their glare.

Saddling up, we marched some twenty miles through narrow valleys which acted like flues for the wind. This came off the ice-covered slopes of the hills, and as it swept in our faces it made our teeth chatter and our horses dance sideways, and we hardly knew we were possessed of feet.

We looked forward to another miserable night in our sodden blankets, but a stroke of luck befel us.

We halted at a farm called Doorn-bosch (Thorn-bush), and found the family had removed into the town for the winter, as is the custom amongst the more well-to-do farmers living in these bleak hills. It was a large house of twenty-one rooms (nearly all Dutch houses consist of but one storey), and we took possession of these, and for one night at least we felt ourselves independent of the weather.

As we rode up, a solemn procession was just issuing from the house towards a small grove of trees. It was the funeral of one of the Bushmen. Yesterday two squadrons had left the camp on a reconnaisance. One had been surprised at a farm some miles further on, and the second came up just in time to extricate them from a very serious position. During the fight, one of the Bushmen—Trooper Moore of the V.I.R.'s,—to quote the 'orders,' " gave his life whilst performing a gallant action."

The men say he literally threw his life away to save some of his comrades. He had galloped almost into the enemy's ranks and, after turning their flank, was again mounting, when he was shot through the stomach as he swung his leg over the saddle. Even then his teeth were not drawn, for he shot two of his foes after he was down. The poor fellow had to ride some miles in the saddle through the storm, held up by his chums. They used every care they knew, but he died during the night. In every isolated Dutch farm-house the coffin of the farmer is kept ready, often for years before his death, and the coffin found at Doornbosch was used for the dead Bushman. We halted and ' carried arms ' as the cortege passed, the coffin followed by a long string of Bushmen, bearded and fully armed, whilst around the others held the horses, ready saddled for the march.

A party of newly-raised Midland Mounted Rifles were also bivouaced at the farm. They were a very mixed body, both in nationality, age and appearance. Some had the seamed and hardened faces of veterans of many a fight, others were nothing but boys of 15 and upwards, with high-pitched feminine voices. They had had a skirmish with the Boers a day or two previously, and it was amusing to hear of the " particular h—l " these boys had knocked out of the enemy on that particular occasion. They went about telling our fellows the details and more particularly their own deeds, till it was wearying to hear them.

Outside, their sentry stamped his chilled feet and rubbed his red nose as he tried to keep warm, and a Company of them were being instructed in the ' manual exercise.' It seems as though these later Colonial corps are first brought into the field, and then taught their rifle exercises and other drill when the intervals between the trekking and fighting leave them leisure to do so.

One of the sergeants, a Swede, was a great swell. He was clean-shaven, save for two small whiskers at the side, and looked something between a young cabby and a waiter from a third-class restaurant. His dress was as follows: Black shiny Hessian boots reaching to the top of his calf; tight black breeches *à la* Cape Police; khaki serge tunic, with gold stripes on shoulder-strap (and I never once saw him without his polished leather bandolier); a stiff white linen collar one inch above the collar of his tunic; and a khaki field-service cap set very much on one side of his head, with the thin leather chin-strap coming down his cheek and round the point of his chin. And this in the midst of the guerilla fighting in the snow-covered Sneeuwberg Mountains.

More trekking amongst the hills, and at Stockdale—the home of a loyal Dutchman burnt to the ground by the Boers—the squadron again fell upon good fortune. For they secured a large sheep-pen surrounded by stone walls, half of it covered by corrugated iron sheets supported on rough pillars. The men slept under the roof and turned the horses into the open part. I was on Cossack post that night, some mile away on the edge of a coppice of birch, and when we came in at dawn over ground white with hoar frost, the men were still sleeping snugly under the roof. They said the arrangement had only one drawback. During the night the horses would come under the roof, and stepping over the sleeping forms, wander about after stray fragments of biscuit left from the evening meal.

Several times had the Colonel been reminded by our officers of the Witmoss telegram, but he said it was not safe for a single squadron to go wandering amongst the hills alone; but he would let us go when we reached the railway. And to-day his opportunity came. A convoy of empty wagons had to be sent to within twenty miles of Cradock, to meet a full convoy and bring the stores back to the column. Here was our chance, and when we heard the rumour that the 65th were to go with the convoy, we blessed the name of Colonel Henniker.

But the evening orders were read, and we learned that " the 65th would accompany the empty wagons, and *escort them back again.*" And there was wild talk, born of bitter disappointment, which happily went no farther than the ranks.

It had to be done, so turning out before the light, we rode

through the passes for twenty-eight miles on the way to Cradock to a farm where our instructions told us to wait for the laden convoy. To illustrate how nicely these movements are fitted together by the telegraph (which ran by Doorn-bosch), I may mention that before we had finished outspanning the mules, we saw far out on the plain the laden convoy coming from Cradock which lay twenty miles farther on.

And so transferring the loads, we remained there that night, and at dawn rode back to the column.

Pearston—and Sunday again. And momentous news again fly through the camp. A peremptory wire has come. Our boat sails in five days, and at last we are to be released from the column. Five days. The question is—Can we get there in time? Fifty miles away lies the railway, and to-morrow it must be reached. Can we do it? How our played-out steeds will stand it, we cannot tell; but it will be our last ride, and the horses must be sacrificed—anything rather than miss the boat.

Long before dawn we are on the way. No wagon is taken. A man keeps one blanket if he wishes, everything else has been given or thrown away.

As the horses trot along, it is easy to see the change in the men. The horses are going well, and we are going home, and song after song rises from the files as the miles are covered.

It is done. The saddlery is in store. The horses are left in a kraal waiting for new masters—and more trekking, poor brutes!

And we. As the train starts upon its seven hundred miles run to the Cape we sing the favorite song of our concerts, the song that has oft brought us sweet longings by the camp-fires—longings now to be fulfilled :—

> "Rolling home—
> Rolling home—
> Rolling home across the sea;
> Rolling home to dear old England,
> Rolling home dear friends to see."

PART III.

THE STORIES OF THE SQUADRONS.

Leap up, mailed myriads, with the light
   Of manhood in their eyes ;
Calling from farmstead, mart and strand :
   "We come ! and we ! and we !
That British steel may hold the land,
   And British keels the sea."

        *   *   *   *

From English hamlet, Irish hill,
   Welsh hearths, and Scottish byres,
They throng to show that they are still
   Sons worthy of their sires ;
That what they did we still can do,
   That what they were, we are,
Whose fathers fought at Waterloo
   And died at Trafalgar.
Shoulder to shoulder see them stand
   Wherever menace be,
To guard the lordship of the land
   The trident of the sea.

        *   *   *   *

Comrades in arms, from every shore
   Where thundereth the main,
On to the front they press and pour
   To face the rifles' rain ;
To force the foe from covert crag
   And chase them till they fall,
Then plant for ever England's flag
   Upon the rebel wall !
What ! Wrench the sceptre from her hand
   And bid her bow the knee !
Not while her Yeomen guard the land
   And her ironclads the sea.

                      ALFRED AUSTIN.

THE 17TH BATTALION OF IMPERIAL YEOMANRY.

CONSISTING OF

50TH (HAMPSHIRE) SQUADRON,

60TH (NORTH IRISH) SQUADRON,

61ST (SOUTH IRISH) SQUADRON,

65TH (LEICESTERSHIRE) SQUADRON.

Officer-Commanding ... LIEUT-COL. R. ST LEGER MOORE,
    Late Captain 5th (Royal Irish) Lancers.

Second-in-Command ... MAJOR T. J. DE BURGH,
    Late Lieutenant 5th Dragoon Guards.

Adjutant ... CAPT. JAMES BROWNE.
    7th Battalion Royal Munster Fusiliers.

Quarter-Master ... LIEUT. L. HARCOURT COLES.
    5th Middlesex Vol. R. C..

Medical Officer ... SURGN-CAPT. J. E. MARTIN, M.B.
    Gent.

THE STORY OF THE 50TH SQUADRON I.Y

CAPT. A. C. NICHOLSON, *Capt. Hants (Carabineers) Yeomanry Cavalry.*

LIEUT. SIR R. N. RYCROFT, BART, *2nd Lieut. Hants C.Y.C. (formerly 9 years in the Rifle Brigade, also 3 years in 3rd Battn. Hants Regt.)*

LIEUT. DOUGLAS MARRIOTT, *2nd Lieut. Hants C.Y.C.*

LIEUT. H. J. FULLER,* *Late 2nd Lieut. 3rd Battn. East Kent Regt.*

LIEUT. R. LAMB, *Lieut. 1st Volunteer Battn. Hants Regt.*

THE 50th was the Second Squadron of Imperial Yeomanry sent from Hampshire, and the men were quartered in the Artillery Barracks at Christchurch during their training for active service. Each man was expected to provide his own horse, and these were purchased by the Government, but were not taken out by the Squadron, who were mounted in South Africa. The men of the 50th probably received as thorough a training as any squadron that has left these shores, for after considerable mounted drill upon a large tract of ground contingent to the barracks, their operations were widened, and they practiced the tactics peculiar to the mounted branch to which they belonged in the surrounding country for many miles around. This was made more valuable and interesting from the fact, that instead of practicing the attack upon an imaginary enemy, their own draft, reinforced by the local volunteers, on many occasions acted as an opposing force. The New Forest was near, and many an invaluable lesson in reconnoitring and

---

* Lieut. Fuller was sometime attached while in Rhodesia for service on the staff. He was afterwards Provost-marshal on the Kimberley Column and finally remained in South Africa as Adjutant to the new 17th Battalion I.Y.

THE STORY OF THE 50th SQUADRON I.Y.

other work was learned amongst its treacherous bogs, many ditches, and hidden rabbit holes.

At length came the order to embark on the *America* upon March 14, but at the last moment—the kitbags had been actually sent on to Southampton—the vessel was condemned; and it was not until April 6, after thirteen weeks hard and useful training, that the Squadron entrained for the docks at Southampton, and embarked on board the *Galeka*.

Southampton being a Hampshire port, the men received a most enthusiastic send-off from the docks; bands discoursed sweet music, while crowds of friends patiently waited to see the last of their 'boys in khaki,' as the vessel cast off from the dockside,

On April 11, the *Galeka* cast anchor off the picturesque little town of Santa Cruz, in the island of Teneriffe, where a short stay of eight hours was made. Thence, after a voyage through seas scarce broken by the white crest of a wave, Table Mountain was sighted at noon on April 27, but no call was made. And on May 3, after a twenty-eight days run of nearly eight thousand miles, the *Galeka* entered the mouth of the Pungwe, and casting anchor off Beira, her long voyage was over.

From the port of Beira to the Base Camp the history of the 50th is the history of the whole battalion and has been told in the first part of this book.

The Squadron suffered heavily from the fever foe during their progress through the low land near the coast, and of their sick sent to the Umtali hospitals, three — Troopers Blackden, Bloomfield, and Burden—were carried there only to die. At Marandellas yet another one—Trooper Davis—died from blood-poisoning, and was buried in the little graveyard, newly formed in the bush on the outskirts of the camp.

The sickness and mortality in the Rhodesian Field Force arose solely from the break in the guage of the line sixty miles from the coast, which caused the congestion of men, horses, and stores at Bamboo Creek, and the consequent delay in moving them to the healthy uplands at the Base Camp. When we know that the conversion of the whole line into one—the broad guage—was afterwards actually completed in three days, surely it is to be regretted that this could not have been done *before*, instead of after the moving of the men through Portuguese territory.

The following figures, given by Sir Charles Metcalfe, enable one to realize the enormous difference which the prior conversion of the narrow guage would have made to the speed with which the troops could have been moved.

" On the 2-feet guage each locomotive could only haul twenty tons, and it took three days to make the journey from Beira to Umtali. With a 3 feet 6 inch guage, one locomotive could haul 160 tons and make the journey in *sixteen hours.* Hence on the broader guage sixteen trains could do the work which now needed three hundred and seventy-five."

It is not for me to say whose was the blame. Suffice it the change was not made until too late; and the Rhodesian Field Force paid the price for the neglect in a score of precious lives, and the shattered health of hundreds more.

At Marandellas the Hampshires received their horses, and after a stay of nearly four weeks at the Base Camp, on August 3 they entered upon the long march to Buluwayo, which they reached a month later, on September 3.

Three weeks at the Matabele capital soon came to an end, and the Squadron received the 'route' for Tuli, 160 miles away, near the Transvaal northern border. The first part of the journey ran through the Matoppo Hills, and the scenery was at once bold and interesting; but water was scarce during the latter part of the march, and on many occasions could only be procured by digging in the sand of the river-beds.

Tuli was visited by the whole of the 17th and 18th Battalions (with the exception of the 65th Squadron), and I think the men are unanimous in the opinion that they were never in a more undesirable place during the whole of the time they spent in South Africa. The district was a notoriously unhealthy one, and soon disease laid its fell grip upon the squadrons. The supply of provisions was very irregular and often inadequate, and the men were for part of the time upon half rations. It is a well-known axiom that a fully occupied mind and body is the best preventative to fever, and the Officer in Command of the Battalion had evidently great faith in this. Day after day the men, often hungry, were turned out for parades, musketry instruction, and big field-days on horse and foot. But however well these were meant, they were intensely unpopular with the men, and the following lines—written on the spot by one of the Hampshires whose extempore songs have enlivened many a camp-fire concert—though they do not perhaps breathe the spirit of the strictest discipline, yet eloquently voice the prevailing opinion of the camp.

A Voice From Rhodesia.

Bards at home may sing of heroes
    Fighting on a foreign shore,
Fighting for their Queen and Country,
    As their fathers did of yore;
Carrying terror to the despot,
    'Neath the flag of Love and Right,
Caring not for foemen's bullets
    Face to face with Death's dark night;
Bringing honour to their country
    Thro' the noble deeds they've done;
Heedless of their lack of comforts,
    Happy o'er the victories won.

Yet these Bards forget the many
    Far behind the battle's din,
Far from all the joys of victory,
    Far from all their kith and kin;
Working worse than bloomin' niggers
    From the early break of day,
Working hard on empty stomachs,
    Till the daylight fades away;
Digging trenches, fighting battles
    'Gainst a foe who is *non est*;
Fooling like a lot of schoolboys,
    'Cause it suits their O.C. best
Would he'd let his men, who're hungry,
    Take things with a little ease,
'Stead of jumping o'er the country
    Like so many parched peas.

> These are they who left their homes
>   To do their share, and never shirk;
> Fighting for their Queen and Country—
>   'Stead of which they have to work.
> Robbed of every chance of glory,
>   To a soldier always dear;
> Robbed of every joy and comfort,
>   Worst of all—their chance of Beer.
> Never mentioned in the papers,
>   Lost to friends and light as well,
> Dragging out a dread existence
>   In a veritable H—l.
>   JNO. B. McCARTNEY.

But at last, to the joy of everyone, Tuli was left behind, and the Squadron retraced their steps to Buluwayo, accomplishing the march in fourteen days. Next day—November 25—they entrained for the South, and passing through Mafeking and Kimberley (where a four days' halt was made) reached Orange River Station upon December 2—and their fighting days commenced.

On the night of Dec. 8, the news came to Orange River Station that Belmont was again in the hands of the enemy. There was hasty saddling up, and the 50th (with one squadron of Irish Yeomanry, and two squadrons of Sharpshooters) made a forced march towards the place, twenty-one miles away. All through the night they rode as rapidly as the darkness would allow, and Belmont was reached about 5-0 next morning, but the alarm proved a false one. The Irish squadron returned to the Orange River, and the others pushed on northwards, arriving at Kimberley on Dec. 11.

Boshof was an isolated little town some thirty miles N.E. of Kimberley, well fortified and held by a British garrison since we took it from the enemy in the early part of the war. But it was entirely dependent upon Kimberley for its supplies, and the work of carrying these stores was both a difficult and dangerous one. For the whole district was infested with lurking bodies of the enemy, and already had one supply column been stopped and the traction-engine and trucks destroyed. Therefore the convoys, which went out at short intervals, had to be sent under an escort of considerable strength.

Two days after the arrival of the Hampshires in Kimberley, one of these periodical convoys was sent out and the Squadron formed part of the escort. The convoy of over fifty wagons was under the command of Col. Parke, of the 18th Battn. I.Y., and several squadrons of the S.S. were also with the column. Leaving Kimberley at 6 p.m. they marched all through a very cold night, nothing breaking the monotony with the exception of a few shots fired at a Boer scout, who escaped. A few hours' sleep, and the convoy again went on, till after midday they off-saddled for a welcome rest. But at 4 p.m. the outposts were fired on, and the troops at once saddled up, and galloping out to the veldt, pushed the enemy before them for five or six miles, till darkness fell, when the pursuit ceased, and the men lay down by their horses for the remainder of the night, kept awake by the occasional sniping bullets which sang over their heads. Next day the convoy pushed on, the mounted troops driving before them the enemy, who continually harassed their front and flanks, but would not make a stand.

But a large party of the Boers were at last located at a farm —Viljoen's Kloof—standing at the foot of a long rugged ridge, and the 50th were ordered to clear them out. Led by their Captain they galloped for nearly a mile across the open veldt. From a tree close by the house fluttered a white flag, which upon a nearer approach they made out to be an article of feminine attire. But upon arriving within a few hundred yards of the house, a heavy fire was opened upon them. At once dismounting, the men took cover behind the numerous small anthills which studded the veldt, and poured in a rapid fire upon the treacherous foe until the Boer fire began to flag, when, fixing their bayonets, they crossed the intervening space at a run, and gained the house. But the Boers did not wait for the bayonets. They mounted in haste, and galloping across the veldt, were lost in the growing darkness. The farmer Viljoen said that the Boers had rushed the house, but his doings on several previous occasions had been more than suspicious, so he was taken into Boshof, and his farm burned to the ground.

The 50th had not come through scatheless. In the attack

P

upon the farm, Corporal Grace was severely wounded, a bullet piercing his thigh, passing through horse and saddle, and wounding him in the other leg.*

At sundown the mounted troops were sent forward to clear the road into Boshof, but little opposition was met with, and the convoy pushed on through heavy rain storms, and reached the town at four o'clock in the morning. The convoy was warmly welcomed by the garrison, as for some time Boshof had been practically in a state of siege; and no provisions being able to enter the town, they were very short of food.

As might be expected from its antecedents, the town was a hot-bed of treachery, and the Commandant had taken the summary though wise precaution of shutting up over eighty of the suspects in the Dutch Church. These prisoners were brought back into Kimberley by the returning column, and the small photograph of the church—(*see illus. p. 228*)—was taken whilst they were taking leave of their friends and relatives through the railings which surround the building.

Taking but twelve hours rest, the troops again left the town and reached Kimberley two days later, on Dec. 18. The latter part of the march was made through blinding storms. The road—it was dark night—was indistinguishable under its covering of water from the surrounding veldt. The guides themselves were at fault, and for some hours the road was lost, and only recovered after expending several boxes of lucifer matches, by the feeble light of which the half-obliterated wheel-tracks of the outward-bound wagons were at last revealed to the shivering troops. At length—miles from the town itself—they saw the searchlights of Kimberley which, from high on the head-gear of the diamond mines, were directed nightly upon the surrounding veldt to guard against surprise.

Again—Dec. 23—upon convoy escort, but this time bound for Koffyfontein. Though this journey was but little interrupted by the enemy, the work was most trying and arduous from a different cause. The rivers and spruits were all in flood from the recent incessant rains, and the drifts were both difficult and dangerous

---

* The part taken by the Sharpshooters will be found under the Story of their Squadrons.

for the wagons. Even before leaving the camp, the mounted troops had to wait at their horses' heads for three cold hours— 4 to 7 a.m.—whilst the wagons, some drawn by thirty oxen, crossed the ford of the Modder.

Jacobsdal was reached the same day, but a man was lost in crossing a swollen spruit near the town. The column remained outside the town until the following morning, but a vigilant watch was kept, as but six weeks before fourteen of the Cape Highlanders had lost their lives by the treachery of the inhabitants. The Highlanders were encamped upon the outskirts of the town, but during the night the people admitted the enemy to their houses; from the roofs of which the Colonials were shot down as they emerged from their tents at daybreak.

One of the little drawbacks incidental to the life of a foot-soldier was here brought home to the men, for in the diary of a Sergeant of the 50th, I read—

—" Have just been down to water with the horses. Saw a number of foot-soldiers crossing the river with their trousers over their arms—nothing on but boots and coat. They were going on guard to a kopje on the other side."

Christmas day was passed in the saddle. From reveillé at 3 a.m. they were marching till 6 p.m., when they halted for the night ten miles from Koffyfontein. They were not altogether without Xmas cheer, for the same diary tells me—under Dec. 26—

—" Last night we had a tot of rum—just about enough to fill a thimble. Quite a farce."

Upon the return journey another man—Gunner Kemp of the Pom-Pom Battery, who had come out with the 75th Sharpshooters—was drowned whilst crossing the treacherous Riet.

The column again reached Modder River upon Dec. 29, and four days later the Hampshires entrained for Fourteen Streams, which place was reached in a most violent storm of thunder, lightning and rain. To men without tents the veldt, after the heavy rain, did not promise as desirable a bed as they could have wished, but worse was to follow.

The troops retired to rest, and all went well until early morning, when, with hardly any warning the storm broke upon them. Thunder, lightning, rain, and hailstones as large as nuts, swept along by fierce winds, were a few of the minor troubles. The wind blew down the officers' tents, and tearing up the frail blanket shelters erected by the men, whirled them away skyward, leaving the men underneath at the mercy of the hail and the pitiless rain. In the midst of the confusion a cow, tethered near the horse lines, was struck by lightning and killed; and the horses, which were tied to the usual long horse line fastened to the ground by picketing pegs, tore up the pegs, and sweeping—still fastened to the rope—right over the row of their recumbent riders, stampeded into the darkness. By the time they were once more secured the surface of the veldt was hidden under several inches of water (*see illustration*) and the wretched troops could do nothing but wait for morning and daylight. That night will long live in the memory of the Hampshires.

The next day was passed mainly in " drying their clothes and cleaning the mud out of their rifles."

On the 6th the column crossed the border into the Transvaal and marched into Christiana ; returning to Fourteen Streams on the following day. Thence they made a large sweep across the surrounding country, completely denuding it of stock, and on Jan. 13, once more they marched into Kimberley, driving nearly ten thousand head of horses, cattle and sheep.

The Squadron were not allowed to rest long upon their laurels amongst the attractions of Kimberley, for after two days' rest— bivouaced upon the outskirts of the town—they once more started upon the familiar road to Boshof. A long march was made upon the first day, and a considerable portion of the distance covered; but meanwhile another long train of supplies, drawn by six traction engines, had started from Kimberley, and the 50th Squadron I.Y. were ordered to return alone and bring them on to the column. Turning out at 2.15 a.m. they marched back to within several miles of the town before the convoy was met; and all through that day and far into the night they marched, continually delayed by the breaking down of the engines, until at midnight the column was reached.

But they were not to reach Boshof without serious opposition

Photo by *C. W. McKechnie*
THE VELDT AFTER THE STORM—*p. 228.*
THE CHURCH-PRISON AT BOSHOF—*p. 226*

(sniping they had every day), for the column had not been marching many hours the next day, when they were subjected to a fierce attack from the enemy, who were strongly posted on a long range of kopjes which commanded the road. The fight continued for over three hours before the enemy were dislodged from their position by a frontal advance on foot of the Hampshires and other troops, and at 2 p.m. the Boer position was in our hands. During the engagement the 50th had no casualties, except five horses shot in the early part of the fight —Capt. Nicholson's, Lieut. Marriott's, and three others—and one man—Trooper Suter—being made prisoner. Suter was carried to the ruins of Viljoens Kloof—burned by the Squadron upon their former visit—and told he would be shot in the morning; but during the night he effected his escape and rejoined his comrades in Boshof.

The troops were followed to Boshof by the discomfited Boers, and it was not until the Pom-Pom again went out and spoke to them that they retired.

But though the Hampshires came through the fight unscathed, Death the Destroyer had laid his hands upon them elsewhere. For on this day died Trooper Ford in the hospital at Kimberley, a victim of the soldiers' foe—enteric.

Kimberley was again reached on Jan. 21, the journey being slow and wearisome owing to the repeated breakdown of the returning engines. Next day the Squadron assisted in the apprehension of a number of suspects; suddenly surrounding the market-place until their arrest was effected.

They left the same afternoon for Koffyfontein, with a large convoy of some 100 wagons—oxen and mule—and arrived at their destination on the 27th, without a shot being fired, or having seen a Boer, except at a distance.

At 2.30 the next morning the men were quietly aroused from a well-earned sleep, and saddling up silently—noise and lights being forbidden—they stole quietly out from the camp to surprise a Boer laager known to lie a few miles to the south-east of the town. But their journey was a bootless one. The traces of the laager were there, but the Boers had by some means been apprized of their visit, and had gone. And the Squadron reached camp near midday, bringing in nothing beyond a clamorous appetite. Another night at Koffyfontein, and the return journey commenced.

The column had not covered more than four or five miles when the advance guard was received by a heavy fire from the enemy concealed amongst the ridges. The Hampshires, who were divided at that time into three troops—under Captain Nicholson, Lieuts. Rycroft and Marriott—were ordered to turn the left flank of the Boer position. They galloped for nearly a mile until clear of the front fire from the kopjes; but suddenly another body of the enemy opened fire upon them from a line of ridges not half-a-mile to the left of the Squadron.

" Left about wheel "—came the order from the Captain, and it was obeyed coolly as upon parade, and the Squadron retired at a gallop. One of the men—Trooper Ponsford—fell wounded from his saddle, but afterwards succeeded in reaching the column.

Retiring to a safer range, the Hampshires made a large sweep and came up in rear of the Boers who had so discomfited their former movement. These, seeing themselves outflanked, mounted and galloped off in hot haste followed by the Yeomanry, to a small kopje where they again halted and opened fire on their pursuers. Dismounting, the men again poured a steady fire into the Boers until they compelled them once more to seek safety in flight. But unfortunately, seven of the 50th horses broke away, and galloping after the flying Boers, were lost. The remainder continued the pursuit for several miles until they had to return, their ammunition being nearly all expended. The result of the fight as far as the Hampshires were concerned, was eight horses lost and one man wounded, while the Boers had four men killed, two wounded, and one horse killed.

Encamping for the night some miles farther on, the column next morning marched towards Petrusberg, halting at a farm called Holijan. Here an outlying Cossack post was attacked and lost their horses, the three men having to run to the camp for their lives.

Again on the following morning the column was attacked before it had proceeded two miles upon its way. Its movements were greatly hampered by the immense herds the men were

THE STORY OF THE 50th SQUADRON I.Y.

driving, collected from the country they passed through. After two hours' fighting, with the guns in action most of the time, the enemy were driven off, having sustained a loss of seventeen killed.

Resting for a few hours, at 10 p.m. the column started for Petrusburg and marched steadily on through the night. Till 1 a.m. when their progress was arrested by the enemy, who opened fire at a very short range. Quickly wheeling off the road in the darkness, the column diverged several miles into the veldt and remained halted until dawn, when they pushed their way into the town through a strong opposition, which the guns broke down after an hour's fighting. A number of the inhabitants whose neutrality during the recent fighting was more than suspected, were carried away as prisoners, and the column returned towards Kimberley. Several times they were fired upon during the march, especially at Paardeberg—Cronje's Paardeberg—where they were subjected to a most galling rear attack as it grew dark. But at last after ten days of the hardest work they had yet seen, they entered Kimberley on February 4, bringing in 15,000 sheep, 2,000 head of cattle, and near 1,000 horses.

Their arduous work had not been unnoted, and two days later the following telegram was received from Lord Methuen.

To O.C. Kimberley Flying Column. Feb. 5th, 1901.
Please tell the Kimberley Flying Column how pleased I am to hear of the good work it has performed.
METHUEN.

On February 9 De Wet crossed the Orange on his second invasion of Cape Colony, and on the same day the Hampshires left Kimberley for Modder River, to again become attached to the Kimberley Flying Column, and to take part in the strenuous but abortive attempts which were made to capture the guerilla chief. Marching through Honey Nest Kloof, Graspan, and Belmont (where a day's halt was made), Orange River Station was reached at 7 a.m. on February 12, and here they stayed until the following morning.

Upon February 15, the day upon which the Boers made their disastrous crossing of the railway near Potfontein, the column marched into Krankuil, twenty-three miles farther north.

Then came a fortnight of reconnaisance and patrol ; of night marches through heavy rain-storms, of days of sixteen or seventeen hours passed in the saddle ; and of the necessary work of convoying provisions to Plumer's and the other columns taking part in the chase ; until upon March 2, after De Wet had made his escape across Lilliefontein Drift, they marched into Colesberg with the rest of the seven or eight baffled British columns.

It was during this period that Trooper G. G. Allen of the Hampshires was severely wounded whilst upon a little patrol of four men under Lieut. Sir Richard Rycroft.

And it was two days after that—on February 25—that an incident occurred which illustrates one—and not the least—of the difficulties met with in a chase of this kind—the danger of mistaking a distant friendly column for the foe.

De Wet had slipped by Hopetown, and the Kimberley Flying Column came in hot pursuit. Sudden they saw far out on the veldt the dust of moving men and horses. The enemy at last ! and the guns galloped to within long range, unlimbered, and in another moment would have opened fire—when over the plain from the dust-line in front came two mounted men at furious speed. And explanations followed.

Corporal Pickford, of the 50th—one of the advance guard—was that morning wearing a helmet given to him by a non-com. of the Artillery, to replace his own slouch-hat which he had lost; and this helmet saved the column from possible disaster. For the distant dust was raised by Bruce Hamilton with ten big guns. He also had mistaken the Kimberley Column for De Wet, and would have opened fire upon them with his ten guns, when luckily a keen-eyed officer caught sight of the khaki helmet on the head of the Yeomanry scout. Though the Boers sometimes adopt the khaki tunic, they have hardly yet taken to the big British helmet, and two officers were sent across hot-foot to make enquiries. And the two columns went their separate ways, kept from each other's throats by nothing but the Corporal's borrowed plumes—the Artilleryman's helmet.

With De Wet across the Orange, there was work elsewhere for the Kimberley Flying Column, and upon March 6, they left Colesberg on the return march ; and passing through Philipstown and Krankuil, reached Orange River Station upon March

THE STORY OF THE 50th SQUADRON I.Y.

11. To pass the next few days in beating storms of rain and a flooded camp. Under these circumstances the order to move northwards was a welcome one, and once more they reached Kimberley and their old campaigning ground.

Upon March 26, the Squadron marched upon their last—and what was destined to be their most fatal—journey to Boshof. The object of the column was to collect and drive into Kimberley all the stock still left on the farms, and to clear the neighbourhood of the enemy, who had of late rendered themselves most troublesome to supply columns and small bodies of troops passing through that part of the country. Those of the enemy who were not accounted for by the column were to be driven, by skilful manœuvring carefully prearranged, into the hands of Lord Methuen, who was advancing from Warrenton along the banks of the Vaal River to receive them.

The main body of the column advanced along the beaten road with Denison's Scouts thrown out as an advance guard. Upon the right flank rode the New Zealand Roughriders, upon the left the Hampshires, and the rearguard was furnished by the Diamond Fields Horse.

So the column crept slowly through the darkness, hoping to come upon and surprise the enemy, who were known to be in strength in the vicinity.

The dawn broke at length, and the 50th found that in the darkness their distance from the column had considerably widened, and they were then nearly four miles away from the road and the main body.

All around as far as the eye could see stretched the level veldt, the only elevation being a long low-lying ridge on the left flank of the Squadron. And at the far end of this ridge several horsemen driving a number of horses could be seen.

" C " Troop—eleven men in all, including the officer, Lieut. Lamb—were at once sent in pursuit, and rode swiftly over the veldt after the Boer raiders. Passing along the foot of the ridge, they were fast overhauling the chase, when a far-stretching wire fence barred the way. The cutting of this delayed them a few seconds and again they went forward at a rapid pace. But before they were many yards past the wire, suddenly, from the silent ridge not seventy yards away, broke a heavy fusillade of rifle fire. The whole of the crest was lined with the ambushed enemy, and wheeling on the instant, the little troop rode at top speed away from the hill. At the first fire Sergt. Montgomerie had fallen mortally wounded. and a number of horses were hit.

But they found that those few horsemen had decoyed them into a trap, for after galloping less than a hundred yards, another wire fence confronted them. They were in a large wired-in enclosure and practically at the mercy of the pitiless marksmen on the hill, not two hundred yards away.

" Dismount and lie flat "—was the only order that *could* be given, and with each man's foot through his reins, they lay and fired volley after volley at their concealed foes. It was whilst lying there that Corporal (afterwards Sergeant) Pickford saw one of the men struggling to disentangle himself from his horse which had fallen on him at the place where Sergt. Montgomerie had been shot. Quick as thought he jumped to his feet, mounted and galloped back to the man ; and dismounting—not more than seventy yards from the ridge—extricated the fallen trooper, put him across his saddle, and again mounting, coolly rode back to his troop through the hail of bullets, untouched.

For some fifteen minutes did the unequal fight continue, and one by one the devoted little band were being silenced. Trooper W. Fryer, and then two others—S. Parsons and R. de R. Roche —were dangerously wounded. But sudden, to their amazement the firing ceased, and the Boers ran helter-skelter down the far side of the ridge. Immediately the few that were left mounted, and galloping up the kopje, saw their enemies riding over the plain for their very lives. And now was seen the cause of the sudden flight, for hot-foot over the veldt—attracted by the firing—the column was coming to their aid.

The tables were turned, and for a time the flying Boers made a splendid target for their rifles. Then, the remainder of their squadron coming up they joined in the chase after the enemy, clearing them from several large patches of bush in which they had taken refuge. The guns now opened fire, and sent the Boers in scattered groups in all directions over the plain, where they were pursued by the mounted troops till long past noon.

And the column encamped at Kameelfontein Farm, where the

THE STORY OF THE 50th SQUADRON I.Y. 235

last tributes were paid to one of the New Zealanders who had fallen in the fight.

But the enemy had not yet been broken, for during the afternoon an outpost of the New Zealanders, posted not 500 yards from the camp, was driven in by a stray body of Boers. Hurriedly flinging on their bridles, the Hampshires did not wait to saddle up, but rode out bare-back to their assistance, only returning to the camp at dusk, when no further traces of the enemy were to be seen.

Yet again at 1 a.m. the tired troops were aroused by several volleys fired into the camp by a body of the enemy who had crept up within short range; but it was known they would decamp after firing a few rounds, so pursuit was not attempted in the darkness. A number of the horses were hit by the chance bullets, and another of the Hampshires—Trooper R. A. Allen—was dangerously wounded.

Before daybreak the column once more took up the chase, driving the Boers northwards towards the Vaal River; and at length they heard the sound of Methuen's guns far ahead. Their drive had been a complete success.

But Sergeant Montgomerie and Trooper Fryer succumbed to their wounds, and on March 30 the Squadron fired the last sad volleys over the graves of their comrades.

And upon the same day, though they knew it not, died one of their officers, Lieut. Douglas Marriott, at Deelfontein, two hundred miles away.

From Boshof a night march was made to surprise a laager fifteen miles north-east of the town, but the expedition was fruitless. The Boers had gone.

Then came the return march—a tale of daily harass from Boers on flanks and rear; of the compulsory slaughtering of whole droves of the sheep they were driving, dead-beat with fatigue and constant trekking—until at last, upon April 2, the column reached Kimberley, sniped at to within three miles of the town.

And in Lord Kitchener's despatches from Pretoria, dated May, 1901, appeared the following—

"Mentioned by Captain Nicholson, 50th Co., Imperial Yeomanry, special report forwarded by General Pretyman, April 30th, 1901.

Corporal Pickford, 50th Co., I.Y.
Near Boshof on March 28th, 1901, a man lost his horse. Corporal Pickford went back for the man under a heavy fire, and got him away."

April 7 was Easter Day—a glad Easter Day for the Hampshires. For they were under orders for Springfontein, and at Springfontein they would be relieved by the new 50th Squadron which had come out to replace them. And they watched the Kimberley Flying Column again march out, but this time they were left behind.

Five days later, amidst a vast amount of challenging from the numerous sentries—for the New Yeomanry were intensely keen in the discharge of their novel duties—the time-expired squadron marched into the mobilization camp.

It was not, however, until a month afterwards that, having handed over their horses to the relieving squadron, they entrained for Worcester, where the old Yeomanry were mobilizing for home.

They did not leave Springfontein without giving a big 'smoker' to the new men, and the feature of the concert, the extempore songs of Corpl. McCartney, would undoubtedly have brought down the house—had it not been held in the open air.

Most popular of all was—

THE OLD 50TH TO THE NEW.

We're just going home on a ticket of leave—
    Rom-tiddley-om-pom-pom.
We're 'time-expired,' as you'll all perceive.
    Rom-, &c.
We joined the British Army when we heard our country's call,
To fight our nation's battles—do our best, however small.
Don't think that we are funking—We don't want to do it all.
    Rom-, &c.

We did'nt join the regulars, our physique was not the best ;
    Rom-, &c.
We couldn't swear sufficient, and we couldn't 'chuck a chest.'
    Rom-, &c.
But we 'chucked' our situations, and sallied forth with glee,

LIEUT. MARRIOTT. CAPTAIN NICHOLSON. Photo taken at Fourteen Streams.
LIEUT. SIR R. RYCROFT, BART. LIEUT. LAMB.
OFFICERS' QUARTERS ON THE VELDT.

THE STORY OF THE 50th SQUADRON I.Y.

We knew the way to ride and shoot, so joined the Yeomanry ;
And Hampshire County's proud of us. And so she ought to be.
   Rom-, &c.

We'd thirteen weeks in Barracks, and they worked us very hard.
   Rom-, &c.
When we couldn't groom our horses we were sweeping out the yard.
   Rom-, &c.
But when evening came and work was done, we went out on the spree,
A livelier lot of characters I never wish to see:
If a man chanced homewards *sober*—he got 14 days C.B.
   Rom-, &c.

At last, our larking ended, we were ordered out to fight,
   Rom-, &c.
We were shipped away like convicts in the middle of the night,
   Rom-, &c.
For a month aboard our lugger we were bounding o'er the main,
We cut some sorry figures, and experienced awful pain,
But in spite of that, we all agree *we'll risk it home again.*
   Rom-, &c.

Of the country called Rhodesia, I think we saw enough,
   Rom-, &c.
There's not the slightest shade of doubt, we had things pretty rough,
   Rom-, &c.
We were packed like bloomin' kippers in the Beira slow express,
With collisions, fever, lions, we'd enough, I must confess;
Its no wonder that so many lost the number of their mess.
   Rom-, &c.

At last we left Rhodesia—to the fighting line were sent,
   Rom-, &c.
We sallied forth from Kimberley; to Koffyfontein went,
   Rom-, &c.
When the Boers commenced their firing, we thought it glorious fun,
As we madly charged the kopjes—oh! I wish you'd seen 'em run,

That morning seventeen corpses showed the damage we had done.
  Rom-, &c.
Since that most eventful morning, we've been at it every week,
  Rom-, &c.
We'd a big trip down the Colony, the great De Wet to seek.
  Rom-, &c.
We got him in a corner, sure *no* troops were ever nigher,
We'd have had him then for certain,—but were ordered to retire.
To catch De Wet, a General to the honour did aspire.
  Rom-, &c.
It would take me hours to tell you all the fun and fights we had,
  Rom-, &c.
You'll agree we've had our portion—to go home we're mighty glad,
  Rom-, &c.
Before we go we thank the men who take our places here,
We wish you all the best of luck throughout the coming year,
At home we'll not forget you—we'll drink your share of Beer.
  Rom-, &c.

The stay in the mobilization camp at Worcester—with its eucalyptus groves and snow-topped mountain ring—was not a long one; and upon April 16 the good ship *Avondale Castle* left Capetown, having on board the whole of the 17th Battalion, save the Leicesters, who were still in the field.

And as the great converted liner steamed slowly across Table Bay, there spread before the men the wondrous sickle of Capetown, backed by its giant wall of rock; and they watched with strangely mingled feelings the sinking into the sea of that land which had given to them a whole life of experience crowded into one short year—of sickness and broken health for some, of trials and hardships for all; yet mixed with many happy days between.

Before the bows stretched the waste of waters—and beyond lay England—and Home—and the life they had laid aside fifteen long months before.

THE STORY OF THE 50th SQUADRON I.Y.

In the despatch from Earl Roberts, K.G., G.C.B., &c., to the Right Hon. the Secretary of State for War, dated London, Sept. 4, 1901; amongst the names of Regimental officers, N. C. officers and men of the Regulars, Militia, Yeomanry and Volunteers, who, with their various units, have rendered special and meritorious service, appeared the following:—

17TH BATTALION I.Y.
  Captain A. C. Nicholson (Hampshire Imperial Yeomanry).
  Lieut. Sir R. N. Rycroft, Bart. (Second Lieutenant, Hampshire Imperial Yeomanry).
  4748 Squadron Sergeant-Major J. Miles.
  4720 Squadron Sergeant-Major C. C. Fowler.
  4790 Corporal T. Yeomans.

THE STORY OF THE IRISH YEOMANRY.*

60TH SQUADRON I.Y.

CAPT. R. LEO MOORE, *Captain 4th Battn. Royal Inniskilling Fusiliers.*
LIEUT. H. C. HARVEY, *Capt. 3rd Battn. Royal Irish Rifles.*
LIEUT. HARVEY DALE, *Gent. (formerly Natal Police).*
LIEUT. A. MCDONNELL CALWELL, *Gent.*
LIEUT. T. S. MURLAND, *Gent.*

THOUGH Ireland possesses no Yeomanry or Volunteer Regiments of her own to draw upon, yet, when the 17th Battalion sailed, she had contributed seven squadrons to the Imperial Yeomanry Force.

The 60th was the third contingent raised in Belfast—the two former being the 46th and the 64th, both belonging to the 13th Battalion. The men were stationed at the Victoria Barracks, and received a considerable amount of foot drill under the instruction of the sergeants of the Royal Irish Rifles. This with musketry practice at the Kinnegar Ranges at Holywood, and a week of mounted drill upon the horses of the 3rd Dragoon Guards, under Captain Magee (17th Lancers) prepared them for their work upon the African veldt.

At two o'clock on April 5 they entrained, but so enthusiastic was their send-off by the people of Belfast, that an ordered march was out of the bounds of possibility, and they arrived at the station by twos and threes. Crossing to Holyhead, they here joined the 61st Squadron, and reaching Southampton before noon on April 6, at once embarked upon the waiting *Galeka*.

The 60th were the only squadron on board equipped with helmets in lieu of the familiar slouch-hat, and they wore as their badge the Red Hand of Ulster on a white shield.

---

* As the 60th and 61st followed the same route through Rhodesia; and, after leaving that country, they were never separated in their work, but were combined under the title of The Irish Yeomanry, I have thought it best, in order to avoid useless repetition, to treat their Story as one under this heading.

THE STORY OF THE IRISH YEOMANRY.

61st SQUADRON I.Y.

CAPT. H. C. CARDEN *Captain Reserve of Officers (late Devon Regiment.*

LIEUT. W. C. NEWTON, *Lieut. 4th Battn. Connaught Rangers.*

LIEUT. SIR ANDREW H. ARMSTRONG, Bart., *late Captain 3rd Battn. Prince of Wales's Leinster Regiment (Royal Canadians).*

LIEUT. ARTHUR J., EARL OF FINGALL, *late Lieut. 5th Battn. Prince of Wales's Leinster Regiment (Royal Canadians).*

LIEUT. E. O. WARD, *late Lieut. 5th Battn. Royal Irish Rifles.*

THE 61st—the Headquarter Squadron of the 17th Battalion was the second contingent of Imperial Yeomanry raised in Dublin; the previous one being the 45th, which formed part of the 13th Battalion. The Corps was raised in January, 1900, by the Earl of Longford, 2nd Life Guards (commanding the 45th I.Y), and was then handed over to Captain de Burgh, who was responsible for their training and equipping. Two days before they embarked, Captain de Burgh was raised to the Second Command in the Battalion, with the rank of Major, and the command of the Squadron devolved upon Lieut. Carden, who a week later was gazetted to Captain's rank.

Early in February they proceeded to that great Irish centre of military life, the Curragh, and the men settled down to two months' hard training for the life before them. Mounted drill was obtained each day upon the horses of the 3rd Dragoon Guards, the 21st Lancers and the 14th Hussars, under sergeant-majors detailed from those regiments.

Through the thoughtful influence of Col. St. Leger Moore, they were permitted to wear a brass shamrock on their hats; enjoying the proud privilege of being the first unit of Imperial troops to adopt the shamrock as their badge. Yet another honour was reserved for them. On April 4 they proceeded to Dublin to assist in keeping the streets during the passing of Her late Majesty the Queen through the city, and were—with a half-squadron of the 74th (3rd Dublin) I.Y.—the only Imperial Yeomanry present, and the only troops in khaki. Moreover it was the first occasion upon which Her Majesty had ever passed through a line of Irish Yeomanry.

Upon April 5, amidst a scene of wild enthusiasm, they left North Wall on the s.s. *Banshee*, and joining their forces with the 60th at Holyhead, proceeded to Southampton, and the *Galeka*.

After laying a week in the harbour at Beira, the two Squadrons of Irish Yeomanry disembarked, and proceeded direct to Twenty-three Mile Creek, where they remained until the 23rd of May.

It was at their first camping-place that one of the 61st was the victim of an accident, which at one cruel stroke cut short his military career. A young officer of the Sharpshooters was returning one evening from shooting in the jungle, and near to the camp he fired at a moving object in the bed of the little creek, half hidden by thick trees. But to his sorrow he discovered that he had shot a trooper of the 61st, who was bending over the stream. The charge entered the leg of the unfortunate man just below the knee, and eventually the limb was amputated. The mishap was doubly sad, as the man—Trooper Flude—had fought throughout the Spanish-American War untouched.*

The evils of Bamboo Creek did not spare the Irish Squadrons, and they had not been encamped at that place many days before half the men were in the fell grip of dysentery and fever, the fatal effects of which were shown a little later in the Umtali hospitals. Six young lives were claimed as the dread toll for their stay in the Portuguese swamps — Trooper McCarron of the 60th and Troopers Franklin, Stone and McCann of the 61st died at Umtali ; while Troopers Walters and McNally of the 60th were invalided, but died on their way home.

The fell disease claimed indiscriminately the strong and the weak as its victims, for Trooper Stone—the first to succumb— was well known in Dublin gymnastic circles, and was perhaps the strongest and best developed man in his squadron. Others

---

* Trooper Flude recovered from his injury—with the exception of the loss of his limb—and upon the return of the Squadron, he was waiting at the Southampton dock to receive them

came through the ordeal with broken health, and amongst these, the 60th lost the services of one of their officers, Lieut. Harvey, who was invalided home from the effects of the pestilential climate.

The vagaries of the railway between Bamboo Creek and Umtali lent a spice of excitement to the journey of most of the squadrons, and the 60th had a narrow escape from disaster. A short distance in advance of the train which conveyed the Squadron and its fortunes, was another laden with stores. Whilst slowly ascending one of the many steep gradients upon the line, the last two trucks of the goods train broke away and ran back down the slopes, gaining every moment added impetus from their pace. On they came towards the 60th train at a terrific speed and a catastrophe seemed inevitable. But a short distance in front was a sharp curve in the line, and this the runaway trucks could not turn; but jumping the metals, they were hurled down a steep embankment, and though two of the Kaffirs on the trucks were killed and several more badly injured, the 60th were saved.

Over a month was passed at the Umtali camp, punctuated and saddened by the funerals of the men from the various squadrons who died in the hospitals.

Though the conditions of life in the Umtali camp were far from unpleasant, the Irish squadrons were eager and impatient for sterner work, especially as they saw train after train of Colonials, bringing their own horses and ready for the field, pushed through before them. The Bushmen greatly excited the admiration of the Irishmen, both by reason of their splendid physique, and from other qualities they possessed. I quote the opinion of a member of the Dublins, who writes—" The social relations which existed between officers and men were, in the light of our own experience, more or less a revelation, and the apt and appropriate language and wonderful facility of expression of all commanded our envy and admiration. Indeed, it is said that General Carrington himself, no novice in the gentle art of vituperation and no stranger to the variety of its intricacies, was on one occasion obliged to remonstrate with a sturdy scion of Greater Britain who was arguing the point with a team of bullocks stuck in a drift. " Language, man ; language " he murmured, and from that instant his reputation sunk several degrees in the estimation of the sturdy pioneers."

At length—June 25—the 61st were removed to Marandellas and were placed in charge of the Remount Camp for a few days, until, upon July 5, they were relieved by the 60th. Though the work amongst the horses was hard, it was interesting; and the Irish Squadrons look upon the time spent at Marandellas as one of their happiest periods. Now and again the unbroken animals gave them rather exciting chases, as will be seen from this extract taken from the diary of one of the Belfasts.—" The horses were driven from the station in a mob, and this was good sport to us. But one morning they smelt the water in the stream which ran at the base of the hill upon which the camp was situated. We could not keep them in hand and they stampeded straight down the hill. Near the bottom was a sluit or empty watercourse about twelve feet deep and four feet wide, and into this the foremost horses blundered, whilst the others galloped right over them on to the water. We had to use pick and shovel to get them out, and marvellous to relate, though they were three deep in the hole, none of them were seriously injured."

After the Yeomanry received their horses, several large field-days were ordered, in which the I.Y., the Colonials, and the newly formed batteries of the Rhodesian Field Force Artillery, all took part. Taking a distant kopje as the object of attack, the guns would pour a hot shell fire into the position, and then the mounted troops would gallop over the bogs and plains; till, within a few hundred yards, they would continue the advance on foot by short rushes, and take the kopje at the point of the bayonet. Off course real shell and ball cartridge was used. It was after one of these charges on foot—a very long one—that a breathless officer of the Irish asked one of his panting men if he felt equal after that to killing the enemy.

" Shure, sir "—replied the man—" I might if I *fell against him* with me bayonet."

At Marandellas died one of the Dublin Squadron—Trooper Armstrong—and he was buried in the little enclosure newly formed within the edge of the woods westward of the camp.

But at last the Squadrons were equipped, and both horses and men were considered sufficiently advanced for a furthur move. Upon August 3, the Dublins commenced their march to Buluwayo; followed four days later by the 60th, whose work at the Remount Camp was taken over by a Company of Victorians. Col. St. Leger Moore marched with the headquarter squadron as far as Enkeldoorn, but from that place he proceeded to Buluwayo by coach, and his health unfortunately having broken down, he shortly afterwards left upon his return to England. Upon his departure the command of the Battalion was assumed by Major de Burgh, who sometime afterwards was gazetted Commandant with the rank of Lieut.-Colonel.

The seeds of disease had not yet been eliminated from the ranks of the Irish Yeomanry, and several men were left behind in the hospital at Enkeldoorn. One of these—Trooper Austin of the 60th—his comrades never saw again, for he died a week after their departure. At Gwelo the 61st rested for three days, and were joined by the Belfast Squadron; and together (with the Hampshires, who were marching with the 61st) they continued the march to Buluwayo, arriving at the Hillside Barracks in the early morning of September 3.

General Carrington was in Buluwayo during their stay, and several field-days and reviews upon the Race Course were held under his keen eye, and before the assembled people of the town. Their work was also agreeably diversified by cricket and football matches with the local clubs, and by sports in which events of a military nature took a prominent position; and in all of these the Irish Yeomanry gained fresh laurels for their corps and their country.

But the most pleasant time must have an end; and upon September 21st, the 50th and 60th Squadrons, under Major de Burgh, paraded and moved off *en route* for Tuli. They were followed five days later by the 61st and a Pom-Pom Battery, under the command of Major Giles, R.A.,* an officer who had accompanied Lord Randolph Churchill in his tour through Rhodesia some years before.

Marching through Manzinyama, Pourri-Perri, and Reitfontein,

---
* Three months later, this officer proceeded on his way home to England on sick leave, but was found dead in the train at Kimberley.

the Squadrons reached Tuli in the early part of October. At Manzinyama Trooper Madden of the 60th had to be left behind, suffering from pneumonia. He did not again join the Squadron for upon their return by the same route, his comrades rode a little out of their way to visit his lonely grave.

Though this march was unmarked by great events, the everyday occurrences recorded by the men in their diaries eloquently tell of the wild undeveloped lands through which they were passing. A few short extracts from a 60th diary I give without comment—

Sept. 29.—Water beastly to-day. Scarcely drinkable even when boiled.

Sept 30.—Was on advance guard to-day. Saw lots of buck. It was very irritating not to be allowed to fire at them.

Oct. 1.—Arrived at Pourri-Perri this morning. Water here very bad and very scarce. We lost a man last night, but found him after some firing and blowing of bugles.

Oct. 2.—Was put on baggage guard to-day. We left four men in charge of the water till the next squadron comes along. We have 32 miles to go to Reitfontein, and no water for that distance. Were able to get a couple of buck and some koorhaans. One of the men named B—— got lost in the bush and was only found after long searching. He had given up hope, and the spoor of a lion was seen not a hundred yards from him.

Oct. 3.—Got to Reitfontein, and were able to enjoy a drink of fairly good water.

Oct. 5.—Inspanned about 5 p.m. and started off again. Just at sunset someone shouted 'There's a lion.' We loaded our magazines and started into the bush after him. Could not see him till someone suddenly discovered that he was between us and the road. The horses had winded him and were all snorting in terror. So we doubled back to the road, and had just time to give him a couple of volleys as he cleared off. As it was getting dark I do not think we hit him.

Oct. 7.—Arrived at West Drift Camp on the far side of the Shashi River this morning. Had great difficulty in getting the wagons across, having to attach double teams (32 oxen) to haul them through the 800 yards of sand in the river bed.

The men were kept busy during their month's stay at Tuli with field days, fortifying the camp, rifle practice at the ranges and field-firing at temporary tin targets erected away in the bush. But the wet season was fast approaching. During the last week they were subjected to heavy tropical storms which turned the camps into temporary shallow lakes ; and this, added to the shortness of food—for, like the 50th, they were upon half-rations part of the time—soon again brought disease amongst the men, and the hospitals became full.

Upon Nov. 10, Battalion sports were held, including events combining instruction with pleasure, such as digging trenches, and turning out in marching order—both against time. These were brought to a close by a big concert. But needless to say, the enjoyment of these relaxations was greatly enhanced by the fact that the Squadrons had received orders to move; and upon Nov. 12, they left Tuli without regret, on the return march to Buluwayo, which was reached upon Nov. 26.

Their stay in the capital was but a short one, for orders arrived almost immediately to proceed southwards by train, and upon Nov. 28 and 29, the two Irish Squadrons bade farewell to Rhodesia. Some were however left in the Buluwayo hospitals —men whose constitutions had been sapped in the low tracts of the Tuli district, and one—Trooper Victor Ringwood of the 61st —after lingering for more than two months, died worsted in the hard struggle against the enteric foe which had seized him in its grip. The following 'appreciation' written by a comrade, ably shows the loss his squadron sustained by his death.

"Death took from us one of the best of our most popular comrades, one of the 'smartest' soldiers in the Squadron—aye, in the Battalion—poor Victor Ringwood! His unvarying cheerfulness under difficulties, his quiet humour, his unselfish solicitude for the comfort of others; these and many other estimable traits which I cannot paint in words, had endeared him to us all. From the commencement of our campaign he had acted as Colonel's orderly with credit to himself and the approbation and high opinion of his superiors. Had he been fated to pursue arms as a profession, he must have gone far. Had the Ruler of our destinies seen fit to grant him a soldier's death with his face to the foe, he himself would have been the last to complain. But, oh the pity o't! After months of suffering, with its past to be proud of, with its future full of promise, far away from everyone held dear, on the hillside at Buluwayo his young life closed. Until the last bugle call may the sod lie lightly on his grave!"

A few hours halt at Mafeking to water and stretch the legs of the horses, and at Vryburg they were detained till morning, as travelling by night south of this town was neither safe nor permitted. Kimberley was not reached without adventure, for at Border Siding, 60 miles north of the mining town, the line was found to be torn up and the wires cut. The Yeomanry were at once turned out and searched the surrounding country—on foot —for traces of the enemy; but without success. From Vryburg they were accompanied by an armoured train, which as a rule carries facilities for repairing obstructions of this nature, and by evening Kimberley was reached. Next day the Irish Squadrons reached and detrained at their destination, Orange River Station.

Here the Yeomanry were constantly employed in patrolling the surrounding districts and in bringing in stock. Upon the occasion of the night march on Dec. 7—described in the Story of the 50th—the Dublins formed part of the hastily despatched force which marched to Belmont, only to find that the rumoured presence of Boers was unfounded. Leaving the remainder of the troops to continue their march to Kimberley, they returned to the camp on the Orange River.

At length, on Dec. 18, the two Squadrons entrained for De Aar; but they had been camped there barely a day, when— at 3 a.m.—a sudden move was made northwards towards Philipstown. Hertzog and Brand had invaded the Colony.

Marching by the side of the railway, they found their advance barred by the Brak River, which was in flood; and as the spaces between the sleepers on the railway bridge were open, they were compelled to wait upon the banks until a train came out from De Aar, bringing planks to fill up the gaps in the bridge. And at daybreak on Dec. 21, the troops pushed on to Houtkraal, to find there the 18th Battn. of Sharpshooters, who had attacked and driven off the invaders upon the preceding day.

Next day the two Irish Squadrons, about 120 strong, taking two mule-wagons, rode out at daybreak to follow the movements of the Boers attacked at Houtkraal. It was near midday, as they were winding through a long valley, enclosed by hills, that the flankers on the extreme left were fired on from a farmhouse. A strong party was at once sent to investigate, and as they

THE STORY OF THE IRISH YEOMANRY. 249

approached, 30 Boers cleared from the farm at a gallop. The house was searched and, hidden weapons and other incriminating articles being found, was burned to the ground.

Two miles or more further on, and far in front a number of the enemy were seen advancing towards them. Twenty-five men under Lieut. Murland (60th) raced to an adjacent ridge and prepared a surprise for the approaching Boers. But

—" the best laid schemes . . . aft gang agley."

The enemy were almost within range, when a man accidentally discharged his rifle ; and the Boers, forewarned, withdrew from the trap. By this time the advance guard had arrived in the proximity of the farm (Matjesfontein) at the head of the valley. Here the flanking patrol came under a heavy fire from a kopje upon their right. Extending to wide open order, the Yeomanry advanced, keeping up a hot fire, until they found they were being outflanked by a second large body of the enemy who appeared on the opposite side of the narrow valley. They therefore retired to the river-bed, and leaving their horses under cover, again advanced in skirmishing order under heavy fire. The Boers had the range correctly, but their aim was bad. The Yeomanry were practically in the open, as very little cover was to be had in the valley, while their assailants were invisible, all being hidden behind the rocks on the surrounding kopjes. An hour or more went by, and several men were wounded, including Major de Burgh, with a bullet through his shoulder. Again the enemy were outflanking them, and seeing this, they retired on their horses in the river-bed. Taking the best cover available, a hot resistance was offered to the encircling enemy. A further advance was clearly impossible and Lieut. Murland took a score of men and rode hard for an adjacent kopje to try and cover the retreat of the wagons. But when within short range they were met by a murderous volley from its crest. It was already occupied by the enemy.

Turning at once, they galloped out of range; and from this point the retreat became general—save for the little body in the bed of the river—and shortly developed into a *sauve qui peut* for Houtkraal. Every effort was made to save the ammunition. The wagons were lightened of sacks of corn and nearly everything save the precious boxes, and the mules were pushed on by voice and whip. But it was in vain. The wheels were hampered by the heavy veldt, and they were overhauled and at last taken by the pursuing Boers.

A hot fire was still kept up from the river, where the little party was still holding out, thus securing the retreat of the rest. A white flag was sent in by the Boer Commandant, with a demand to surrender, which was curtly refused by the officer in command. But whilst this was taking place, the Boers were creeping to better positions, and those in rear coming up and strengthening the firing line. Thrice as many rifles were now bearing on the river bed as before, and the little party were enfiladed on both sides. Again the firing ceased, and a second summons carried over under a flag of truce. The note ran—

> The Officer Commanding.
> Sir,
> I herewith beg to ask you to surrender within 5 minutes. I think enough blood has been spilt, so be reasonable and surrender.
> Yours truly,
> Geo. Brand,
> Comdt.

Their position was desperate. Further resistance useless. And the little party gave up their arms.

The fight once over, the treatment of the captives by the Boers was considerate and even kindly. Though their arms, field-glasses, and in some cases leggings were taken, they were permitted to retain their water-bottles and overcoats and to fetch their blankets off the wagons. The Boers were evidently not short of these articles themselves, as all those not claimed were burned. The prisoners were then taken to a farmhouse about a mile distant, and now their numbers were counted and attention given to the injured.

Forty-four in all—fifteen of the 60th and twenty-nine of the 61st. And of these seven were wounded, though none seriously. The one whose hurt was most severe was Major de Burgh, with a bullet through his shoulder. The others were Troopers Crynible and Floyd of the 60th; Corporal Rowland and Troopers Cleary, Kirkwood, and Nash of the 61st.

Upon one of the captured wagons was a keg of rum, and the prisoners being called round, a substantial 'ration' was served out to them by their captors. Then, first exacting a promise from Major de Burgh that they would not move from the farm before eight o'clock next morning, a whistle sounded, and in less than 15 minutes the commando had gone, and there was not a Boer left in sight.

After a night of much needed rest, the released Yeomen started upon their twenty-mile walk to Houtkraal. During the morning they met the 18th Battalion coming in pursuit of the Boer commandoes. With the column were those of the Irish Squadrons who had escaped capture on the previous day. These went on with the Sharpshooters, while the released prisoners continued their walk into Houtkraal, and from thence they went by train to De Aar to refit. It was nearly four months before they rejoined their comrades.

The stern chase which now took place after Hertzog and Brand, first under Col. Parke, and continued by Colonel Thorneycroft has been described elsewhere. The Irish Yeomanry, who were under the command of Captain Leo Moore of the 60th, reached Britztown with the column upon Christmas Day, but here they parted company with the 18th Battalion.

Upon Dec. 26, twenty men of the Squadrons, which were now combined, were sent out under Lieut. Murland to join Col. De Lisle, who was some miles away. They arrived just in time to participate in an engagement with the Boers at Vogoteras; and later on in the same day, in the capture of Brand and Hertzog's convoy at Houwater Drift. The remainder of the Irish Yeomanry caught them up on the following day by leaving the road and making across the veldt.

Colonel De Lisle's column consisted of the 6th Battalion Mounted Infantry, called for short the 6th M.I.; the New South Wales Mounted Rifles, whose commanding officer, Col. Knight, was severely wounded at Houwater on Dec. 26; Loch's Horse and the Irish Yeomanry; with one Pom-Pom and two 12-pounders of 'R' Battery, R.H.A. The men were all 'veterans' who had been trekking and fighting for over a year—some had actually marched over seven thousand miles. They were adepts in the Boer style of fighting, and hard as nails. It need hardly be said that the reputation of Lieut.-Col. De Lisle as a dashing leader stood second to none; therefore the Irishmen could not have been more fortunate either in their companions or their leader, who moreover, was born in Dublin.

The Boers had fled to the south-west after the fight, therefore the column marched in the same direction. Towards evening their position was located and an attack fixed for 4 a.m. the next day.

"*L'homme propose, mais—*" the Boers decamped during the night in the direction of Vosburg. After them went De Lisle, to find them at last in position on a range of kopjes just beyond the town. Then he adopted the peculiar style of tactics which he had made his own, to which I shall have to refer more fully later on. Extending his horsemen at wide intervals— some 50 paces—they went forward at a mad gallop, swept right through the town, with the 12-pounders playing upon the kopjes over their heads, and arrived at the position, to find the sight of the approaching horsemen had been too much for Dutch nerves, and the enemy were in full flight. At Vosburg the column remained all night, to perform a 28 miles march next day in the direction of Carnarvon, after the routed commandoes.

Again in the saddle before dawn, and another march of 36 miles brought the column to within six miles of Carnarvon; but Hertzog had once more doubled and was now heading southwards. Ninety horses were left by the roadside from start to finish of this day's march.

Once more they came in touch with the Boer rearguard at a farm. Two of De Lisle's black scouts were captured, but the Boers fled in haste, leaving behind a number of sheep ready cooked for their pursuers.

Upon Jan. 7 the column was compelled to go into Victoria West Road to refit.

The following little ' pen picture ' of the leader under whom the Irish Yeomanry were serving, culled from the correspondence of one who accompanied the column, will not be out of place, nor without interest :—

" Colonel De Lisle himself is almost an unique figure in our Army. Before he took part in the present war he was perhaps the most famous man in India. Not to know De Lisle was to argue oneself unknown. Acting as Adjutant of the Durham Light Infantry, he organized a polo team which beat every other in India, and for the first time in the history of polo an infantry regiment carried off the prizes of the polo tournament. This magnificent result was due simply and solely to systematic training and a radical change in the tactics of the game. When he was ordered out here he was Captain of a Mounted Infantry Company. By a stroke of luck he was given the command of a regiment, and during the fighting round Colesberg he distinguished himself greatly, and was much appreciated by General French. He is of medium height, with brown hair and moustache, and possesses a pair of keen brown eyes, which seem to have a further range of vision than most eyes. Although he is a strict disciplinarian, his grand handling of his men in the field has won him the admiration of his command. It may not be uninteresting to state that Colonel De Lisle is a man of great piety, and often preaches to his men on Sundays in the absence of the chaplain.

"But perhaps the chief claim of his column to distinction is the fact that its tactics entitle it to be called the 'galloping column.' Colonel De Lisle's plan of attack differs from that of most of our commanders. When he wishes to attack a Boer position he gallops at it, his men extended fifty paces apart. This form of attack was used at Doorn Kop, Pretoria (where De Lisle turned the Boer southern position), Diamond Hill, and lately at Houwater. In every case the attack has succeeded admirably, and I believe that in all these attacks and other galloping tactics De Lisle has not lost more than ten men, if so . The theory is that galloping men, fifty apart, can hardly be tion of the line is hands which proved invaluable in times like these. I refer to the railway. De Lisle was again ready for the field, and instead of several weeks weary marching across the almost waterless veldt after the Boer commandoes, the column entrained and in less than two days had covered the 350 miles between, and on Jan. 10 detrained at Picketberg Road, 70 miles from Capetown, and in a position to head off the march of the invaders.

Their short stay here was not without incident, for, to quote the diary of a 60th man—

> *Jan. 11.*—Last night we encamped a little way from the station. The Scottish Horse were on outlying picket beyond our camp. About 11 p.m. they became excited, thought they saw Boers, and blazed into our camp. Luckily they hit no one. We rubbed it into them afterwards.

Four days later they marched into Picketberg, a pretty little town shaded by trees, where the ladies entertained the troops to afternoon tea.

After several days' patrolling, upon Jan. 23 De Lisle marched into Clanwilliam.

> *Jan. 28.*—Did 22 miles this morning into Clanwilliam, where we are to stop for a while. Coming into the town, we were surprised to see the flag half-mast. It was with great sorrow we heard that The Queen was dead. We did not believe it at first.

The column stayed nearly a week in Clanwilliam, waiting for their wagons which had gone to Lambert's Bay on the West coast for supplies. But sterner work was before them.

A party of Bethune's Mounted Infantry rode into Clanwilliam and reported the presence of the Boers at Eland's Vlei, eastward. Therefore next day the column marched over the hills and halted at the foot of the Pakhuis Pass, which was held by a patrol of the Western Province Mounted Rifles. Upon the 30th the Pass was crossed, the enemy retiring before them. A small party of the Gordon Highlanders were however cut off, losing one officer (Lieut. Clowes) killed, and another officer and one man severely wounded. The Boers had taken up a position on a line of ridges which the Irish Squadrons were sent forward to turn. This they succeeded in doing without much difficulty, and the enemy retired, shelled by the Pom-Poms until out of range. Then came the descent of a fearfully steep and rugged

THE STORY OF THE IRISH YEOMANRY.

pass, where the wagons had to be let down by ropes, and even then five of them were overturned.

But the trials of the column were not over. Before them rose another ridge, worse than the one they had crossed. Although only several miles across in actual distance, it took 42 hours hard work before the wagons and guns were over. In many places the road had first to be widened, and as the men worked through the night by the light of the moon, Colonel De Lisle was here, there and everywhere, encouraging by word and by deed, more than once himself handling a pick or a spade. The guns were hauled up laboriously by ropes. Each wagon was unloaded, its contents carried up the steepest parts of the pass, and the wagons themselves drawn up by the ropes. To add to the dangers of the crossing, the road " ran along the edge of a dizzy precipice, and had in places fallen away or been destroyed by the enemy."

The work of the Irish Yeomanry is tersely though most graphically told by the diaries of the troopers :—

Feb. 1.—We were sent out this morning at 2 o'clock to occupy a position commanding the pass. We made three attempts to reach it on horseback. In the end we had to leave our horses and go down into a ravine and climb the kopje. It was a terrible climb in the dark. When we reached the top, we found to our disgust that we were not on the right kopje after all. But we were too dog-tired to go any further, and threw ourselves down where we were and slept for hours, of course keeping a man on watch. We were there all next day without anything to eat or drink till 3-30 p.m., when we got a few biscuits which we were too dry to eat. We got into camp at 7 p.m. after assisting to haul wagons up a steep part of the road for two hours.

Feb. 2.—Went on five miles this morning, and then waited for rest of wagons to come up. . . . . Started at 7 p.m. and did a night march of 20 miles, camping at 2-30 a.m.

Feb. 3.—Marched at 4-30 a.m. for a few miles to a farmhouse with a large river near. Halted all day.

Feb. 4.—Marched at 5 a.m. and covered 18 miles to very bad water. Started again, the I.Y. being advance guard, and went on for 12 miles, seeing the Boers clearing as we went on. There was no water where we camped except in a well, to which there was no pump. Accordingly we had a very hard time watering the horses. Jack S—— and I volunteered to butcher for the Squadron, and had a terrible time killing and cleaning five sheep.

The enemy had retired into the fastnesses of the sombre Roggeveld Mountains, which now rose before the column in precipitous masses, 5000 feet in height. Through the hills ran a narrow pass, broken and difficult of access, and this De Lisle knew was held by the Boers. At 9 p.m. a detachment of the New South Wales Rifles, by making a wide detour over almost unclimable paths, gained the far end of the pass, and thus it was hoped the retreat of the Boers was cut off. This night march of the Australians was a splendid piece of work. They had to lead their horses nearly the whole way, and several of these were dashed to pieces by falling over the sheer precipice which bordered the edge of the narrow broken path. To quote one writer, one part of the way, which was crossed by ten of the troopers was " up a rock face, as steep and long as the famous eastern front of the Swiss Matterhorn."

In the early morning the remainder of the column pushed into the pass ; no fires were lit, and smoking and talking were forbidden. But it was all in vain. The enemy had by some means suspected the trap that was being laid for them, and had vacated the pass a short time before the Australians closed the other end. Pushing on, the column came in sight of Calvinia the same day, just in time to see the dust of the last Boers clearing out of it.

" — The majority of the townspeople were delighted to see us, for the enemy had been living on them for five weeks. They had set all the tailors making clothes, and all the private houses baking bread for them. And they had completely looted all the stores. The natives were especially glad to see us, as the invaders had treated them very cruelly, sjamboking several of them and shooting one named Esau."

Mr. H. W. Wilson recounts how " The full story of Esau's murder was told by the residents to the indignant troops. It when the Boers were retreating, their victim was prison in a state of collapse and placed on a horse, ile from the town, he was murdered as treacher- Captain Elliot in the first Boer War. The Boers orters in England pretend that this man, with his .ted, and in a state of collapse, attempted to refore, they say, he was shot. The fact remains Boers had killed him, they kicked the inanimate

A FARM IN THE KARROO.

Photo by *Edgeome, Beaufort West*

Feb. 19.—Did the 15 miles into Carnarvon. Raining heavily as we came in. Encamped over a mile on far side of the town. We had a wretched day and a worse night.

De Wet was in the Colony, and every effort was being made by the column to prevent Hertzog's commandoes from effecting a junction with him. Through Vosburg, Britztown and the surrounding districts marched the indefatigable De Lisle in chase of the Boer invaders. His horses were worn out and their bodies formed grim milestones along his track.

Feb. 21.—My horse, which was done up, I had to leave in Carnarvon. Had to walk and steal a ride on a wagon occasionally.

Feb. 23.—Some remounts came in to-night, so I may expect a horse to-morrow.

Feb. 24.—Got a pony to-day with a lame leg. We went 11 miles out on the Hopetown Road.

Feb. 25.—Marched 30 miles. We are not far from Prieska. My new pony is done up. I had to get another to-day and lead the old one.

Feb. 26.—Started at 3 a.m. and by 4-30 p.m. had done 32 miles. I shot my old pony this evening, as it broke its back in getting out of a river. Started again at 8 p m. and lost our way in the dark. Camped in heavy rain.

Notwithstanding their efforts, the columns did not prevent Hertzog from fording the Brak, and carrying a supply of remounts to the harried De Wet, and upon March 2 De Lisle marched into De Aar.

The Midland Districts of Cape Colony were to be the next campaigning ground of the Irish Yeomanry, and at 8 p.m. on March 2, the same day on which they arrived at De Aar, Col. De Lisle's column entrained for Cradock, where they arrived late upon the following day. At De Aar were left behind the New South Wales Rifles, who were under orders for home, and a hearty good-bye was given to the Irish Yeomanry, amongst whom they had made many friends.

At Cradock the orders were changed, and they continued southwards by rail as far as Cookhouse, and from there marched into Somerset East. The warmest welcome and hospitality was extended to them by the people of the town.

" We were royally feasted by the inhabitants in the Town Hall. Had a smoking concert at night in the same building, of a pronounced Irish flavour."

On March 6 they started for Pearston, but were stubbornly opposed by the enemy, who were not driven off till nightfall. Several hastily made graves were passed upon the march next day, which seemed to indicate that the enemy had lost more lives during the fight than they cared to own to. Continuing their march eastwards they reached Adelaide on the 13th, and Tarkastad three days later.

The Boers under Kritzinger were known to be holding in force a strong position at Magermansberg, some twelve miles from the town. Indeed, upon the preceding day the Town Guard of Tarkastad had sent out to some of their men on duty, who were eight miles out, a quantity of rations carried in two Cape carts driven by Kaffirs and escorted by eight of the Town Guard. These the Boers had captured, shooting the black drivers after driving them with whips before their horses for several miles. Two of the Town Guard were then ordered to drive the carts, and were released after a time.

An attack was made upon the position the following day, March 17, St. Patrick's Day, in which the Irish Yeomanry were given the post of honour—and of danger—by Colonel De Lisle, who was himself born in Dublin. The story of the fight—including a graphic description of De Lisle's 'galloping' tactics—can best be gathered from a letter sent home by one of the 61st (Trooper Earls) which I have received courteous permission to include in these pages:—

"On Saturday evening, the 16th, we received an order at 4 p.m. telling us that we were to be ready to march off at 6 o'clock. . . . as there was a large force of Boers about 12 miles from here holding a strong position. We marched off at the appointed time, bringing two 12-pounders, a Pom-Pom, and some wagons with forage and food for ourselves. The rain had started about 5 o'clock and continued until about 1-0 the following morning. Such a march I never experienced; thunder, lightning, and continuous rain, along with an intense darkness that might be felt. It was so dark from about 7 o'clock until the rain ceased that I could not see the head of the horse I was riding. This is in no way exaggerated. The only time I could see before me was when the lightning flashed, and then I could see the head of the column as plain as if it was daylight.

COLUMN ON THE MARCH.

Photo by Edgcome, Beaufort West

Having drawn fresh horses and been re-equipped, on Dec. 28 these men escorted a large convoy of provisions, stores and ammunition—of a total value of some £35,000—to Britztown; returning to De Aar on New Year's morning without having met with any opposition.

For the next six weeks they formed part of the garrison of De Aar; and as they were the only mounted troops stationed there, upon them fell most of the more distant outpost work at night and all the patrolling by day. During one of these patrols Trooper T. Wood, of the 60th, was slightly wounded.

But the officers and men chafed under the inaction of garrison life, and when an opportunity of again 'going on column' presented itself it was eagerly seized. On the 16th of February Col. Munro's column marched into De Aar. The Berkshire Yeomanry with the column were greatly in need of rest, so Major de Burgh volunteered to march in their place with the Irish Yeomanry under his command. The offer was accepted, and on Feb. 18 they once more took to the vicissitudes and excitement of column work.

Westwards—through Britztown, Houwater, Strydenburg—striving to cut off the commandoes of Hertzog and Brand on their return from the western invasion. Eastwards — to Paauwpan, Petrusville, Philipstown—searching and clearing the country through which had passed the hordes of De Wet; until on March 3, the column marched into the pretty little town of Colesberg, and for a few days rested fron its labours.

On March 7, the column entrained and proceeded to Aliwal North, from thence to be instruments in carrying out the Commander-in-Chief's policy of clearing the country and rendering it incapable of supporting the wandering Boer commandoes. Their instructions—corn to be destroyed, farmhouses stripped, stock of all kinds, cattle sheep and horses, driven in, and women and children brought on in their own wagons to the nearest refugee camp. One of the men writes—

"These drastic measures, painful to us all, were carried out with all possible humanity, though many a severe castigation at the tongues of Dutch viragos did we undergo. . . Sometimes on the line of march the column would halt for a day to permit of parties being sent out in different directions to carry out the work in hand, and bring in the refugees. Once on the move the latter seemed to take things most philosophically. They travelled in large covered wagons, drawn by oxen driven by their own Kaffirs. They camped alongside us, usually at some distance away under an efficient guard, and Heaven help any man attempting to gratify his curiosity by viewing them at a closer range. As night fell they would commence singing psalms, sandwiched with snatches from patriotic melodies, a form of entertainment continued for a couple of hours or more. The light of the many camp fires, oftener than not, the illumination of a glorious moon playing on the majestic kopjes, the rise and fall of the voices in measured cadence, furnished a scene at once pathetic and impressive."

Northward through Rouxville—a town deserted and desolate; through Wepener, until within a few miles of Ladybrand, when the column turned in its course and upon April 1, having been often sniped at but met with no serious opposition, they marched into Springfontein.

A week later and a little force rode at daybreak from Dewetsdorp. It consisted of all the available men of the Irish Yeomanry, under Captain Carden, and a squadron of Bethune's Mounted Infantry—180 in all. They soon came in touch with the enemy, and aided by some guns belonging to White's brigade, which was co-operating with them, a vigorous attack was made. As usual, the enemy would not stand, and a running fight was maintained for several hours. The result was a gratifying one. The little force of 180 men marched into camp at midnight, bringing in 86 prisoners. The B.M.I. had three men killed and one wounded, but the Yeomanry had no casualties.

"It was a creditable capture. Captain Carden himself, accompanied by Sergeant Manico and four men, "held up" thirty in a bunch. They were making the best of their way from the scene of the conflict along the base of a small kopje, when the Captain showed himself on the top and called 'Hands up.' So far as the Boers knew, they were covered by a hundred rifles. They were not taking any risks and did not require a second invitation. Down went their rifles, and up went their hands. The average panned out at five prisoners

TO
THE LEICESTERSHIRE YEOMANRY.

(From a Brother in Exile.)

Where the old brook winds babbling o'er the lea ;
   Where the grand elms cast down their glorious shade :
Where the broad beeches don their purple hue ;
   There have ye often rode or idly strayed.

Shade of Whyte-Melville ! Conjure up some scene
   Where willowy meads, replete with lowing kine
Form a bright foreground to some deep-brown copse—
   A landscape to a huntsman's eye divine.
There have our Yeomen learnt to ride and shoot
   To tend the crops and gather in the hay ;
To welcome in, with ardent fancies bright,
   The sharp clear morn of a November day.
So saddle up; and follow in the wake
   Of the Quorn beauties to old Reynard's haunt ;
We'll follow them to Quorn, or Barkley Holt,
   To Badby, Whissendine, and John o' Gaunt.

Ye love to rouse the rabbit from his seat,
   To flush the partridge from the turnip crop,
And now ye volunteer for England's sake
   To fill the place when England's foemen drop.
Ye ride, but not on hunting pleasures bent,
   'Tis yours to bear the fighting and the brunt :
In England's name ye fight for England's fame,
   All honour to our Yeomen at the front.

Umtali, 31st May, 1900.   E.J.C.

On May 11 the 65th Squadron disembarked at Beira, and encamping in turn at Twenty-three Mile Creek, Bamboo Creek—where they suffered equally with the other Squadrons from the pestilential climate; Umtali, where came the first break in their ranks by the death of Trooper J. Brooker; on June 7 they reached the Base Camp at Marandellas. Here they received their horses, and being the first of the eight squadrons to move to the Base Camp, they were allowed to have their choice of the 3500 Hungarians shipped through Beira, and the manner in which the animals answered to the calls which were afterwards made upon their strength and endurance proved that in the choice of these mounts a more than ordinary knowledge of horse-flesh had been evinced. And the work of training their half-broken steeds went on.

But there was another cause for the eagerness they infused into their work. Far north of Salisbury, near the valley of the Zambesi, mischief was brewing amongst the natives, and even before leaving Umtali the news had run through the Squadron that they were to be sent northwards to assist in quelling the disturbance. Therefore they worked doubly hard to shape their steeds for the work in hand, and three weeks after reaching the Base Camp the result of this was seen, for they were entrained for Salisbury, 60 miles further up the line, from thence to march northwards on the punitive expedition against the recalcitrant chieftain.

The story of the expedition has been told in the early part of this work. In the fight against the Chief Mapondera and his bandits there were no fatal casualties in the ranks of the little force. One or two of the Mashonaland Native Police— familiarly called the ' Black Watch '—were severely wounded, and there were three men slightly wounded in the Leicestershire Squadron—Sergt. Munn and Troopers David and Gittens.

In his summary of the fight in ' orders ' next day Lieut.- Col. Flint published the following:—

" The O.C. is very pleased and will report to the authorities the gallant conduct of the Imperial Yeomanry under Captain Peake, and the B.S.A. Police as well as the Mashonaland Native Police; which were attacked by Mapondera after a long and hard day's march. It is regretted that Mapondera himself

HORSE-LINES—SEPULLO KRAAL.
A HALT IN THE FOREST.
A ROUGH TRACK—LOMAGHONDA.

Photos by *Lieut. H. T. Munn.*

horses, were inspected by General Sir Frederick Carrington. My impressions of the Head of the Rhodesian Field Force I take without alteration from my diary, written at the time :—

"About 4.30 General Carrington drove up accompanied by a staff-officer, in a rather shabby-looking hired landau kind of conveyance, drawn by four second-hand looking mules, which were driven by a second-hand looking nigger sitting on the box. The Captain met him in the road and he came across to our bivouac amongst the trees. We were at stables, and stood to our horses' heads, brushes and rubbers in hand, as he went round. Resting his hand familiarly upon the Captain's shoulder he came into the camp and walked across to the two Maxims, one of which was draped round with blankets, for S—— lay under the shafts sick with fever. He then sauntered slowly through the horse-lines, taking in everything with a keen eye, however, as he passed. Dressed in drill khaki tunic and slacks, with the new pattern Rhodesian helmet on his head, but with brims more narrow than usual. The insignia of his rank upon his shoulders, and a touch of bright colour at his neck. With the two bottom buttons of his tunic undone and his hands thrust either into his belt or pockets underneath—I could not see which—there was nothing exceptionally military in the appearance of our General. Halting at each troop-lines to shake hands and speak to the officer, and in one instance to the troop-sergeant, who, like himself, was an old Cheltenham scholar, the inspection proceeded. At the end the troops were formed up in quarter column, and General Carrington addressed the Squadron as follows.—

'Captain Peake, officers, N.C. officers, and men of the 65th Squadron of Imperial Yeomanry.

I congratulate you warmly upon the appearance and condition of your horses, which reflect great credit upon you. During the last few months you have had some very hard work to do. Though you have had no very serious fighting, you perhaps do not realize the great importance of the work you have done. By the celerity with which you marched with your horses and your wagons northwards of Salisbury to the districts which were disaffected, and by the show of force you were able to make before the natives, you have undoubtedly nipped in the bud

were but twelve miles from the nearest bend of the Orange River, and were constantly employed in patrolling for many miles along its banks, and throughout the district for a long distance round their central camp. Several times Boer laagers were located on the far banks of the river and were shelled by the Australian guns, and once a patrol of 20 men was hotly attacked—at Grootverlangen Drift—by a strong party of the enemy, who withdrew after several hours' fusillade. The men were exposed to miserably inclement weather for several weeks, and being at first without tents, their condition was far from enviable; but towards the end of their stay at Petrusville their lot was ameliorated by the arrival of a few tents from De Aar. Even these were levelled to the ground on one particularly stormy night.

From Petrusville two of the officers of the Squadron—Captain Peake and Lieut. Challinor—were invalided, their health undermined by the exposure and the hard vicissitudes incidental to campaigning. Lieut. R. B. Muir took over the command of the Squadron, and shortly afterwards was promoted to the rank of Captain.

It was soon after this that Hertzog and Brand crossed the Orange, and hard and constant patrolling was the daily lot of the Leicestershire Squadron.

So Christmas drew near. And the men looked forward to a little mild festivity upon this, the most curious Christmas they had ever spent—a little break in the wearing patrols and the hard fare of the veldt. For in the coolest corner of a tent rested a barrel of beer given to them by the officers, and snugly hidden away were sundry plum-puddings—real English plum-puddings, sent from over-sea—but both to be kept religiously intact until Christmas Day should dawn. Meanwhile the patrols went on.

One three days patrol will be long remembered by the score of men who took part in it. The object and composition of the party was as under—

" A strong patrol of 20 men and an officer, will proceed at 1 p.m. to-day (Dec. 20) to reconnoitre the country to the west. The route taken should be roughly Jakkalkuil, Plessis Dam, and Paauwpan Station. Returning, if no opposition is met with, from 5 to 10 miles to the south of the line. If possible it

GRAZING-GUARD ON THE MARCH TO BULUWAYO—*See* p. 269.
Photo by *C. W. McKechnie.*
'D' TROOP MAXIM ON THE MARCH TO BULUWAYO—*See* p. 269.
Photo by *Lieut. E. C. Challinor.*

services rendered in connection with these operations by (*amongst others*)—

Lieut. H. T. Munn.

12010 Tpr. W. Sopp."

Trooper Sopp, for his daring ride, was promoted to Corporal by the Commander-in-Chief and received the medal for Distinguished Conduct in the Field.

Upon the day following the attack on Philipstown, another patrol of the 65th, consisting of a Lieutenant and 20 men, were not so fortunate. At the farm at Wolvekuil they suddenly found themselves surrounded by an overwhelming force of the enemy, and after several hours resistance, were captured. One —Corpl. Wade—was slightly wounded.

On Feb. 14 a mishap occurred to another little patrol who ran against the Boer commandoes twelve miles north of Houtkraal. The broken remnants of the little party reached the camp at Houtkraal by hard riding, but they left several of their number in the hands of the enemy, two of whom were wounded— Tpr. Piggott severely and Tpr. Harrison slightly. The news these men brought turned out the column before daybreak next morning, to complete the demoralization of De Wet's broken hordes, and to commence the long relentless chase which has been elsewhere described*.

It was during the chase of De Wet that Shoeing-Smith H. Brazier of the 65th met his death. For a time the columns had lost touch with the flying Boers, and on Feb. 21 were marching by Driekoppen, with their scouts feeling in all directions for the enemy. Brazier, the outside left flanker, rode to the Elsie Vlaakte farm and suddenly found himself in the midst of five of the enemy, who sprang from their concealment not ten yards from his horse's head, with pointed rifles and a peremptory summons to "Hands up." Brazier was riding a favourite horse 'Marmalade,' an animal of which he was very proud†. Indeed before starting on this, his last ride, he had patted the neck of his steed saying, "I shan't be captured whilst I have you under me." Trusting in the fleetness of his horse, when suddenly

---

* Part II., Chap. 7.
† For portrait of Shoeing-Smith Brazier and ' Marmalade ' see page 128.

day. The men were most hospitably treated by the people of Grahamstown—the most English town in Cape Colony—who pressed on them gifts of fruit and tobacco, and organized teas and other innocent dissipations in their honour. They were not, however, permitted to stay long to enjoy them. On the 17th they moved northwards, and detrained at Rosmead. A week's ceaseless pursuit of the roving commandoes in the district, during which they were several times in action with the slippery foe, and the running out of their stores brought them again into the railway at Schombie.

On March 21 a new officer was taken on their strength, in the person of Lieut. Gill. This officer had come out with the 7th I.Y. (first Leicestershire contingent) as a trooper. He was promoted to Sergeant, and then his opportunity came. He had been sent out in charge of a patrol of 20 men to reconnoitre a line of Boer trenches, in order that, if not too strongly held, they might be stormed on the following night by the column to which he belonged. Creeping up to a position from which his glasses would command them, he saw that just then they were but weakly manned. He therefore decided to attempt their capture with his little patrol, and the bold *coup* came off with brilliant success. For his deed he received the Medal for Distinguished Conduct in the Field and a commission, and was transferred to the 65th Squadron[*].

Another week on the veldt, and on April 9 they encamped at Steynsburg; where they were joined by the comrades whom they had not seen for near four months—the patrol which had left them at Petrusville on the 20th of December of the year before. We will briefly follow the fortunes of this little troop.

This patrol—twenty-one all told, including the Lieutenant in command (Sir Frederick Fowke)—reached Paauwpan Station without mishap—if we except the washing from his saddle of one of the men—unfortunately the author *in propriâ personâ*—whilst crossing a deep spruit, much swollen by the rain. None of the enemy were found there, but it was evident that they were expected. For first came an armoured train, with a number of Munster Fusiliers Militia. Half of them patrolled the line whilst

---

[*] When the Squadron sailed for England, Lieut. Gill remained behind to command the new 65th Squadron.

THE STORY OF THE 65th SQUADRON I.Y.

the remainder removed the provisions and stores from the railway 'winkel' to the train. Evidently it was intended that if the place was raided, the Boers should find nothing worth the taking. Shortly afterwards a second train arrived, bearing the 71st Squadron of Sharpshooters, with Sir Savile Crossley in command. They halted at the station for the night, and next morning slowly marched southwards along the railway, searching the veldt and the kopjes on either side. And the Leicestershire patrol went with them. We then heard for the first time of the fight at Houtkraal which took place on the day we left Petrusville.

Houtkraal was reached on Dec. 22, and we renewed our acquaintance with the Sharpshooters, whom we had not seen since Marandellas. The subsequent march of events was rapid. First came the news of the Irish mishap, followed by the instant commencement of the long chase, during which the 65th patrol were attached to the column of Col. Thorneycroft. Their return to their own Squadron had by this time become most problematical.

The further history of the troop vividly illustrates the career of so many small parties which have from some cause become detached from their Squadrons. Once this occurs, and it is a matter of chance, or rather of the exigencies of war, if they again rejoin their comrades before the order for mobilization collects the scattered units. Hardly a squadron of Imperial Yeomanry but was wiring all over the Seat of War for the men or the little detachments they had lost, when the magic word 'mobilize' appeared in their instructions.

During Thorneycroft's long march, the Leicestershire troop were attached to the 71st S.S. With them they remained during the move from Victoria West to Prince Albert—during the march over the Zwartberg Pass, until on Jan. 28 the 71st marched southwards, to be cut up two days later, and the 65th troop took up a position in the mouth of the Meirings Poort which they held until the close of the fight at Klaarstroom on Feb. 2.

They were now transferred to the 67th S.S. and accompanied Colonel Grenfell on the march which—through Zeekoegat,

twice about attempting on foot. The Boers clambered after them, sometimes having to use their hands as well as their feet. And so the summit was reached, and the mystery of the *cul de sac* explained.

Next day, and for several days afterwards, came heavy rains, and the heavy roads and the hill-climbing, together with the wet and cold at night—for they had no blankets—made these days terrible ones for the foot-sore captives. Sometimes no food could be procured, and one whole day neither they nor the Boers had anything to eat but the leaves of the 'spek-boom' which they tore off the trees as they passed. These trees bear small rounded fleshy leaves, which taste very much like the 'sorrel' that grows in the English meadows. One of the Leicester men—Trooper Mills—was seized with rheumatics, and could go no farther; so he was left at a farm, and afterwards picked up by a British column and sent on to the hospital at Graaff Reinet.

The prisoners had now been eight days in the hands of their captors, and no hope of release was in sight. On the ninth day hurried movements amongst the commando showed that something out of the common had taken place. Major Mullins, V.C., with a small column of troops was very near, though the prisoners did not know it then. It was 9 p.m. when the Boers at last off-saddled at a farm at Uitkomst. The prisoners, who had been warned not to strike any light, sat against the outside wall of the farm. Inside the room they could see Fouchee writing at a table. Suddenly an old man employed on the farm crept up in the darkness, and said in a whisper—" Are you the prisoners ? " " Yes ! " they replied in the same tone, and he pushed into their hands a box of matches and a finger's length of tobacco for each ; then making a sign for silence, stole away into the gloom.

Next day, at 4 p.m., the British column was upon the commando, and a fierce attack was made which only ended with the darkness, when the Boers fled through the hills, and the British column retired to a farm near by—Krugerskraal—to await the dawn. From their camp they could see the flames of the farm at Uitkomst, which the Boers had set fire to before they stole away.

that they were free from the column, they firmly resolved they would find their Squadron if such a thing was humanly possible. But they did not know to what column the 65th were attached, and no one else seemed to know, so for the next fortnight they were employed in searching the Midland districts of Cape Colony for their lost Squadron, often running a narrow risk of being commandeered on the way and attached to another column.

From Naauwpoort to Rosmead—where they were attached to the 1st (King's) Dragoons, and for several days garrisoned a little loop-holed fort ; to Steynsburg—where they heard at last that their Squadron was with Colonel Herbert and expected at Knapdaar in two days. As they left Steynsburg, they passed a column encamped on the veldt, which, upon enquiry, they found was Col. Henniker's. But they wanted Herbert's, not Henniker's. At Knapdaar (some twenty miles from Bethulie), they waited two days until Col. Herbert's column came in, but found the 65th were not with them. In fact, they did not know there was such a squadron. To Burghersdorp—where a night was spent in order to pick up information. Back to Steynsburg —to find that the 65th were there with Colonel Henniker's column, and that they had passed within a mile of them when they left the place three days before.

The Squadron was once more complete, and the next day moved by train to Fish River with the column.

From Fish River, the column marched westwards to Bethesda Road, and from there entrained for Aberdeen Road. They formed the escort into Aberdeen to a convoy of stores drawn by donkeys, and never do they wish for a slower, more monotonous journey. The twenty-eight miles were covered in thirteen hours.

An attack by Malan upon the station at Kendrew took the Squadron, by a forced march through the night, to that place, but the Boers had gone long before they arrived.

From Kendrew, the 65th rejoined Colonel Henniker's column near Pearston, and the same day the Boers were encountered in a narrow valley at Middlewater. The column had halted near midday and was preparing to form camp, when a heavy fire was opened on them from the surrounding kopjes where the enemy were concealed. The guns were soon in action and, aided by the rifles of the mounted troops, drove the Boers before them after four hours' firing. The day nearly proved disastrous to the Leicesters. They were advance guard, and had dismounted on the open space where the camp was to be formed. Cossack posts had meanwhile been sent to the surrounding hills. Suddenly they and the Posts found themselves in the midst of a storm of bullets. Two men—Tprs. Edge and Saunders—were wounded at the first volley, and another—Tpr. Light—injured by the fall of his dying horse. Quickly taking cover they were able to return with interest the sudden fire from their assailants. Captain Muir displayed the greatest coolness under the surprise, and paying no heed to the hail of lead hurtling around him, by his orders and cool example, quickly restored to his Squadron the discipline which the sudden volleys had for a moment shaken.

During the engagement Trooper Doran volunteered to ride through the fire to bring medical aid to the wounded men. This he safely performed.

My own experience in the fight may illustrate the work of the columns in this latter-day part of the war; this guerilla fighting which bristles with little skirmishes, hardly one of which attains to the [dignity of an ' engagement'; yet which entails as much wearying work, and is fraught, I think, with equal danger to the soldier as the ' battles ' of the earlier stages of the campaign. I have copied the following almost literally from my rough notes made in the failing light when the last echoes of the guns had not long died in the hills.

" For the last two miles we, the advance guard, had to force our way through thick groves of prickly pear, full of blind alleys, which filled our knees and maddened the horses with cruel spines. Therefore our progress had been slow; and when at last we reached the camping place, the column were close on our heels. Cossack posts of four men were hurriedly sent to the kopjes fringing the narrow valley. I went with one of them. We stopped at the river to fill our water-bottles, as we might be on the hill all day, and then splashing through, cantered by a farm-house along a lane formed by the hedges

In the despatch from Earl Roberts, K.G., G.C.B., &c., to the Right Hon. The Secretary of State for War, dated Sept. 4, 1901.

Amongst the names of Regimental officers, N.C. officers and men of the Regulars, Militia, Yeomanry and Volunteers, who, with their various units, have rendered special and meritorious service, appeared the following :—

17TH BATTALION I.Y.

Captain W. A. Peake (Major Leicestershire Imperial Yeomanry).

1070 Sqdn.-Sergeant-Major G. Hobden (10th Hussars).
12848 Farrier-Sergeant H. Hill.
12124 Trooper E. Knowles.

War Office, Sept. 27, 1901.

The King has been graciously pleased to give orders for the following appointment . . . to the Distinguished Service Order; and for the grant of the Medal for Distinguished Conduct in the Field to the undermentioned Officers and Soldiers, in recognition of their services during the operations in South Africa. The whole to bear date Nov. 29, 1900 :—

17TH BATTALION I.Y.

D. S. O. :

Captain Walter A. Peake.

D. C. Medal :

Sqdn.-Sergeant-Major G. Hobden (10th Hussars).

NOTE.—The lines " To the Leicestershire Yeomanry," on page , 266 appeared anonymously in the *Rhodesian Advertiser* during the stay of the Squadron in Umtali

THE STORY OF DUNRAVEN'S SHARPSHOOTERS.

AMONGST the many patriotic offers made to the Government during the closing months of the year 1900, when England's greatest need was for men able to cope, on somewhat equal conditions, with her enemy in South Africa, none was more magnificent or of more value than the offer of the Earl of Dunraven and Mount-earl to raise and equip the now historic Battalion of The Mounted Volunteer Sharpshooters.

Needless to say the offer was gratefully accepted by the War Office, and under the following Committee of officers and gentlemen, the work of organization went forward rapidly.

GENERAL COMMITTEE.

THE EARL OF DUNRAVEN, K.P.
THE RT. HON. SIR JAMES FERGUSSON, BART., M.P.
COLONEL THE RT. HON. E. SAUNDERSON, M.P.
SIR JOHN DICKSON POYNDER, BART., M.P.
THE RT. HON. HORACE PLUNKETT, M.P.
H. SETON-KARR, ESQ., M.P.
BRUCE VERNON-WENTWORTH, ESQ., M.P. (Grenadier Guards).
LIONEL PHILLIPS, ESQ.
MAJOR THE HON. T. F. FREMANTLE, A.D.C. (1st Bucks R.V.C.
CAPTAIN ALFRED CHRISTOPHER (late Recruiting Staff Officer, N.W.D.)
SIR RALPH PAYNE GALLWEY, BART.
LIEUT.-COLONEL T. A. HILL (late commanding 12th Lancers).
BRIGADIER-GENERAL SIR HENRY FLETCHER, M.P.
THE LORD CLONCURRY.
GENERAL HENRY STRACEY.
COLONEL MELLISH.

THE STORY OF THE SHARPSHOOTERS.

LIEUT.-COLONEL R. PILKINGTON, M.P.
COLONEL WYNDHAM MURRAY, M.P.
MAJOR F. C. RASCH, M.P.
A. K. THARP, ESQ. (Derbyshire Yeomanry).
(*With power to add.*)
HON. SECRETARY.
J. A. G. HAMILTON, ESQ.

The great value and importance of good rifle shooting in the campaign in which the men were destined to take part was fully realized by the Committee, and, as far as possible, everything was subordinated to this end. Therefore a standard of rifle shooting higher than that required from the Imperial Yeomanry was fixed, after conferring with some of the highest rifle shooting authorities in the Kingdom.

The following were the Special Conditions and Equipment of the Corps.

1. Only thoroughly good rifle shots will be accepted. Members of this Corps will be required to satisfy the Committee in this respect, either by past records or by actual shooting at the range, in addition to the ordinary Yeomanry marksman's test.

2 In addition to the Government allowance for horse and outfit and the Lee-Enfield Government rifle, each member of this Corps will be provided, if he desires, with a good field glass and possibly a pistol.

3. Each member with dependants will receive, if he desires it, a Life Insurance Policy for a year for £250. All members will also receive a Special Bounty of £10 (in addition to any Government Bounty) at the expiration of service, which is to be for one year or the period of the War.

4. Other conditions and pay as per Imperial Yeomanry Regulations.

Creek; but the Scottish Squadron was stationed for several weeks at the Remount paddocks at Beira, where they took charge of the large quantities of horses destined for the Rhodesian Field Force. The New Zealanders whom they relieved were pushed rapidly up country for Mafeking, but arrived a few days too late to take part in the relief.

They were not many days in camp before many of the men were down with dysentery and fever; and little wonder, between the number of horses, scarcity of water, and dense malarial fogs at night. In addition there were the land crabs, which swarmed over the camping ground. Each morning the floors of the tents would be all pock-marked by them. The fresh soil these crustaceans brought up, the effluvia from which the sleepers inhaled, made breakfast almost impossible. To add to these horrors, there were the mosquitos by night and the plague of flies by day. It is no exaggeration to say that the tents were literally black with the latter pests.

Of the hardships endured by the 70th S.S., and the manner in which they were borne, the following extract from a letter written by the Officer in command of the Squadron throws sufficient light:—

"Even before starting upon the march, I have had time and opportunity to test pretty well the stuff of which the Squadron was composed. We had had no fighting, but we had had something much harder to endure. For some weeks we were camped in a pestilential swamp near Beira, guarding 1500 horses. The work both by day and night was incessant, and carried on under the greatest difficulties. The only food was bully beef and biscuits, the only drink putrid water. The result was that before a fortnight had elapsed, nearly 50 per cent of the Squadron were suffering from fever and dysentery. When at last we were sent to the base camp at Marandellas many of the men had to be left behind, some on the hospital hulks in the harbour at Beira, others in the hospitals of Umtali. Neither then nor at any other time was there any grumbling or complaining at the work. Even when half the Squadron were on the sick list, and double duty was thus thrown on the remainder, the work was always done, not only thoroughly but cheerfully."

THE STORY OF THE SHARPSHOOTERS.

Upon May 22 the Squadron was moved and joined the remainder of their Battalion at Bamboo Creek.

Sad memories will ever cling around Bamboo Creek. Disease —the disease which comes from the fever mist and the swamp— swept over the Rhodesian Field Force, as I have related elsewhere; but Death had respited the Squadrons as yet—all save one. Of the 67th, two were left behind at Bamboo Creek.

In a letter home, an officer—a fellow-townsmen of one of the men who died—writes:—

"The camp has been in gloom all day, for we have lost two men. Poor young Apps died this morning about 7 o'clock, and another man, also of the 67th, named Shaw, to-night. I am awfully sorry for poor young Apps. He was a good fellow— one of the best in his section. We buried him with full military honours in a pretty little spot where lie several other Englishmen. I went out into the jungle and got some green leaves and the few flowers I could find, and made a little wreath which I placed on the coffin, and had a photograph taken of the grave."

Thence to Umtali, where the time was spent in useful route-marching amongst the surrounding hills and passes; and health was once more blown into the weakened frames of the men by the rare mountain breezes. All save those on whom disease had taken too firm a grasp; for in the Umtali graveyard were buried four men of the Sharpshooters—Trooper Dunne of the 67th; Troopers Hinton and Pugh of the 71st; and Trooper A. E. Shaw of the 75th. Lieut. Andrew of the 70th was carried to Salisbury, but died in the hospital there. It was the death of this young officer which called forth from the Rhodesian Press that strong protest which I have quoted in full in the early part of this book.

During the stay of the Sharpshooters, various shooting matches were arranged between the officers and the Umtali Rifle Club; and between the men of the Squadrons and the strong local Company of Volunteers. But the men from over the seas proved worthy of their name, and invariably inflicted defeat upon their hosts. Indeed, in the final match the Sharpshooters eclipsed their former efforts by scoring 700 points against 500 gained by their opponents. In this match, the

—only pursued the same route as far as The Range; from thence proceeding to Buluwayo by the road followed by the whole of the 17th Battalion.

An unpleasant incident befel the Scottish Squadron during this march. After leaving The Range, they lost the track. For hours they marched and countermarched, until men and horses were wearied out, and a halt was decided on until daybreak, when their bearings might be studied with a greater chance of success. The men had filled their water-bottles in the morning, but they did not husband their little supply very carefully, depending upon reaching a stream before the end of the day. But no water was found, and that night when the men sought their pillows—*i.e.* their saddles—there was not a drop of water to be had in the camp for love or money. It was their first experience of real thirst, and troopers were offering five shillings for half-a-cupful of water, but it was not to be had. It was not till 11 o'clock next forenoon that water was reached. But there was very little complaining, and the set faces of the men, made hardly distinguishable by sweat and dust, showed their officer what kind of stuff the Edinburgh lads were made of when their powers of endurance were called upon.

And so, by short stages, the march to Victoria was accomplished. In order to save the horses as much as possible the men walked and rode alternately, nearly half the distance being covered on foot. Most of the journey lay across vast level tracts, mile upon mile of continuous plain, broken only by the sky-line. The country was very sparsely populated until nearing Victoria, round which the native Mashonas cluster very thickly. Nearing the end of their march, the ground became more broken, and abounded in giant fig-trees, some of which must have been of great age. The 70th encamped under two of these large trees upon the night before they reached Victoria. A number of magnificent cacti and huge boulders of granite made the spot an ideal and picturesque one for a camp—or a picnic.

Victoria lies some 1200 feet lower than Marandellas, and though quite as bracing, the climate was perceptibly warmer, the town being surrounded on three sides by mountains covered with foliage to their very summits. A

acres) will be granted to *bona fide* settlers who will personally occupy and farm with stock and agriculture.
1. For five years subject to a quit-rent of 10s. per annum.
2. After five years' occupation as above, settlers to have the following option :
    (a) Of purchase at 1s. 6d. per morgen.
    (b) Of leasing the land for five or seven years at a rental of £5 per annum, the quit-rent in both cases to continue at 10s. per annum.
3. The British South Africa Company will obtain and distribute breeding cattle up to 50 to each settler, who shall have the option :
    (a) Of purchasing outright at cost price, or if it is preferred, in four annual instalments with interest at five per centum per annum on the unpaid instalments.
    (b) Of farming with the said cattle on halves with the British South Africa Company, who retain the ownership of the cattle.
4. The British South Africa Company will pay each settler £25 per annum for at least five years; in return for which the latter will agree to be liable to be called out for military service when required, and to attend for training and drill as ordered by proper authority. During such period of training an allowance will be paid at the rate of 5s. per day."

It was the general opinion at the time that the Squadron would see no fighting, and that, figuratively speaking, their swords could be turned into plough-shares almost immediately; but the sterner work farther south, I think, partly ousted any colonizing schemes they may have had from the minds of the men. Whether any have accepted the offer of the British South Africa Company since their disbandment I cannot say.

Within eighteen miles of Victoria lay the ruins—undoubtedly the most interesting in the length of Africa—of the Great Zimbabwe*, and a number of the Sharpshooters were allowed the privilege of visiting these relics of thirty centuries ago.

---

* The natives now living at the ruins pronounce it *Zimbabge* (the "g" having a deep guttural sound), and in the Tshikaranga language, spoken by them, the word means the "houses of stone." There are more than five hundred of these 'Zimbabwes' scattered throughout Rhodesia, but far the most important group of these ruins is the 'Great Zimbabwe" near Victoria.

What romance can equal the all-engrossing mystery of those snake-infested walls, built by a people the very memory of whom has crumbled like their dust? Of the mazy labyrinths of its temples—the sacred enclosures approached by a granite passage with walls thirty feet in height, open to the sky, like all these Nature-worship temples, and yet so narrow that in places two men can hardly walk abreast : or of the hill fortress, standing on its granite kopje, 500 feet above the plain, guarded by sheer precipice, and accessible only but from one side ; and even there protected at every turn by traverses and ambuscades.

What histories are wrapped in those silent granite sets, square-hammered with infinite labour, and reared in numberless tiers without the aid of mortar or cement ? In its decorated pillars, its huge monoliths, its soapstone carvings ? How many have bled on those crumbling altars, human sacrifices offered in the pagan worship of its Priests ? As one stands on the crest of the Zimbabwe Hill under giant cacti and fig-trees whose age would shame the noblest of our oaks at home, and looks over the far stretches of pregnant soil, o'er miles of waving grass and rich foliaged trees ; one ponders on the mysterious race which peopled this land ages beyond the utmost backward stretch of the traditions of those in the clustered kraals below. But ponders vainly. Who can tell ? Scientists may guess, but who can prove ?

In an outlying angle of the ruined walls, lay the remains of Major Wilson and the men who fell with him seven years ago; here brought from the far spot on the Shangani where they died, making the English-speaking world ring with the manner of their death. And in the creepers trailing o'er his grave, a little bird had built its nest.

Shooting matches were held 'twixt the troops and the Victorian teams, also cricket on cocoa-nut matting. On the range, as was but natural, the Sharpshooters were unassailable, but with the bat the settlers more than held their own.

At Victoria a Maxim battery was formed—four Maxims, each manned by six men, who volunteered for the work from the various squadrons of Sharpshooters. The battery was placed under the command of Lieut. Seagrave* of the 71st.

---

* Lieut. Seagrave was a few months afterwards promoted to Captain, and on May 25, 1901, was made Second-in-Command of the new Battalion with the rank of Major.

FORT TULI.

Photo. *B.S.A. Company.*

day it would be tolerable ; the next almost unendurable from the intensity of the enervating heat. To cross the sand of the river bed on days like these was an experience in heat endurance. The river was fringed with groups of lordly palms, numbers of which were tapped by the natives for the palm-oil they contained.

The 75th Squadron arrived on September 20, but only stayed for a week, continuing the march southwards on Sept. 27 for the Limpopo River and the Transvaal border. On the 24th the 67th Squadron arrived from Buluwayo. They had completed their long march from Marandellas in 28 days, but only stayed a week in the Matabele Capital, marching for Tuli through Manzinyama, Pourri-Perri and Reitfontein. Troops were fast coming in. Squadrons of Australians, batteries of Artillery, the 17th and 18th Battalions of Yeomanry, and other details brought the total garrison up to near a thousand men. It was intended that this force should march southwards through the Transvaal and occupy Pietersburg, then in the hands of the Boers. From Pietersburg the railway ran to Pretoria, and it was thought the advent of this force threatening the Capital from the north would make a material difference to the Boer resistance. But the march of events further south rendered a total change of tactics advisable, and the original intention was never carried out.

Halting for a night at Bryce's Store—a dilapidated collection of buildings, wrecked by shell and spattered with bullet marks—the 75th Squadron marched on to the Limpopo, and encamped in a strongly defensive position within a mile of Pont Drift. Here they remained for nearly a month. There was no lack of interest for those with a taste for natural history. The camp abounded with tarantulas, scorpions and small snakes. In and over the rocks darted the less noxious lizards, from the brilliant little fellow with green body and orange tail some four or five inches long to the sluggish monitor—or ' legovaan,' as the Dutch call them—sometimes measuring a yard in length. Harmless little chameleons appeared in the light of the camp-fires, and occasionally the camp was disturbed by the unwelcome presence of a puff-adder (one was killed under Colonel Parke's bed). The country around abounded with the Cape guinea fowl. This handsome game-bird with crimson head and wattles and pale blue neck was found in large flocks, and the natives were very expert in snaring them. Near the Drift were the littered sites of old camping-grounds, some nearly ankle-deep in places with the feathers of the guinea fowl.

The vicinity of the Limpopo was more tropical in its vegetation than any part of Rhodesia the men had yet seen. The road wound through a jungle of luxuriant tree-life, many of them of great width and size; their branches linked and interwoven with trailing loops of parasitic flowers and foliage. The northern border of the river was clothed with groves of palm, and away to the south stretched the broken plains of the Transvaal.

Embedded in the sandy bed lay the large pontoon which had formerly been used to cross the river in the rains, and had been sunk by Plumer many months ago. This was raised to the surface and repaired by the 75th during their stay; and on the 26th of October—having previously sent an armed party to search for water—the Squadron marched across the Drift and penetrated into the unknown land beyond. They were followed the next day by the 71st Squadron and part of the Pom-Pom battery; and their post at Pont Drift was taken by the 67th.

The road through the Zoutpan district was very rugged and the water supply scarce, and when found, often brackish and unpalatable. And small wonder; for they were skirting the great salt-pans which lay at the western foot of the Zoutpansberg (Salt Pan Mountain) Range. In many places the ground was white with a coating of the salt, and the exhalations from the pan are said to be peculiarly deadly to Europeans during the summer months.

Wegdraai was the farthest point to which the two Squadrons penetrated in the Transvaal. It stands near a bend of the Brak River, some forty miles from the Rhodesian border. In this camp the troops were very short of food and were upon half-rations until two days before the return march was commenced. One of the 75th writes :—

"Do you know what it is to be hungry? I mean a hunger that gnaws at you all day; a hunger that your daily ration of food refuses to appease. A half-pound of flour with no baking-

In the former Boer trenches around Fourteen Streams the men found many relics of their whilom occupants; but none more suggestive—none which could a better tale unfold—than the innocent-looking empty whiskey case, bearing the name of a well-known firm of merchants, and consigned *via* Algoa Bay—but neatly fitted inside for the accommodation of six 15-pounder shells.

A part of the Battalion of Sharpshooters were taken to Orange River Station, and took part in that night march on Dec. 8, told in the " Story of the Hampshire Squadron." Continuing their march from Belmont, they reached Kimberley on Dec. 11, and there rejoining the Squadrons from Vryburg and Fourteen Streams, the 18th Battalion was once more complete.

On Dec. 13 the whole of the 18th Battalion formed part of a force sent to escort a large convoy of some fifty wagons to Boshof, which had been practically in a state of siege for some weeks, and therefore cut off from supplies. The little force was under the command of Col. Parke (commanding Battalion of Sharpshooters), and consisted, in addition to the S.S., of the Hampshire Yeomanry, and five guns escorted by the Kimberley Regiment; and the wagons were directly under the charge of part of the Somerset Regiment.

Marching through the night no opposition was met with until the afternoon of the next day. On the 15th the column lay encamped, when at 3 p.m. three of Harding's black scouts galloped in bringing the information that a large number of Boers were lying behind a little range of kopjes some two miles from the column. Sergt. Kerr and six men of the 70th S.S. were at once despatched to reconnoitre their position. It seemed but a short time before the advanced outposts in that direction heard faintly a continued crackle of musketry, and a little knot of horses came tearing across the veldt at top speed. And all but three of them were riderless.

The little body had run unwittingly into a strong outpost placed in front of the Boer position. The enemy opened a murderous fire upon them, under which Sergeant Kerr fell, shot through the thigh. Trooper Campbell's horse was shot and he lay stunned by the fall, to find, on regaining consciousness, that he was being relieved of his arms and his watch by a couple of rough-looking Boers. Though injured by his fall (he was invalided to Capetown for a time with slight concussion of the brain) he bound up the Sergeant's leg, and was then allowed by the enemy to go in quest of an ambulance. Trooper Walker's horse was also shot, and in his fall he was pitched into a hole in the ground, where he lay unobserved by the enemy for some hours, and afterwards made his escape. The outposts were withdrawn at sundown and a combined movement made to clear the road into Boshof. The town was reached at four o'clock in the morning, and after two hours' rest for the horses, the Sharpshooters were again in the saddle, and moved on the position from which they had been fired upon. The Boers made no stand, but galloped off upon the approach of the horsemen. Sergt. Kerr was found where he had fallen, and was carried into Boshof by the ambulance sent out with the Squadrons. Tpr. Davis, of the 75th S.S., was also slightly wounded on the same day.

On Dec. 18 the column again reached Kimberley, bringing in a large party of Boer prisoners—seventy-eight white and three coloured—who were marched to the gaol under the escort of the Kimberley Regiment. They were chiefly suspects gathered in from Boshof and the district, and since their capture had been temporarily confined in the Boshof Church. (*See p. 226.*) Amongst them were two who had been concerned in the recent firing on the convoy. Sergeant Kerr was brought into Kimberley by the ambulance, and at first it was thought he would recover from his injuries, but these hopes proved vain, for some weeks later, on Jan. 22, he succumbed to his wounds received in his first engagement.

On the day after their return to Kimberley, the 18th Battn. again entrained. Their destination was De Aar. De Aar had been their destination when they left Buluwayo, and the journey to the dusty little station had come to be looked on by the men as something of a joke. They were always entraining for De Aar, but they seemed fated never to get there. And in this instance, too, their scepticism proved to be well founded.

It was whilst watering their horses at Potfontein that a goods train passed with the startling news that they had been fired on some miles to the southwards, and that the wires were trailing

HEAD OF THE COLUMN ENTERING BEAUFORT WEST.

Photo by *Edgeome, Beaufort West.*

reason had to be left at a farm, was snapped up by a party of Boers only a few hours after his comrades had left, and promptly relieved of his horse and arms, after which he was released.

On Jan. 15 these two squadrons of the Sharpshooters moved by rail to Prince Albert Road, and marched the twenty-eight miles into the pretty little village of Prince Albert, at the mouth of the Zwartberg Pass. They were joined by the 67th S.S. from Beaufort West and two days afterwards by the 70th Squadron who, since moving to De Aar on Dec. 26, had been patrolling and guarding the hill passes in the vicinity of Frazerburg. Thus the four Squadrons were once more united.* There had been several changes amongst the officers of the Scottish Squadron. Their commander, Captain Hill, had left to take up staff work in Bloemfontein, and the command of the Squadron was given to Captain McDowell (Adjutant of the 18th Battn.). Also Lieuts. Younger and Wellwood had taken up their commissions in the Regular Army (*see footnote p. 295*) and two Sergeants of the Squadron—A. E. Borthwick and H. J. Aitcheson--were promoted in their place.

Let us look for a moment at the causes which had brought the troops hurrying so far southwards into the Colony. On Dec. 16 Kritzinger, with 700 men, had crossed the Orange at Rhenoster Hoek Drift, and after threatening Burghersdorp, Middelburg, and Richmond, and fighting an indecisive engagement with Colonel Grenfell at Plaisterheuvel, he succeeded in evading several of the British columns, and penetrating into the southern districts of Cape Colony. On Jan. 18 he attacked Willowmore, but was beaten off by the Town Guard and a party of Australians. Then, after tearing up the rails of the line near Willowmore, burning the sleepers, and doing all the damage that lay in his power, his force split into two bodies, and moved towards Oudtshoorn, by the north and south sides of the Kammannassie Mountains. Hence the hurried pushing of the troops southwards—and *inter alia*, the 18th Battalion of Sharpshooters.

---
* From this point the Squadrons were very much split up into troops, or patrols of twenty men or less, which would, in some cases, be attached to one or two different Squadrons before again rejoining their own. The wanderings of these detachments form a network of movements which would but be bewildering, could they be described. I shall therefore, in noting its movements, confine myself to the main body of each Squadron.

The loyalists of Prince Albert received the troops with kindly hospitality, providing tea and fruit for them upon their arrival, and placing the village reading-room and the schoolroom at their disposal until they left. With Kritzinger in the vicinity of course patrols were sent out every day, and every approach to the town had its little Cossack post a mile away from the outskirts. Probably these unfortunates did not relish the idea of subsisting on the regulation 'bully beef,' whilst their comrades in camp were having the run of the stores, for I note in the diary of one man who was on a twenty-four hours outpost—

Jan 18.—Sent on outpost at 9 p.m. for 24 hours.

Jan 19.—Much rain last night. Cold wind to-day with heavy showers of rain. Bully beef was sent out to us for our dinner, and we decided to have a change. So purchased a pig for five shillings, and killed and stewed the same. Was relieved soon after 8 p.m.

I think the happiest person in Prince Albert when the troops marched in was an old grey-bearded man, who soon made himself known to the men. He was a Crimean veteran of the old 13th Foot (the Somersets). He had been badly wounded in his side, and his injury had afterwards made a residence in a warmer clime necessary to the prolonging of his life. So for thirty years he had lived with his niece in this placid little Colonial 'stad.' With tears of joy in his eyes, he wandered by the aid of his stick in and amongst the rough bivouacs of the men, saying again and again that this was a proud day for the loyalists of Prince Albert. His beloved regiment was ever in his mind, but he had never dreamed of again seeing English troops after he left his native shore.

Troops were hurried into the threatened town of Oudtshoorn, and the 67th and part of the 75th S.S. marched through the Zwartberg Pass, to assist in frustrating Kritzinger's intentions. They were warmly received by the people of Oudtshoorn, who loaded them with fruit and tobacco. But they had come for sterner work than fêting, and after staying two days in the town they marched to Kruis River and there encamped. That night a smoking concert was held in the camp, but it was rudely broken up by the advent of a despatch rider from Colonel Williams, asking for reinforcements, as his force

they pointed across to the sheep which were running about, and said—'Catch one!' Worn out as we were we had a sheep killed, skinned and half-cooked in no time. We made a fire of the veldt-bush, and put the sheep (cut into pieces) upon the fire just as it was, and when half-cooked—we could wait no longer—we set to and made short work of that sheep."

Next day, after a consultation between their officers and the Boer Commandant, they were escorted several miles on the way to Willowmore and then released, the Boers saying if they set eyes on them again they would shoot them 'on sight.' But they had better luck this time and eventually arrived at Willowmore, where they were lodged in the diminutive Town Hall. Retiring early to rest, they at last promised themselves a night of sleep absolutely free from care—the sleep of the thoroughly wearied.

But it was not to be. It was nearing midnight, when suddenly the discharge of a sentry's rifle on a kopje near by turned out the little garrison, for the town was hourly expecting attack; and with rifles pushed into their hands, the half-rested Sharpshooters were hurried to the trenches to take part in the defence of the town. But it was a false alarm. Two officers had gone out some hours earlier in a Cape cart, and returning after dark, had not replied to the sentry's challange. The Town Guardsman without more ado opened fire on them. Hence the alarm. Luckily his bullet passed between them as they sat in the Cape cart, and the little garrison returned to finish their sleep.

After several days at Willowmore, the Sharpshooters entrained for Graaff Reinet, where they were once more equipped and mounted; and again entraining, reached Houtkraal on February 14, where we will leave them for the present.

It was at Prince Albert that the Sharpshooters received the sad tidings of the death of Her Majesty the Queen, and a gloom seemed to lie upon the camp for a time. A cricket match and subsequent concert had been arranged, but of course both were cancelled.

Troops were still pouring in. On January 21, five guns

that the report of the enemy's presence had been correct, for within several miles of the place Lieut. Borthwick and Trooper Bethune pluckily captured three of the enemy's scouts, but this did not deter Capt. McDowell from leading part of his men right into the village itself. Here they obtained all the information they wished, and as the enemy were massing in numbers at a short distance, and there seemed a danger of being outflanked, the retirement began. Immediately they left the village the Boers gave chase, and the tactics of the patrol were to hold the enemy in check by turns, one party taking a position and keeping the enemy busily engaged, to allow the other troop to gallop further back, and in turn cover the retreat of the first. Once disaster nearly overtook them. One of the little troops delayed its retirement too long, and when making for their horses, suddenly found themselves under a cross fire from less than 200 yards away. Colonel Parke himself had joined the party, and but for the pluck and presence of mind of Sergt.-Major Jackson and Trooper Mobsby, he would have been shot or captured. But these two, seeing the Colonel's peril, dismounted and covered him with their rifle fire until he was in the saddle. His self-sacrifice caused the Sergeant-Major his liberty, for he was captured before he could get away himself. The only casualties which the Squadron sustained occurred at this point. Lce.-Corporal Boyd* was killed, and eight men, whose horses were shot, were taken prisoners.

So the risky work went on. The two officers handled their men perfectly, and at last the guns were sighted, and the patrols knew they had admirably succeeded in carrying out the intentions of their commander. The enemy were allowed to flock out over the last ridge within 3,000 yards (the Howitzer's best range) and then the first shell came hurtling, with a grand upward curve, right into their midst. They did not fire another shot, but raced back the way they had come in a panic-stricken horde, pursued until out of range by the huge bursting lyddite shells. But Klaarstroom was no resting place for them. For

---

* Corporal Boyd was the first man enrolled in the Scottish Sharpshooters. Born in Ireland, though of Scottish extraction, he had spent most of his life in Queensland. Patriotic to a degree, with a patriotism which his knowledge of Greater Britain had but intensified, when the opportunity came, he hastened to take up arms in the service of that country he loved so well; and, as was his dreed, in the faithful fulfilment of his duty, for his country he gave his life.

COLUMN CROSSING THE GAMKA RIVER, NEAR PRINCE ALBERT.

Photo by *Edgcome, Beaufort West.*

of Scheepers. Therefore had they paid him a visit, had taken £350 worth of goods and practically cleared his store.

Hot-foot by long forced marches went the columns after the raiders, and every day the distance lessened between them, but at last the pursuit came to the usual end. The column ran short of supplies, and although but a few short miles separated them from the quarry, they were obliged to turn to the railway, and encamped at Letjesbosch, on a farm owned by two colonists of American descent. These men farmed 20,000 morgen (about 40,000 acres) of land, principally devoted to sheep. But by erecting an immense dam across the Gamka, which flowed by the farm, they were able to irrigate many acres of garden, and the troops during their stay revelled in purple grapes and other luscious fruit. The farmers had been hourly expecting a visit from the Boers, and outside the granaries was an enormous pile of forage which would have been burned upon their approach. Needless to say their relief was great, when the dusty line they saw approaching their dwelling turned out to be a British column in place of the dreaded marauders. On Feb. 12 the column marched at 2 p.m. by the side of the rail for Beaufort West, 26 miles away, arriving there two hours before midnight.

After staying here for two days—two days spent in a quagmire of mud on the outskirts of the town -- they again entrained, and on Feb. 18 once more reached the village of Prince Albert, to find the 70th and 75th encamped at the foot of the frowning rocks which guarded the mouth of the Zwartberg Pass.

After the ruse played so successfully upon the Boers on Feb. 2 (related on p. 316), the 70th and 75th remained for a short time in Prince Albert, to guard against any meditated descent on the village on the part of the enemy. Outposts and patrols came in rapid succession, and to be on duty for several nights in succession had come to be a common experience with the men. Some pleasures, however, were interposed between the numerous duties, and a cricket match and gymkana was held, in which the more athletic inhabitants vied with the hardened troopers in friendly contest.

The country south of the mountains was well watched, and part of the two Squadrons, with a few of the 71st, were sent as

column of Col. Crabbe, which had left Houtkraal that morning before the dawn. The Yeomanry attached to this column was composed of the 65th (Leicesters) and the 71st S.S. Together the two squadrons took part in that heart-breaking chase after the broken bands of the invaders, which only ended with the escape of De Wet across the Orange, and the marching of the worn-out columns into Colesberg on March 2.

In Lord Kitchener's despatch, dated March 8, 1901 ; describing the operations against De Wet, amongst those he " desired to bring before the notice of the Secretary of State for War for their valuable services rendered in connection with these operations" occur the following names. —

Captain Sir S. B. Crossley, Bart.
Sergeant A. H. Day, 71st Co. I.Y.

On March 6, the 71st left Colesberg with Col. Crabbe's column, which was still working in conjunction with Col. Henniker. Passing through Gansgat, Karbonaatjeskraal, and Petrusville, Orange River Station was reached on the 10th. Here the two Yeomanry squadrons were transferred to Col. Henniker's column, and continued with it until the expiration of their service.

The next move of the Squadron was a distant one. An attack on Grahamstown was feared, and Col. Henniker's column was hurried by rail over the intervening three hundred and seventy miles and detrained at Grahamstown on March 13. The advent of the column saved the threatened town from the raiding of the enemy, and the people were proportionately grateful. The camp had hardly been formed when a Scotch cart loaded with luscious pine-apples drove into the lines for the troops, and during their short stay the people showered on them gifts of fruit and little luxuries, doubly welcome to men fresh from the hard chase of De Wet. On March 17 the Column entrained for Rosmead Junction, and for the next two weeks were in the saddle from dawn till dark scouring the Midland districts after the elusive Kritzinger. No less than seven columns were operating in this chase, directed by General Jones. On March 29, Col. Henniker's column had a sharp brush with the enemy, but did not succeed in inflicting heavy loss upon him, and on April 7, the column halted at

Steynsburg. From Steynsburg they entrained for Fish River, and from there marched westward, through a district where disloyalty had been most rampant. A number of farms whose owners had gone on commando were burned and the families brought in to the Refugee camps. On April 15 the column reached Bethesda Road, where they entrained, and passing through Graaff Reinet, reached Aberdeen Road the same day.

The trekking and the discomforts of the veldt were drawing to a close. On April 22, after another week of seemingly aimless marches, the column were attacked by an ambushed body of the Boers at Middlewater. After a three hours struggle the enemy were beaten off into the hills, and the column remained encamped for some days. Here the 71st squadron left them, for on April 28, they received orders for Worcester, and marching to the nearest railway, entrained for the mobilization camp, and on May 8 sailed from Capetown on board the *Mongolian*.

To return to the 70th and 75th Squadrons, which we left encamped at the village of Klaarstroom on Feb. 20. Troops were concentrating here for another move against the mischievous Scheepers, and the little village was a busy scene of parked guns, of lines of horses, and of half-loaded wagons; and in between a pulsating, restless crowd of rough-looking, veldt-worn, khaki-clad men. On Feb. 22 the preparations were complete, and under the command of Sir Charles Parsons, the long column moved eastwards—seven guns—Howitzers, Hodgkiss, 15-pounders, and Pom-Poms; 2nd Brabant's Horse, the I.Y. consisting of the 70th, 75th, and a troop of the 65th; and a detachment of the 6th (Inniskilling) Dragoons.

By making a forced march of thirty-six miles the column reached Toverwaterpoort and encamped for the night. At daybreak on the 23rd several troops of Brabant's Horse went out to reconnoitre towards Zoetendalspoort. Several hours later the sound of fierce firing came from the Poort, and shortly the patrol was seen riding back for their lives. The camp was pitched behind a low range of hills, but through a break in these, through which ran the wide dry bed of a river, the country beyond could be seen. There was hasty saddling

Kidd, had been forming a connecting link between the two patrols, was captured. In their dash for liberty, they divided. The Corporal safely reached his comrades, but Wilson was unfortunately stopped by a wire fence, and was surrounded by the enemy before he could get through. He was for eleven days in the hands of the Boers, and the story of the hardships endured by him and his fellow captives will be found in the history of the Leicestershire Squadron.

The story of the 75th is more tragic. When, as related in the chapter above referred to, the Captain of Dragoons found himself under a heavy cross-fire, the only men with him were Lieut. Edlmann and six men of the 75th. Lance-Cpl. Benson had fallen, mortally wounded, as they were headed off from the plain onto the fatal kopje. Cover there was none—or next to none. Each man dismounted, and flinging his rein over the nearest stone or bush, threw himself down and opened a hopeless fire on the ridge from which the raking bullets were coming. Captain Anstice shouted " Blaze away at them, boys " and they needed no telling. Trooper Watt* was killed whilst taking aim for his first shot. A few moments afterwards Ritchie was wounded to the death, for he lived but three days after he was carried back to camp. Still the devoted few kept up a steady fire on their concealed foes. Suddenly Reading called out " I'm shot!" then putting his hand to his head said " But it's only a graze." He got up and ran back, but had not gone ten yards before he fell, and died an hour after he was found by the ambulance. Then Legg, the only unwounded survivor, heard the Captain say " Keep it up, Edlmann " but knew by his tone he was wounded. He had five wounds, but eventually recovered. For some time longer they held out, but the situation was desperate, and the Captain cried " Retire and take what cover you can." Murray rose to obey the order, and almost immediately fell disabled, shot through the arm. Only two were now left in the firing line, and soon one of these was silenced, for Lieut. Edlmann was wounded, and only Legg was left. The rest has been told.

---

* Lance-corpl. Benson and Trooper Watt were originally enrolled in the 70th Squadron, but were subsequently transferred to the 75th. By a curious coincidence Trooper Watt was born at Aberdeen, Scotland, and met his death at the Colonial town bearing the same name.

COLUMN HALTED IN THE KARROO. Photo by *Edgcome, Beaufort West.*

THE STORY OF THE SHARPSHOOTERS.

The remainder of the troops and the guns were out by this, the men advancing in extended order on foot, and two hours afterwards, the broken commandoes had fled to the hills with their prisoners.

The following is an extract from ' orders ' issued next day.

" The O.C. troops writes to congratulate all ranks of the 6th Dragoons and 18th Battalion I.Y. on their splendid behaviour yesterday, 6th March, under most trying circumstances."

From Aberdeen the column moved to Murraysburg, the mounted troops making a long and fatiguing night march to forestall the Boer commando, only to find that this had been accomplished by Kitchener's Fighting Scouts, who had arrived during the night. At Murraysburg a welcome rest of a week was enjoyed, at the end of which the two squadrons of Yeomanry left, with Major Warden of the 75th in command; and marching over the Sneeuwberg Mountains, entered Graaff Reinet on March 19, where the prisoners captured at Aberdeen —amongst them Trooper Wilson of the 70th—were found. Their release had been forced several days before by the hot pursuit of a small British column under Major Mullins.

At Graaff Reinet the men obtained a fresh supply of much needed clothing, and in three days were again on their way out to the veldt, engaged in running down the scattered and elusive bodies of the enemy in the Midland Districts. On the 24th they arrived at Pearston, to find that the town had been captured and looted only a day or two before. Learning the direction in which the enemy had gone, they left in pursuit the same evening ; but after chasing them for two days, it was found impossible to take the guns and transport over the mountain cattle-paths by which the Boers had fled, and the column returned to Graaff Reinet.

On the 29th Colonel Scobell moved out from Graaff Reinet at the head of a strong column of 1200 men and six guns, and with him marched the Sharpshooters. A large commando of the enemy were known to be in the neighbourhood, but beyond a slight skirmish, in which three of Brabant's Horse were wounded, the expedition met with small success, and on April 1 reached the village of Aberdeen, the scene of their action some

one man and one horse, checked the enemy till the rest of the force arrived. Had they occupied the kopje considerable loss would have been caused to our men."

Middleton formerly belonged to the Black Watch, and had seen service in Egypt. At Rietfontein another of the 75th—Trooper Busby—was wounded.

Upon May 1, Colonel Scobell's column marched into Cradock, where it was reconstructed, and the Sharpshooters left it.

For the next three weeks the Yeomanry were employed on escort work, taking convoys to the different columns working in the vicinity, but they invariably returned to the town when their charge had been safely handed over. Several times they had to repel slight attacks from the enemy, but they sustained no further losses in the field. One of the 70th Squadron—Trooper Gilbert—was accidentally severely injured in the camp, losing the sight of one of his eyes.

At last they received the welcome order for mobilization, and on May 24, the 70th and 71st—or what was left of them, for their ranks were sadly depleted from various causes—arrived at Worcester, there to join the 67th S.S. The 71st had embarked nearly three weeks before.

Lieuts. Aitcheson, Parr and Drummond (who had been promoted from Sergeant) remained behind to command squadrons in the new Battalion of Sharpshooters, and Lieut. Poulteney, who had formerly held the rank of Quartermaster-Sergeant, became its Adjutant. Many of the Lieutenants in the new Sharpshooters were taken from the ranks of the time-expired squadrons.

And on June 3, the good ship *Hawarden Castle* carried them from the shores of South Africa, where for twelve long months they had suffered, and fought, and fulfilled their duty as became England's Yeomen. Where moreover, whenever occasion offered, they had carried out the behest of their King, and had ' shot straight ' as became the men who bore the cognomen of ' Dunraven's Sharpshooters.'

To be Lieut.-Cols. in the Reserve of Officers :
Major C. Barton.
Capt. C. W. Warden (Maj.-Reserve of Officers).

D.C. Medal :

Sqdn.-Sergeant-Major T. Jackson.
Sqdn.-Sergeant-Major A. Giles.

LIST OF CASUALTIES.

"No branch of His Majesty's forces in South Africa has shown greater gallantry or done more valuable service than the Imperial Yeomanry, for out of a force of 10,921 officers and men sent out last year the casualties up to date have numbered 3,390 —of which 703 have been killed or died of disease— amounting to about 30 per cent., which I believe is the highest casualty percentage in any branch of the forces that has served in South Africa. This testimony, I feel sure, speaks for itself."—[*Extract from letter from the War Office, published in the Press, June 15, 1901.*]

LIST OF CASUALTIES OF THE 61st (South Irish) I.Y.

11288	Tpr. C. Flude	acc. sev. wdd.	May 18, 1900	23 mile Peg	
11191	Major T. J. de Burgh	wounded	Dec. 22, 1900	Matjesfontein	
11219	Corpl. R. Rowland	slightly wdd.	Dec. 22, 1900	Matjesfontein	
11282	Tpr. E. J. Cleary	slightly wdd.	Dec. 22, 1900	Matjesfontein	
11309	Tpr. W. C. Kirkwood	slightly wdd.	Dec. 22, 1900	Matjesfontein	
11204	Tpr. G. Nash	slightly wdd.	Dec. 22, 1900	Matjesfontein	
11283	Lce.-Corpl. J. Oliver	severely wdd.	May 6, 1901	near Smithfield	
	Tpr. F. Allen	severely wdd.	May 6, 1901	near Smithfield	
11289	Tpr. J. Stone	died	June 12, 1900	Umtali	Dysentery
11262	Tpr. D. C. Franklin	died	June 5, 1900	Umtali	Mal. & dys'tery
11300	Tpr. J. McCann	died	June 12, 1900	Umtali	Dysentery
11254	Tr. T. G. B. Armstrong	died	Aug. 7, 1900	Marandellas	Meningitis
11242	Tpr. F. J. Madden	died	Oct. 18, 1900	Gwanda	Pneumonia
11311	Tpr. T. Miller	died	Feb. 7, 1901	De Aar	Enteric
11190	Tpr. Victor Ringwood	died	Feb. 9, 1901	Buluwayo	Enteric

LIST OF CASUALTIES OF THE 67TH (SHARPSHOOTERS) I.Y.

12399	Tpr. G. Smith	wounded	Feb. 18, 1901	Palmietfontein	
12468	Tpr. E. R. Apps	died	May 29, 1900	Bamboo Creek	Mal. & dys'tery
12449	Tpr. G. F. Shaw	died	May 29, 1900	Bamboo Creek	Enteric
12469	Tpr. A. J. Dunne	died	June 24, 1900	Umtali	Dysentery
7001	Lce.-Cpl. G. F. West	died	Oct. 22, 1900	Mafeking	Enteric
12498	Tpr. C. Olney	died	Oct. 28, 1900	Victoria	Enteric
7005	Tpr. R. Jefferies	died	Jan. 28, 1901	Deelfontein	Enteric

LIST OF CASUALTIES OF THE 70TH (SHARPSHOOTERS) I.Y.

12617	Sergt. J. A. Kerr	killed in action		Died, Kimberley, Jan. 22, 1901, from w'nds rec'd Boshof, Dec. 15, 1900	
12535	Lc.-Corpl. J. Boyd	killed in action	Feb. 2, 1901	Prince Albert	
12625	Sgt. J. E. Liddiard	killed in action	Feb. 23, 1901	Toverwater Poort	
12586	Tpr. W. A. Gilbert	acc. sev. wdd.	May 10, 1901	Cradock	
	Lieut. H. Andrew	died	July 9, 1900	Salisbury	Dysentery
12580	Tpr. B. Grey	died	Oct. 15, 1900	Victoria	Enteric
12612	Tpr. R. B. Russell	died	Dec. 3, 1900	Tuli	Enteric
12636	Tpr. J. B. Deas	died	June, 1901	Pietermaritzburg	Enteric

BRAK—Brackish, salt.
BREEDE—Broad.
BRUINTJES HOOGTE—" Brown's Ridge."
BUFFEL—A buffalo.
BULUWAYO—" The Place of Killing."
BURGHER—Every male over sixteen years of age possessing the franchise.

CALEDON—Town named after the Earl of Caledon, Governor of Cape Colony, 1807-11.
CARNARVON—Town named after the Earl of Carnarvon, Sec. of State for the Colonies, 1874.
CHAP—Snap, flash.
COLESBERG—Town named after Sir Lowry Cole, Governor of Cape Colony, 1828-33.
CRADOCK—Town named after Sir John Cradock, Governor of Cape Colony, 1811-14.

DAAR—There.
DAM—An artificial lake or water supply.
DE WET (De Vet)—Boer guerilla leader.
DISSELBOOM—The pole of a wagon.
DONGA—A river bed—often dry. A deep ditch or water-hole with steep sides. A gaping crack in the ground.
DONKERS—Dark.
DOORN—Thorn.
DOP—Cape brandy.
DORIESFONTEIN—Dry or barren spring.
DORP—A village.
DRAAI—Turn, corner, twist.
DRAKENSBERG—" Dragon's Mountain."
DRAKENSTEIN—" Dragon Stone."
DRIE—Three.
DROOGE—Dry, arid, dull.
DUIVEN—A pigeon.
DURBAN—Town named after Sir Benjamin D'Urban, Governor of Cape Colony. 1834-38.
DWING—Force, power.

ALPHABETICAL GLOSSARY.

EENDRAGHT MAAKT MAGT—" Right makes might," the motto of the South African Republic.

ELANDS-LAAGTE (Ee-lands-*laarg*-te)—" The Valley of Elands " a South African antelope.

ENKELDOORN—" Single Thorn."

FISKAL—Boer name for a species of shrike, or " butcher-bird " —the Fiscal, or Crown-Prosecutor, being in the old days of the Batavian Government an officer by whose exertions criminals were brought to justice and executed. The association is obvious.

FONTEIN (*fon*-tane)—A spring.

FRANSCHE HOEK—" French Corner." Town so called because it was the home of the Huguenot refugees who came to the Cape in 1686-88, after the revocation of the Edict of Nantes.

GANS—Goose.

GAT (haht)—A hole or narrow passage.

GEDACHT—Think, consider.

GELUK—Fortune, luck.

GENADENDAL—" The Dale of Grace." Town in Cape Colony. The oldest Mission Station in the Colony. It was founded in 1737 by the Moravians.

GOED—Good.

GRAAFF-REINET (Grarf-*ren*-net)—Town in Cape Colony also called " The Gem of the Karroo." Named after Governor Van de Graaff and his wife Reinet.

GRAHAMSTOWN—Town named after Col. Graham, commander of the British forces in the war of 1811.

GRAS—Grass.

GRIQUALAND (*Gree*-ka-land).

GROENE—Green, verdant.

GROOT—Great.

GROOTE-SCHUUR (Grewte Skoor)— " The Great Granary." Residence of the Hon. C. Rhodes, at Newlands, near Capetown.

GROOTVERLANGEN—Great desire, or longing.

GRUIS—Dusty.

NEK—The saddle connecting two hills.
N'GAMI—Giraffe.
NIEUW—New.
NOOITE—Never, did not.
NYLSTROOM—" Nile Stream." A tributary of the Limpopo, so called because when first seen by the emigrant Boer farmers, they supposed they had reached the head waters of the Nile.

OLIPHANT—Elephant.
OLIVE—Olive.
ONDERSTE—Undermost.
OORLOG—War.
ORANJE VRYSTAAT—Orange Free State.
OTTER – Otter.
OUDEDAG—Old, old-aged.
OUDTSHOORN—Town named after the Baron von Rheede von Oudtshoorn, Dutch Governor appointed 1773, but died on the voyage out.
OUTSPAN or UITSPAN—To unharness. Also applied to the camping-place.

PAARD—A horse.
PAARL—A pearl.
PAAUW—Largest of the South African bustards *(Otis Kori)*. called by the Boers ' gom paauw '—literally ' gum-peacock.'
PALAPYE (Pal-*larp*-swe).
PALMIET—Date palm.
PAN—A sheet of water.
PAS OP—Look out, beware. As in ' Pas op voor zakken-rollers ' (Beware of pickpockets.)
PATROLJE—A patrol.
PHILIPSTOWN—Town named after Sir Philip Wodehouse, Governor of Cape Colony, 1861-70.
PIETERMARITZBURG—Named after two famous leaders of the emigrant Boers in 1836—Pieter Retief and Gerrit Maritz.

SEA-COW—Same as the Dutch ' Zee Koe,' a hippopotamus.
SJAMBOK (*sham*-bok)—A hide whip, usually cut from the skin of the rhinoceros or hippopotamus.
SLUIT (sloot)—A ditch on the veldt, usually dry.
SNEEUW—Snow.
SOMERSET EAST—Town named after Lord Charles Somerset, Governor of Cape Colony, 1814-28.
SPEK-BOOM—' Spek ' literally ' fatty ' or ' feeding '—A tree, the small fleshy foliage of which is eaten by horses and cattle, and sometimes by the Boers at a pinch.
SPITZ—Sharp, pointed.
SPOORWEG—Railway.
SPRUIT (sproot)—A small river or stream.
STAD or STADT—Dutch town or village.
STELLENBOSCH — Town named by Simon van der Stell, Commander 1679, Governor 1699.
STERK—Strong, hard, firm.
STOCKENSTROOM—Town named after Sir Andries Stockenstroom, appointed Lieut.-Governor of Cape Colony, 1836.
STOEP (stoop)—A raised stone-paved platform, sometimes covered, sometimes open, at the front of nearly every Dutch house.
STORMBERG MTS.—The home of Storm, a noted Bushman chief.
STROM or STROOM—A stream.
STRUIS or STRUIS-VOGEL—The ostrich.
STRYD—A fight, dispute.
SWELLENDAM—Town named after Hendrick Swellengrebel, Dutch Governor of Cape Colony, 1739-51.

TAAI—Flexible, pliant.
TAAL (Tarl)—The low-Dutch language, spoken by the Boers; as distinct from the high-Dutch or Dutch proper, as it is written in Holland.
TAFEL—A table.
TANDTJESBERG—" Little Tooth Mountain."
THABA BOSIGO—" Mountain of Night."
THABA INDUNA—" Chief's Mountain."
THABA N'CHU—" Black Mountain."

ALPHABETICAL GLOSSARY.

Touw—Rope, cord.
Toverwaterpoort—" The Pass of the Bewitched Water."
Trek—To travel.
Tugela (Too-*gay*-lah)—" Startling the bathers by its force and depth."
Tulbagh—Town named after Ryk van Tulbagh, Dutch Governor of Cape Colony, 1751-71.
Twyffel—Doubt.
Tyger—Tiger. The Leopard (*Felis pardus*) is erroneously called a 'tiger' by nearly all South Africans, though curiously enough the Boers call the cheetah (*Felis jubata*) a 'luipaard.'
Uitlander (*Oo*-it-lander)—A white resident in the Transvaal not of Boer origin.
Uitspan—See Outspan.
Umgeni—" Flows to the Sea."
Umkomanzi—" Heaped up Water," as by the tide.
Umvoti—" The Milk-giver."
Umzimkulu—" Tshaka's Great Kraal."

Vaal (farl)—Yellowish-brown.
Valsch—False.
Veldschoen (*felt*-schoon)—Rough homemade shoes worn by Boers.
Veldt (felt)—The open plains.
Vet—Fat.
Vierkleur (fear-cloor)—" Four-colour "; the Transvaal flag —red, white and blue flag of Holland, with a broad green vertical stripe next to the staff.
Vlak—Straight.
Vlakke—Shallow.
Vlakte—Plain.
Vlei (flay)—A pond, small lake, or a marsh.
Voetsak (foot-sack)—A common expression signifying 'Get away' or 'Clear out.'
Volksraad (*fokes*-rard)—The Legislative Assemblies of the Transvaal and the Orange Free State.
Voorlooper (*fore*-looper)—The man or boy leading the first couple of an ox-team.